To my dear Fri
Don Smith.

Let Justice Be Done

The Life and Times of
Justice
J. Harold Hawkins

David A. Dosser, Sr.

Typography, layout, and cover design
by
Kennth Irvin Storey

Portrait of Judge Hawkins (On Cover)
by
Sarah Garner

Photograph of Judge Hawkins' portrait (On Cover)
by
Maryann Cornett

Printed and bound by Indigo Custom Publishing, LLC

Printed in the United States of America

ISBN 978-1-934144-15-2
1-934144-15-0

Library of Congress Control Number 2007924515

Copies may be ordered from
David A. Dosser, Sr.
www.letjusticebedone.info/

"Dedicated to my dear beloved wife and companion,
Ann Hawkins Dosser."

DISCLAIMER: *In order to retain the original copy of the newspaper articles, only changes in their text occurred when copies of the original were poor and difficult to read. Occasionally words and punctuation were not readable. Usages of that time have remained as written. None of the minor errors altered the basic intent of the articles.*

ACKNOWLEDGMENTS

It is to these special people below that I owe an enormous debt of gratitude.

First, I wish to thank my family for years of support and for complying with my many requests for various bits of knowledge and memories. My wife, Ann Hawkins Dosser, and her sister, Jane Hawkins Ramsey, responded in many ways with stories and facts, which I would not have otherwise been aware. One of the most stressful tasks was the typing of many pages necessary to complete the story. Many thanks to Betsy Berry, granddaughter of Judge Hawkins, who came to the rescue and typed all the memorials we used. This was no small undertaking.

Words are difficult to find to express appreciation to my children and their spouses, David and Kathy Dosser, Jane and Danny Cornett, and Sue and Ed Davison. Each has provided me with better ways to do all manner of things and most of all encouragement to continue the project. Jane was extremely helpful in keeping the computer working, especially the online system where I spent many hours doing research.

A special thanks goes also to Lindell and Ann DeJarnett of Marietta, Georgia, who provided me many times with an attractive room in which to stay when I was conducting research in the area. I am also grateful to Judge Conley Ingram and Sylvia who made suggestions that were most helpful and in particular the introduction so kindly written by Judge Ingram.

There were many subjects that were most difficult for me to develop. Attorney Don Smith devoted much of his valuable time responding to questions regarding identity of subjects in pictures, explaining legal terms and procedures and was always accommodating and kind. I profusely appreciate his generous assistance.

When the manuscript was about two-thirds finished, I began to be concerned about the quality and organization of the story. I am grateful to have found Joy Day, an English teacher, and Public Services Librarian at the Lon Duckworth Library at Young Harris College in Young Harris, Georgia. Her knowledge alleviated my concerns and her suggestions were always helpful. Joy enriched the story by reviewing grammar and kindly suggesting changes in location of subjects or the structure of a sentence, which always made the story read with more force and understanding. She has become a good friend and her enthusiasm and strong support for the book was inspiring.

I appreciate the work of Kenneth Storey, who took on the job of formatting this book. Through Ken's hard work, he has created a book which is a pleasure to read.

Thanks to the Marietta Museum of History for their courtesy in making available historical pictures that added to the book. Also the Cobb County Library in Marietta, Georgia, for their courtesy and help in researching historical information.

In addition, thanks to the *Marietta Daily Journal* for making it possible to get copies of their paper for current and past years in the local libraries.

David A. Dosser, Sr.

INTRODUCTION

Long time Marietta resident and retired banker, David Dosser, has put together a loving and fascinating biographical history of his father-in-law, the late Harold Hawkins. Justice Hawkins was the first citizen of Marietta to serve on the Supreme Court of Georgia and one of the very best judges ever to serve on that court. His life was most remarkable in every sense. He rose to the top of the legal profession the old fashioned way – he earned it. He never graduated from college or from law school, but he became a legal scholar admired throughout the legal community.

After completing his limited education, Judge Hawkins learned shorthand and became a court reporter. He studied law on the side. Through his hard work and applied native intelligence, he learned quickly and became legal secretary to Court of Appeals Judge Frank Jenkins and then became a practicing lawyer. After successfully practicing law in Marietta for a number of years, he was appointed Judge of the Blue Ridge Judicial Circuit, which then included Cobb County, and was re-elected four times without opposition. In 1947, he was encouraged to offer himself for election in 1948 to fill a vacancy on the Georgia Supreme Court to succeed his mentor, Chief Justice Jenkins, who retired to teach at the Emory Law School. For the first time in his life, Judge Hawkins found himself engaged in a hotly contested race against Joe Quillian, well-known and politically connected lawyer from Winder. Joe Quillian was the clear favorite and was expected to win. But his lead was overcome by the hardworking and persistent Judge Hawkins who personally campaigned throughout the state. It was a close race, but Hawkins prevailed and became a legend on the Supreme Court where he served with great distinction and earned the affection and admiration of his peers until 1960 when he retired.

Judge Hawkins' life is the story of a truly self-made great man who gave his best and was rewarded for his fidelity and service by the love and appreciation of all who knew him. It is a great story and should be read by everyone interested in the life of an extraordinary public servant from Cobb County who succeeded against all odds. He remains an inspiration to all of us in the legal profession.

Judge Conley Ingram
Senior Judge, State of Georgia

PREFACE

In 1961 Justice Harold Hawkins had fully served his term as an Associate Justice on the Supreme Court of Georgia.

It is my desire to tell his story so that family and friends will remember him for what he was, a man whose life was an open book of unmistakable integrity. It was my good fortune to become a part of the Hawkins family upon my marriage to Ann Hawkins and to be close to this special man. I say *special* because I too believe everything he did as a citizen, a lawyer, a profound jurist, and a Christian was crowned with marvelous success.

It was my pleasure to have had the opportunity to spend time with the Judge and to listen to his wisdom regarding many subjects and most importantly subjects peculiar to his legal interests. It was especially a joyful experience to observe the twinkle in his eyes, his gentleness, his courage, his fidelity, and his unbridled love for his family. Judge Hawkins showed his Christian loyalty on the bench and in every facet of his life.

None of these qualities diminished his ability and determination to fearlessly make decisions that fairly and justly complied with the laws and the Constitution, to bring equal justice to all who came before him. An associate said that Judge Hawkins' obvious concern and consideration for any defendant would have moved a heart of stone. I am convinced more than ever that these characteristics are the criteria by which we judge a man's greatness. Though I consider it an honor to have had the privilege of assuming this challenge and compiling the facts as I remember them along with research of many matters, I can only wish that someone more qualified than I would have taken on this task.

I will never forget this wise and gentle man

David A. Dosser, Sr.

CONTENTS

CHAPTER ONE

IN THE BEGINNING

JUSTICE J. HAROLD HAWKINS
May 22, 1892 – June 8, 1961

Judge Harold Hawkins was a man dedicated to the administration of justice according to the highest ideals of fairness, impartiality, compassion, and firmness. As he raised himself from a simple stenographer at a small law firm to a seat on Georgia Supreme Court, his life mirrored those qualities. He was truly a self-made man, for his formal education was complete at about the eighth grade level.

The time of his birth was an important era in America. It was when Alexander Graham Bell had recently patented the telephone, electric lights were just becoming familiar to Americans, and the gasoline engine automobile was soon to be a popular means of transportation. At ever-increasing degrees, these events would forever change our lifestyles, our pace of life, and our conception of time, distance, and mobility. Benjamin Harrison was President of the United States and a depression was looming.

When their first son was due to arrive, Perry C. Hawkins and Della G. Bramblett, were married and living in Ball Ground, Georgia. As was common for young ladies at the time, Della went to her parents, Cicero Cronin Bramblett and Mary Thomas Bramblett, in Cumming, Georgia, for the birth of her first son. John Harold Hawkins was born on a Sunday morning May 22, 1892.

John Harold Hawkins' father, Perry C. Hawkins, a veteran of the Spanish-American War, was long engaged in the marble industry as a well respected master stonecutter. He worked for the Georgia Marble Company in North Georgia.

They later had three other children, all girls. These girls were Grace, Winifred, and Zillah. When the girls became adults, Grace married Preston Chaffin and lived in Barnesville, Georgia. Winifred married Albert Turner and lived in Atlanta, Georgia. Zillah was never married.

As long as he lived, their brother Harold was the mainstay in the lives of the girls. This was especially important to Zillah who was deaf. Compassionate as he was and sincerely loving all of his sisters, he soon learned sign language and was forever able to converse with his sister Zillah.

Both Harold's paternal and maternal antecedents were distinguished residents of Georgia.

His maternal grandfather was Cicero Cronin Bramblett, a lifetime resident and farmer in Forsyth County. He was married to Mary E. Thomas. Cicero was the second child of Riley and Margaret Bramblett. Until he got his degree, Cicero's brother, Martin Truman Bramblett, was a medical student who worked on the farm while going to

Atlanta Medical School (now a division of Emory University). When at school he took the train from Atlanta to Buford and walked to the farm. After receiving his medical degree and beginning his practice, Dr. Bramblett made house calls in his horse and buggy. He charged one dollar per call, and this included medicine.

Cicero and Mary Bramblett had eight children, one son and seven daughters, one of whom, Della, was Harold Hawkins' mother. Cicero and Mary lived on Bramblett Road (now Dr. Bramblett Road) in Cumming. When Cicero's mother died, Riley, his father, married Cinderella Bolin in 1860.

John Harold Hawkins' paternal grandfather was the Reverend Frederick (Fed) M. Hawkins, a prominent and distinguished Baptist minister who was first married to Elizabeth Brannon. This union was blessed with ten children. Upon the death of Elizabeth, he married her sister, Samantha Brannon, to whom twin boys were born, Perry C. and Berry C. Hawkins.

Reverend Frederick M. Hawkins is said to have founded and become the first pastor of the Friendship Baptist Church in Cumming. From 1861-1865, he was a member of the Georgia House of Representatives of Georgia from Forsyth County. He was also Justice, Inferior Court Forsyth County, from January 10, 1861 through January 23, 1865. The Hawkins and Brambletts were both pioneer families who played important roles in shaping the religious, political and business developments in North Georgia.

Jane Hawkins Ramsey, my sister-in-law, was familiar with the cemetery at the Friendship Baptist Church in Cumming. Jane, Ann, and I located the family gravesites of Frederick (Fed) Marshall Hawkins, his wives Elizabeth and Samantha, and other family members. Berry, the uncle of Harold, and his wife are buried in this cemetery but in another location near the entrance.

Rev. Frederick M. Hawkins held official positions in Forsyth County and the State of Georgia during the War Between the States. During this period the Union Armies destroyed many public records, and as a result records in many Georgia counties, including Forsyth and Cobb, where my primary research was done, are significantly limited.

In 1901, when he took office upon the assassination of President William McKinley, Theodore Roosevelt, not quite 43, became the youngest Chief Executive in history. This is when the Perry Hawkins family moved from Forsyth County to Cobb County, Marietta. Harold was just a young lad and still in grammar school. During his formative years, he attended the local public schools in Forsyth County and Marietta, Georgia.

As a youth living in Marietta on Powder Springs Street and attending Waterman Street School, Harold had a genuine aspiration to associate himself in some way with the legal profession. He wrote on January 15, 1930, to an uncle, H. G. Hawkins of Ballard & Ballard Co. in Lakeland, Florida, requesting more information on his grandfather, Frederick Hawkins. His grandfather, as mentioned earlier, was in the Georgia State Legislature, served as an Ordinary of Forsyth County, and was actively involved in Georgia politics all of his life. It is obvious that Harold was familiar with this family history. There is very little doubt this knowledge engendered his interest in the law and public service.

Waterman Street School began with the first grade and continued through the eighth grade. While at school, at the age of 12 or 13, he obtained employment as an office boy at the Kennesaw Paper Mill on Mill Street, which runs into the downtown square of Marietta. His work apparently was office work, sweeping floors, and general labor. He learned quickly that to succeed in anything it would be necessary for him to enhance his business skills.

Harold saved his money from his employment at the Kennesaw Paper Mill, and used these funds to go to the business school in Atlanta. Located on Mill Street one block from the town square, it was a short walk to work from his home on Powder Springs Street. After work each day, he would travel by streetcar to Draughon School in Atlanta where he learned the basics of business, including typing and stenography. He used the shorthand learned there to develop his own unique system, which was to serve him well in the years to come. Designed for his personal use, his shorthand system was so complex and intricate that it was of little value to almost anyone else. It was a system of shorthand using the basics of Graham-Pitmanic Shorthand not familiar to those who used the more popular Gregg Shorthand. Later his court law assistant, Harold Glore, learned to translate most of this shorthand notation, but at first it was necessary to ask the Sheriff of the Supreme Court, L. R. Waddey, who was familiar with Graham-Pitmanic, to read the shorthand notes if the Judge were not available.

On February 19, 1910, when he was only seventeen years old, Harold's mother, Della G. Bramblett Hawkins, died after having lived for only 36 years. As described in the local newspaper, the *Cobb County Times* on February 20, 1910:

Waterman Street School

Courtesy of Marietta Museum of History Archives

Kennesaw Paper Mill

Courtesy of Marietta Museum of History Archives

"This community was very much pained to learn of the death of Mrs. Della Hawkins, which occurred at her residence on Powder Springs Street, Saturday morning at ten o'clock. Mrs. Hawkins was thirty-six years old and was married to Mr. P. C. Hawkins at the age of sixteen. She was one of the most useful members of the First Baptist Church, was a persistent Sunday school worker, and was president of the Philathea class. In the death of Mrs. Hawkins the church sustained a great and irreparable loss. The funeral occurred at the First Baptist Church Monday afternoon at three o'clock. Rev. A. R. Bond, the pastor, made a beautiful and appropriate talk from the text, "And God shall wipe away every tear from their eyes."

A beautiful, tender and touching talk was made by Mr. R.H. Northcutt, teacher of the Philathea class, in which he told of the work of charity that Mrs. Hawkins was so much interested in. She leaves a husband, one son, Harold, and three daughters, Grace, Zilla and Winnie, a mother, father, six sisters and many friends to mourn her death".

Mrs. Hawkins was buried in the Citizens Cemetery on Powder Springs Street in Marietta. Perry Hawkins, father of Harold Hawkins, is also buried in this cemetery with Della.

In the 1910 census Harold Hawkins is shown as a "stenographer for law office" at the age of eighteen. The girls, of course, are shown as not employed.

Della Hawkins is not identified because she was not living at the time of the census. The census was taken April 18, 1910, while the family was living on Powder Springs Street in Marietta. Perry's occupation is shown as a "clerk at a furniture store." This obviously was not his choice of work.

During the economic depression a few months after Mrs. Hawkins died, Perry Hawkins moved to South Georgia with his daughters so he could accept work in his chosen profession as a stonecutter.

Harold, at eighteen, was determined to pursue his education and did not wish to move from Marietta. He wanted to continue his study at Draughon School in Atlanta. He also wished to continue his employment at the local paper mill in Marietta, as this would provide funds to pay for his school tuition.

George R. Edwards, a good friend, suggested that Harold temporarily stay with his family. Ms. Ella Edwards, George's mother, invited him to live at their family tourist home.

I have been unable to determine if the arrangement was a business arrangement at the tourist home or just a friendly agreement. It is a fact that "Miss Ella," always a loved and respected resident of Marietta, operated a tourist home. Knowing the close relationship of Harold and George, it was no doubt a favorable arrangement. Some years later, this friendship was manifested again when Harold asked George to be his best man at his wedding.

Blow-up of section covering Perry C. Hawkins, Harold, Grace, Zilla, and Winnie in the Thirteenth Census of The United States 1910-Population.

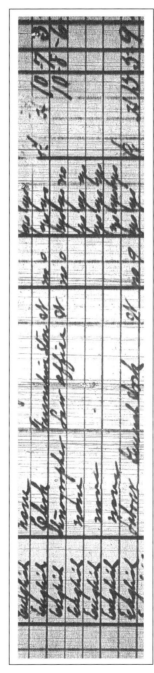

Harold Hawkins is shown as a "stenographer for law office" at the age of eighteen.

Harold's schooling in Marietta and at the Draughon School of Commerce in Atlanta was helpful in that it provided him with a good basic business education. He continued to read law on his own initiative, truly a self-educated man. Measured by present day standards, his formal education was brief and limited. Until his untimely death on June 8, 1961, he relent-

First Baptist Church

Courtesy of Marietta Museum of History Archives

lessly pursued his education through study and observation.

As Harold was growing up in Marietta, he worshiped at the First Baptist Church with his parents. He was regularly in attendance and volunteered to assist the church organist, Mrs. George Daniell, by manually turning the pump handle to fill the bellows with air needed to produce sounds from the pipe organ. With his great sense of humor, along with his proclivity and talent for story telling, he recalled many times how weary and exhausted he would become when "Miss Leila" would play loud and use low notes, which would demand strenuous efforts on his part.

Also during his youth Harold found time to study the violin with a local German violin teacher. He had no intention of playing seriously but became proficient enough that he was occasionally asked to play at the First Baptist Church for Sunday morning services. He enjoyed telling the story that he was ready and willing to perform, but each time it was announced that he was to play, someone would hide his violin.

Youthful Employment and Marriage

Harold Hawkins in the firm offices of Clay and Morris.

Judge Hawkins' files

Harold started his legal journey prior to 1910 when he began the quest that would be the focus of his professional life. He was employed as a legal stenographer by Clay and Morris, a local firm in Marietta. The partners in the law firm were Herbert Clay and Newton A. Morris. Their office was diagonally across the street from the courthouse on the second floor over Allen's Drug store. The 1910 census shows seventeen year-old Harold Hawkins as a stenographer in a law firm. In this photo the name Clay and Morris is on the door.

Shortly thereafter, having become familiar with legal matters and documents, Harold was reading law in the office of Clay and Morris. He would read law and study at every opportunity, night or day.

These experiences strengthened his ability as well as his desire to become an attorney. Morris very kindly permitted him the use of the firm's legal library. This was of great benefit to him in pursuing his mission to acquire the legal experience and knowledge needed to pass the Georgia bar examination.

In 1914 Harold Hawkins requested from the court that he be appointed commissioner to take testimony in and for the County of Cobb. The record of minutes for this date reflects the appointment that was approved by Judge H. G. Patterson. A digital reproduction of the original court record follows:

> Georgia
> Cobb County} To Honorable H L Patterson Judge of the
> Blue Ridge Circuit—
> The petition of J H Hawkins a resident of said County
> respectfully shows;
> First—
> That he desires to be appointed Commissioner to take
> testimony in and for the County of Cobb, and that he is
> Competent to fill said office
> Wherefore. petitioner prays That This Honorable Court
> appoint him as Such Commissioner—
> This 16ᵗʰ day of May 1914
> J H Hawkins
> Petitioner
> The above and foregoing read and Considered It is
> Ordered That J H Hawkins be. And he is hereby appointed
> Commissioner to take testimony in and for said County
> of Cobb for a term of four years from this date,
> It is So this Ordered That This Order be placed—

In the few years prior to the United States being involved in World War I, the Judge was courting a charming young lady by the name of Irene Northcutt. She was the daughter of E. H. Northcutt and Sallie Jane McClain Northcutt of Marietta.

Harold and Irene were both active in the local First Baptist Church

and it was here they first became friends. His faith was a true calling focused through his devotion of his grandfather, Baptist minister, F. M. Hawkins, and the love and respect for his mother, Della G. Bramblett Hawkins. Harold felt a strong loyalty to his faith and Church.

Harold and Irene (left) frolicking during joyful and happy courting days.

The Marietta News

Motto: 'Principles Above Men'
Marietta Ga., April 19, 1914

Northcutt–Hawkins

An interesting event of Wednesday evening April 22 will be the wedding of Miss Irene Northcutt (Right) and Mr. Harold Hawkins, which will be solemnized at the First Baptist Church.

Miss Northcutt will have as her maid of honor Miss Mary Marston of Augusta, and her Matron Mrs. H. Grady Conway of Atlanta and the bridesmaids will be Miss Pauline Collins, Miss Edna Barrett of Acworth and Miss Willie May Blair. Mr. George Edwards will be best man, and the groomsmen will be Col. William Holland, Mr. Norman Collins and Mr. Alvin Smith of Atlanta, and the ushers will include Mr. Ralph Northcutt, Mr. Carl Butler, Col. Lindley Camp and Mr. H. Grady Conway of Atlanta. Sarah Frances and Elizabeth Northcutt nieces of the bride will be flower girls and her little brother Douglas ring bearer.

After a courtship of several years, Irene and Harold were married on Wednesday, April 22, 1914, at the First Baptist Church in Marietta. Following the wedding they traveled to Daytona Beach, Florida, by train for their honeymoon. Upon their return, they stayed with Irene's parents on Church Street in Marietta.

Jane Hawkins Ramsey was born on February 13, 1918. Soon thereafter the Judge built a house on the east side of Church Street two doors from the Northcutt home, and in this house Elizabeth Ann Hawkins Dosser was born on November 13, 1925.

Although the houses were painted white until recently, only minor changes have taken place in the many years they have existed. In the early years, flower gardens and vegetable gardens were always found around these houses.

Northcutt family home is where the Judge and Irene lived following their wedding and after returning from Daytona Beach, Florida.

The first house built and owned by Judge Hawkins (above) is on Church Street in Marietta. It is two doors south of Northcutt home, and across the stree from his final home.

APPOINTMENT AS COURT RECORDER AND PASSING THE BAR

Harold Hawkins' preparation and after-hours late night studies paid off. At the close of the adjourned term of the Cobb Superior Court on January 26, 1915, the Honorable H. L. Patterson, Judge, passed an order appointing J. H. Hawkins to the position of official stenographer and reporter of the Blue Ridge Circuit. The official minutes of the Superior Court of Cobb County are as follows:

Georgia, Cobb County:
January 26th, 1915

It is now hereby ordered that J. Harold Hawkins of said County be, and he is hereby appointed Stenographer and Court Reporter in and for Superior Courts of the Blue Ridge Judicial Circuit, composed of the Counties, of Cobb, Milton, Forsyth, Cherokee, Pickens, Gilmer and Fannin, to hold said position until the further order of the Court. This order to become effective on the 15th, day of February 1915.

Let this order be entered upon the minutes of the Superior Court of Cobb County, and recorded together with the oath of said appointee.
H. L. Patterson,
Judge Superior Courts, B.R.C.

It is now, at three o'clock P.M., Ordered in open Court, that the present session of the Court, take a recess until February 6th, 1915.
Signed, in open Court, this the 26th day of January 1915.
H. L. Patterson,
Judge Superior Courts, B.R.C.

The following article appeared in the *Cobb County Times* in 1915 regarding this appointment.

Cobb County Times
1915

> Mr. Hawkins is the youngest court recorder in Georgia, being only twenty-two years of age, and when the important duties of the office, and the enormous amount of work connected with it are considered, his appointment is an exceedingly high compliment to him. He is a young man of sterling worth, honesty and sobriety, and is regarded by those who know him as one of the best stenographers and typists ever seen in this section of the country.

When Judge H. L. Patterson left the court, he was replaced by Judge N. A. Morris as the Superior Court Judge of the Blue Ridge Circuit. During a special session of the court on January 1917, Judge Morris re-appointed J. H. Hawkins as Court Stenographer and Court Reporter. The minutes of the special session are on the following page.

He served in this position on the Blue Ridge Circuit in the Northern section of Georgia until September 1, 1917.

Throughout the years as court recorder for the Blue Ridge Circuit, from January 26, 1915 until September 1, 1917, Harold continued to read law and study law while working at the firm of Clay and Morris in Marietta. He studied law at night in his spare hours and utilized his every talent and opportunity to prepare himself for being admitted to the Bar. Judge Morris supported his aspirations, and Harold's plans and dreams came to fruition when he took the necessary actions to apply for and be admitted to the Georgia Bar on December 26, 1916.

The procedure by which Harold Hawkins was admitted to the bar was considerably different from the methods used today. The qualifications to become an attorney have changed radically over time. Dr. James A Hunt, Professor at Mercer University, wrote an article on February 22, 2005, in the *New Georgia Encyclopedia* regarding procedures for being admitted to the bar in Georgia.

Minutes, *January Special* Term, 191*7*, Cobb Superior Court.

In Re, J. H. Hawkins

*Cobb Superior Court
January Special Term.*

Georgia, Cobb County.

It is hereby ordered that J. H. Hawkins of said County, be, and he is hereby appointed Stenogr. and Court Reporter in and for the Superior Courts of the Blue Ridge Judicial Circuit, Composed of the Counties of Cobb, Milton, Forsythe, Cherokee, Pickens, Gilmer, and Fannin.

Let this order, together with the Oath of said appointee, be recorded upon the Minutes Cobb Superior Court.

Granted in Open Court, this the 2. day of January, 1917

N. A. Morris
J.S.C. = B.R.C.

Georgia, Cobb County.

I, J. H. Hawkins, do Solemnly Swear that I will, to the Best of my Ability, faithfully perform all of the duties devolving upon myself as Stenographer and Court Reporter in and for the Blue Ridge Judicial Circuit, So help me God.

J. H. Hawkins

Sworn to and Subscribed before me, in Open Court, this the 20th, day of January 1917,

N. A. Morris
Judge Supr. Court, B.R.C.

Minutes of the special session of the court on January 1917 reappointing Harold Hawkins stenographer and court reporter.

The Georgia General Assembly decided in 1789 that an oral examination by a superior court judge and evidence of "moral rectitude" were sufficient barriers. Georgia's lax approach contributed to a rising population of lawyers, who numbered 1168 in 1860. During the Civil War the General Assembly imposed new restrictions. Applicants had to possess state citizenship and good moral character. They were required to have "read law" for some unspecified time and to pass an oral examination in superior court that covered English law in force in Georgia, pleading and evidence, equity, the codes of the state and the Confederacy, and local practice rules. The law limited membership to the "white male citizen." Similar requirements persisted for most of the nineteenth century.

In addition to the kind assistance of Dr. James A. Hunt at Mercer University, John M. Perkins, Reference Service Librarian at the Furman Smith Law Library, researched the methods by which attorneys were admitted to the bar from 1910 until 1933. Mr. Perkins found and copied the applicable Georgia Code. Following are excerpts that were in effect at the time Harold Hawkins was admitted to the bar on December 26, 1916.

The Georgia Bar Association, an organization of attorneys formed in 1883, pressed for higher admission standards. The association's efforts produced laws in the 1890s that required a written examination. The General Assembly undercut the examination's potential when they allowed diploma privileges, which allowed graduates of a law school authorized by the state to be admitted without examination.

In 1910 the Georgia Legislature changed the code for attorneys being admitted to the bar and there were no amendments to the law between 1911 and 1916 except that women were allowed to become members of the Bar in 1916, a significant addition.

Georgia Code
1916

§4931. ATTORNEYS ADMITTED TO THE SUPERIOR COURTS: Those who are admitted to practice in the superior courts may practice in any other court of this State, except the Supreme Court, for which another and special license must be obtained.

§ 4934. APPLICATION AND CERTIFICATE: Any male person desiring to become a member of the bar of this State shall make a written application to a Judge of any superior court, accompanying the application with a certificate from two practicing members of the bar of the State of Georgia as to his moral character, and those certifying to such character shall further state in said certificate that they have examined the applicant upon the various branches of the law and deem him qualified for admission to the practice of the law. The certificate of character and qualification shall be sealed with the number assumed by the applicant, so that said name shall not be disclosed until after the grading of such examination.

§ 4935. TOPICS AND SUBJECTS OF THE EXAMINATION: The applicant must be examined touching his knowledge ...
Of the principles of the common and statute law of England, of force in this State.
Of the law of pleading and evidence.
The principles of equity, and equity pleading and practice.
The Revised Code of this State, the Constitution of the United States and of this State, and the rules of practice in the superior courts.

§ 4936. BOARD OF EXAMINERS: It shall be the duty of the Justices of the Supreme Court to appoint a board of three examiners, designating one of their number as its chairman, whose powers and duties shall be as herein after declared, and the members of which shall be learned and experienced attorneys at law of generally recognized ability and integrity.

§ 4940. EXAMINATION OF APPLICANTS: Each applicant, except as provided in section 4942 shall submit to an examination in writing, which shall be prepared by the board of examiners, covering all the topics and subjects a knowledge of which is, under existing laws, requisite to admission to the bar. Said board shall pass upon the merits of each examination, and as to each applicant determine whether or not he is qualified to plead and practice in the several courts of this State other than the Supreme Court, admission to bar of which shall be governed by existing laws.

All examinations of applicants shall, in accordance with said rules, be conducted under the supervision of the judges of the respective superior courts. Each applicant shall sign his examination paper by number and in a sealed envelope accompanying said paper, shall state the number he has adopted, so that his name shall not be known until after the board of examiners have passed upon the question of his admission or rejection.

§4942. EXAMINATIONS NOT REQUIRED: This law shall not apply to those who have received diplomas from any law school of this State authorized to issue diplomas to students of law, nor shall it apply to those admitted to the practice of law in other States which by comity admit to the practice the duly licensed lawyers of this State.

The above section regarding (diploma privileges) was not abolished until the code was amended 1933.

CHARTER FOUR

Judge Jenkins,
Private Practice and Judgeship

Cherokee Advance
Canton, Ga., 1917

Hawkins Has Resigned Post

Mr. Harold Hawkins, who has been reporter for the courts of the Blue Ridge Circuit for the past several years, has resigned. He will become private secretary to Judge Jenkins of the Court of Appeals at his office in the State Capital building in Atlanta.

Mr. Hawkins is an unusually efficient stenographer and before becoming court reporter was private secretary to Solicitor General Hebert Clay. He is well qualified for this important position and his selection will be a source of much joy among his numerous friends in Marietta and throughout the Blue Ridge Circuit.

The above announce-ment will come as a great surprise to Mr. Hawkins' many friends in Chero-kee County. Col. Harold Hawkins is a fine young man and has any number of friends in Canton who will regret to know that he will not be in attendance upon our courts, but will learn with much interest that his new duties are as a great promotion in life.

Harold Hawkins was secretary to Judge W.F. Jenkins of the Court of Appeals.

> The Advance feels that Col. Hawkins is equal to the occasion and that he will make good in his new duties.

Following his success as the Court Reporter for the Blue Ridge Circuit, the Judge resigned this position in 1917 when he was appointed Secretary to Judge W. F. Jenkins, Judge of the Court of Appeals of Georgia. Harold Hawkins was 25 years old at the time. Judge Jenkins became his friend and mentor and later became Chief Justice of the Georgia Supreme Court. This experience as assistant to Judge Jenkins was invaluable to Harold as he developed skills needed to advance his career. Photo was in September 1935 *Atlanta Georgian*.

A short excerpt from a memorial for J. Harold Hawkins prepared by Robert B. Troutman and presented to the Georgia Supreme Court serves to chronicle the Justice Hawkins' early career. The memorial testament is signed by many distinguished Georgia friends and associates who honored J. Harold Hawkins' courage and perseverance.

> His training for admission to the Bar was likewise informal. He could not afford to attend a law school, but he studied law at night and in his spare hours and was admitted to the bar in 1916. His subsequent career demonstrates how he utilized his every talent and opportunity to prepare himself for his great career as a Member of this Court.
>
> He became secretary to Judge W. Frank Jenkins of the Court of Appeals of Georgia, later Chief Justice of this Court. What an opportunity it was for this neophyte to learn at the feet of one of Georgia's great lawyers and judges the lessons which every truly successful lawyer and judge must learn: industry, integrity, selfless devotion to the cause of truth and justice. He was an apt pupil. Well did he learn not only the principles and rules of substantive law, but also the means of applying them to the case at hand, under orderly procedure.

A. J. Henderson, Sr.	Henry G. Neal	Leon Boling
B. H. Chappell	Herman E. Talmadge	Louie D. Newton
Ben F. Carr	Hubert R. Edmondson	Luther C. Hames, Jr.
Carl N. Nelson	J. C. Davis	Phil M. Landrum
L. M. Blair	J. G. Roberts	R. Carter Pittman
Charles J. Bloch	J. Henderson, Jr.	R. Wilson Smith Jr.

Charles L. Gowen
Claude Joiner Jr.
E. T. Averett
Edwin A. McWhorter
F. M. Bird
Frederick Kennedy
Garvis L. Sams
Grady G. Vandivier
H.B. Troutman Sr.
Harold M. Walker
Hatton Lovejoy

J. Hines Wood
J. Lon Duckworth
James Maddox
James R. Shaw
James T. Manning
John L. Tye Jr.
John P. Cheney
John S. Wood
John W. Davis
Konts Bennett
L. Harold Glore

R. Wilson Smith, Jr.
R.A. Bell
Ronald F. Chance
Sam P. Burtz
Scott S. Edwards, Jr.
Shuler Antley
T. Baldwin Martin
T. H. Crawford
Vance Custer
William Butt

Respectfully submitted
Robert B. Troutman

Harold continued as secretary to Judge Jenkins until March 1, 1920. He then resigned to become engaged in active practice of law. He was associated with Newton A. Morris, who was considered by many as having one of the best legal minds in Georgia. Judge Morris had just retired as Judge of the Blue Ridge Circuit, and this presented an opportunity for Harold to practice law with a retired judge. Harold Hawkins signed a contract to work with Judge Morris for two years.

The law firm was located near the courthouse in Marietta. This short-term contract led to the firm known as Morris, Hawkins and Wallace. The partners in the firm were Newt A. Morris, (right), J. Harold Hawkins and Campbell Wallace. Campbell Wallace was the son-in-law of Georgia Governor Nat Harris. Harold practiced law in Marietta for eleven years, from March 1, 1920, to 1931, after which the firm was dissolved. The practice took him into all counties within the Blue Ridge Circuit and beyond. During part of the time he served as County Attorney for Cobb County and presented cases in the Appellate Courts, including the Georgia Supreme Court. On May 1, 1920, Harold Hawkins was admitted to practice as an Attorney and Counselor at Law in the District Court of the United States for the Fifth Judicial Circuit, Northern District of Georgia.

Judge Hawkins' Files

Authorization to appear and practice in Fifth Judicial Circuit Court.

On December 31, 1931, L. G. Hardeman, Governor of Georgia, sent a commission to Marietta, appointing J. H. Hawkins Judge of Superior Courts of the Blue Ridge Circuit effective March 1, 1931. He would succeed the Hon. John S. Wood, who had been elected to Congress as the representative of the Ninth Georgia District. Judge Hawkins was selected to fill Judge Wood's unexpired term, which ended January 1, 1933. The appointment of the Judge was received with a great deal of enthusiasm by the people of the counties and was reported accordingly by local newspapers. He felt at home with the Superior Courts of the Blue Ridge Circuit as he had been associated with these courts for years as the court recorder and handled cases in the courts either alone or in association with his partners in Morris, Hawkins and Wallace. It speaks well that he was re-elected to the position as Superior Court Judge of the Blue Ridge Circuit four times without opposition.

Hawkins swearing in as Blue Ridge Judicial Circuit Superior Court Judge.

Judge Hawkins' Files

Cobb County Times
January 1, 1931

Judge J. M. Gann, Ordinary, is shown swearing in Judge J. Harold Hawkins as Judge of the Blue Ridge Judicial Circuit Superior Court. Judge Hawkins was sworn in December 26 to fill the unexpired term of Judge John S. Wood. In the picture with Judge Hawkins are Mrs. Hawkins and two children, Jane and Ann Hawkins. Judge J. M. Gann above was the great-uncle of Harold Glore who later became the Law Assistant to Justice Harold Hawkins during his entire tenure on the Georgia Supreme Court.

On the same day, January 1, 1931, Judge Hawkins was sworn in as Judge of the Superior Courts of the Blue Ridge Circuit, an article appeared in *THE FOUR-COUNTY POST* in Acworth that forecast the coming of the distressing economic disaster of 1930s. The heading read as follows: "S. Lemon Bank Co. fails to open doors Friday. One of Oldest Banks in Georgia Goes Under as Result of Non-Payment of Loans Made." It was apparent that farmers who had made loans to "tide them over" were unable to repay the loans because they could not sell their crops for enough money to service their debts. This phenomenon was all too frequent throughout the country during the following dreadful years of the Depression while the Judge was serving on the Blue Ridge Circuit.

Following is a brief history of the Circuit Court to which Judge Hawkins had just been appointed. An article explaining the history is by Fred D. Bentley, Sr. and Lawrence B. Custer for the Cobb County Bar Association, Inc. entitled, "The Origins Of The Cobb Judicial Circuit Bar Association."

> The Blue Ridge Judicial Circuit was created by an Act of the Georgia Legislature on November 24, 1851. Originally the Blue Ridge Circuit included eleven counties: Campbell, Carroll, Cherokee, Cobb, Forsyth, Gilmer, Lumpkin, Milton, Paulding, Polk, and Union. By 1853 there were 63 lawyers who actively maintained offices in the Circuit, of which 18 were in Cobb County, all in Marietta. Cobb County was included in the Circuit until January 1, 1953, at which time Cobb became a separate unit known as the Cobb Judicial Circuit.
>
> Cobb County, prior to 1953, supplied many able attorneys to the operation of the Blue Ridge Circuit for both Judges and Solicitors General (i.e., District Attorneys). All officials elected or appointed to the Blue Ridge Circuit made outstanding contributions.

Further research reveals that Judge J. Harold Hawkins was honored to serve as the first President of The Blue Ridge Bar Association, created in 1933. The counties included in the Blue Ridge Circuit while Judge Hawkins served on the circuit were Cobb, Milton, Cherokee, Pickens, Gilmer, Fannin, and Forsyth. Milton County was on the Blue Ridge Circuit until 1932 when along with Roswell, it became part of Fulton County.

While the Judge was holding court in the northern counties of the Blue Ridge Circuit, he would make every effort to see that his court convene at the appropriate time and in accordance with the laws. At that time, twice each year, it was necessary for him to hold court in each of the counties that composed the Blue Ridge Circuit. Although it was not unusual for some of these northern counties to have snow or ice storms, he traveled by car as a general rule.

A friend, Judge Watson White, of the Cobb County Superior Court, remembers that in inclement weather it was necessary for the Judge to arrange for his retinue of lawyers, court reporter, solicitors, and equipment to be transported from Marietta to Atlanta by streetcar. There they would board a train from Atlanta to Buford where they could rent a hack for transportation to the county seat. Judge Hawkins used the same train to get to court in inclement weather that his great-uncle, Martin Truman Bramblett, had used a generation earlier. The court could then be in session, on time and on schedule. Swaying and bouncing, for a one-way trip the streetcar ride to Atlanta took about one hour, and made many stops between Marietta and Atlanta. It is sad that it no longer exists.

Courtesy of Marietta Museum of History

A letter on January 1, 1931, responding to a congratulatory letter from Harold Glore, even before sitting on the bench for the first time, Judge Hawkins expresses his dedication to equal justice. He states: "I, of course, realize the responsibilities devolving upon one who undertakes to fill this office and my earnest desire is that I may be able to discharge them with fairness and impartiality. I shall strive to do so." As you will see, this belief was dominant throughout the tenure of his chosen profession.

Cobb County Times, in March, 1931, reports on the appointment of J. Harold Hawkins to be Superior Court Judge of the Blue Ridge Circuit. It was reported: "the appointment of Mr. Hawkins as judge was received with a great deal of enthusiasm by the people of this county who hold the new judge in high esteem." It also included the facts regarding his legal career prior to being appointed, with information regarding his being secretary to Judge Jenkins on the Court of Appeals and his eleven years in private practice as a partner with Morris, Hawkins and Wallace. The *Cobb County Times* observed that he was appointed just fourteen years after being admitted to the bar in 1916.

Below is an additional article regarding Judge Hawkins' first term of court in Cobb County on March 12, 1931. Before coming to the Cobb County Superior Court, he already had handled eighty trials in other counties of the circuit. It was an exciting time for him. A large crowd was present to hear him charge the Grand Jury.

COBB COUNTY TIMES
March 12, 1931

Large Crowd At Opening Court Session Monday
Judge Hawkins Delivered Lengthy Charge to Grand Jury.
Prayer by Rev. Patton

Judge Harold Hawkins was greeted by a large crowd Monday morning when he opened his first court in Marietta. Stating that he knew of no one who needed the "Divine guidance more than a judge," he asked Rev. Patton to open the court with a prayer. It has been some time since this custom was in practice but Judge Hawkins said he felt that it should be done as our forefathers had always opened their court sessions with a prayer.

Following the prayer and regular routine of court procedure, Judge Hawkins made his charge to the jury. It was longer than the usual charge of the judge to his jurymen and in it he told of his idea of enforcement of law. He placed special emphasis on the prosecution of violators of the Prohibition law. Stating that while many of us might not be in accord with the law, never the less it was a law of the land and he felt sure the majority of the people were in sympathy with the amendment.

Judge Hawkins has handled the cases which have appeared before him quickly and efficiently. About 80 cases have been taken care of since the opening of the court Monday. The majority of the cases are small civil suits which have either been dismissed or settled for judgment. A few persons have plead guilty to various minor charges and have been sentenced. The new judge states that he will give out no suspended sentences but that he will parole a man, but if he sentences him he will have to serve the sentence.

During his seventeen years on the Blue Ridge Circuit, the Judge presided over many interesting trials. Most were the usual variety of cases, but some were more exciting and attracted the attention of the press. During his first year on the bench, one murder trial attracted statewide attention.

The Marietta Journal
Marietta, Ga. November 19, 1931

George Goumas Found Guilty, is Given Life Sentence

George Goumas, a former Marietta butcher, was found guilty and given a life sentence Tuesday for the murder of Doyle P. Butler in Marietta on June 3 of this year. Goumas had been denied a change of venue and the trial was called in Cobb County Superior Court Tuesday. Judge Hawkins allowed as many spectators in the room as could be comfortably accommodated without interfering with the progress of the trial. Hundreds had to be turned away because there was no further room. Former Judge John S. Wood in the prosecution assisted Solicitor General George D. Anderson. The trouble started, it is believed, when Goumas was questioned about a stolen automobile from the Forrester Motor Company by local officers, in which he was said to have been seen on Sunday before Wednesday, the day of the murder.

Eyewitnesses testified that Goumas came to the Forrester Motor Company on Atlanta Street and asked for Mr. Forester; when told that Mr. Forrester was out, Goumas turned and called to Doyle Butler, manager of the firm, who was standing outside the Forrester Company office talking with a salesman. As Butler neared the door through which Goumas had called to him, witnesses said, Goumas drew a gun and fired. Butler reeled and fell from the sidewalk to the street, struggling to his hands and knees. Goumas rushed out as Butler tried to regain his feet, saying, "$^#D* you, Doyle, don't you go nowhere," pointed his gun at Butler and fired again. Butler made his way across the street and passing through a filling station he called to Mr. Hurt, operator of the station, to "stop him, he shot me." Hurt started toward Goumas, who was following Butler across the street, calling to him not to shoot again. According to Hurt, Goumas replied: "I will kill him if it is the last thing I do." Hurt replied, "You have already killed him." Goumas then got into an automobile in which there was no key. Hurt told him to get out and go home, that he was in serious trouble. Goumas got out of the car and started down Atlanta Street toward his home. Deputy Sheriff Jack Miller, who had responded to a call, walked down the street with Goumas to his home, where he finally secured his gun before the arrival of Sheriff Sanders and Deputy Algood.

Goumas was taken into custody and carried to Fulton county jail. Butler was carried to the Marietta Hospital and died about eleven p.m. George Goumas read a prepared statement to the jury in which he claimed he had suffered mental lapses from shell shock received during his services with the American Army in France. The statement was not under oath and no witness was introduced to substantiate any of his claims.

The case was given to the jury about 3:30 and a verdict of guilty with recommendation for mercy of the court was reported by the jury about 8:30 after the jury requested and received a recharge regarding insanity laws. Judge Hawkins received the jury's verdict as soon as the jury had announced it and sentence was immediately imposed on Goumas. Goumas was given a life sentence. Augustus F. Lee of Atlanta, L.M. Blair and S. J. Welsh of Marietta defended Goumas. Blair and Welsh were appointed by Judge Hawkins to assist Lee.

WILLIE WHITE, DEATH PENALTY AND ANECDOTES

Judge Hawkins in his office in the Cobb County Courthouse. Circa 1938.

While he was Judge of the Superior Court of Cobb County, there were neither State Court Judges nor Juvenile Court Judges. These cases were all tried in the Superior Court. For the duration of his terms on the Blue Ridge Circuit, his salary did not exceed $6000 per year, and this was in middle of the 1940s. He did not receive supplements from the counties.

My wife Ann (right) remembers a time when she was a child and the family was sitting on the front porch as a prison work gang passed by their home on Church Street. Many of the prisoners yelled and waved greetings to the Judge and seemed to enjoy it. Ann told her father that this was frightening to her and asked if he were afraid. He responded, "No, each of them knows they re-

29

ceived equal justice in my court and a fair trial." Again equal justice of the law was foremost on his mind.

Jane Ramsey, older daughter of the Judge, remembers the times when she would be practicing her typing in the office of her father. She had no typewriter at home and would use the office machine. His office was across from the Sheriff's office where many exciting events occurred. When the Sheriff had "captured" a bootlegger, he would bring the car to a point behind the jail just below the window of the office. At each occurrence, a real spectacle would ensue as the Sheriff's deputies would find the concealed bottles of whiskey, break them, and pour the contents into the drain. It was always a well-attended event as word got around the courthouse. Some bystanders were often seen with cups.

The trial of John Willie White, a Negro who was accused of killing two white men, attracted much attention of the news media in 1934.

In the 1930s the Ku Klux Klan was active in the Atlanta, Georgia, area, and it was a sight to watch when they frequently marched up Church Street in Marietta, Georgia on their way to burn a cross on top of Kennesaw Mountain. The location was a couple of miles from the square in Marietta, Georgia, and the burning cross could be seen for miles. Because of the nature of this double murder, it would not have been unusual for the Klan to create trouble of some kind. There was none.

Following the trial Judge Hawkins made a statement to the press regarding the reaction of the citizens of Marietta, Georgia.

The Cobb County Times
1934

Judge Commends Cobb Countians

"I am proud of the people of Cobb County," said Judge J. H. Hawkins Tuesday afternoon, when the murder trial of John Willie White was completed.

"Though the courthouse was crowded, perfect order was maintained throughout the trial", Judge Hawkins said. He emphasized the fact that it was only through the cooperation of the people and county officials that White was given a fair and decent trial.

The court room doors were locked during the trial, and only people who could find room to sit in the court room were allowed entrance. Guards were placed at each entrance as a precautionary measure, but there was no need for this as all went on quietly.

Shortly thereafter the newspaper wrote another article concerning the trial. This article is presented below.

The Cobb County Times
1934

The County of Cobb has a right to be proud of its judicial authorities for the intelligent fashion in which the trial of one John Willie White, Negro, was conducted Tuesday in superior court. The charge against the Negro was murder—in fact, the brutal murder of two white men—but the court viewed the case in the same calm and dispassionate manner with which it ordinarily handles even lesser cases. Attorneys for the defense and for the state were more than ordinarily careful in making out their cases. The prosecution indulged in very little appeal to emotion or prejudice, but built their evidence on facts from the mouths of many witnesses. The defense, by cross-examination of witnesses and by the defendant's own unsworn statement, fulfilled their duties as counsel in a worthy and creditable manner. The trial stands out as a shining example of intelligently administered justice. The crowd was not allowed to show any disposition to upset the dignity of the courtroom by unseemly demonstration. Quietness and respect dominated the atmosphere. When the verdict was brought in, there was no show of emotion from anyone. Scarcely an expression changed, for every one who had been in the courtroom was impressed with the seriousness of the task which the machinery of law was doing.

The Judge pronounced the sentence—death—after allowing the defendant his opportunity for a statement. The doomed man was led out between two officers and it was all over. The audience remained still and subdued until the judge calmly excused them.

> *The Times* commends Judge J. H. Hawkins and officers of the court for the able and dignified manner in which they handled the trial and wrote into the history of justice in this county a glowing page. Would that such steady hands always hold the scales of justice.

John Will White was executed December 12, 1935, in Milledgeville.

Until 1862 the Georgia death penalty for murder was mandatory. Unless the sentence was reversed by the courts or commuted by the governor, everyone convicted of murder received a death sentence and was executed. Then, in 1863, the Georgia Code of 1861 went into effect, including provisions making capital punishment for murder discretionary. A person convicted of murder could now receive a life sentence instead of a death sentence, but only if the jury so recommended.

The two most important decisions in any capital case were made by the solicitor, (district attorney), who was most always a white man. The solicitor decided whether to seek the death penalty and, if death were sought, whether to withdraw a notice to seek death as part of a negotiated plea disposition. Often the decision of the solicitor reflected the prosecutor's and the community's prejudices.

Judge Hawkins said many times that sentencing anyone to the death penalty was the most difficult responsibilities of any judge. Attitudes of citizens at that time were different from today. In recent years many laws have been applied for the protection of minorities, including racially mixed juries, which have been put in place to address the problem. This will not preclude the race factor but will at least alleviate it considerably.

For the eighteen years Judge Hawkins was Judge of the Blue Ridge Circuit there were 236 death sentences carried out in Georgia. In the six counties of the Blue Ridge Circuit there were 7 death sentences carried out, including John Will White.

Some interesting facts are found in a January 2004 report prepared for the State of Georgia Department of Corrections by the Office of Planning and Analysis. A brief review of this report is as follows:

From 1735 to 1924 the legal method of execution in Georgia was hanging. The sheriff in the county or judicial circuit where the crime was committed carried out the execution. The first person believed legally executed in Colonial Georgia was a woman, Alice Ryley. She was hanged for the murder of her master Will Wise. A male accomplice was hanged the next day. I presume they were not white. The last legal execution by hanging occurred on May 20, 1925, when Gervis Bloodworth and Willie Jones, both white males, were hanged in Columbus, Georgia for murder. The execution was transferred to Columbus because the condemned claimed that the hanging would be public. The law at that time provided for non-public executions. An agreement to move the execution was made because people could stand on the roof of the drug store in Butler, Georgia, and see the gallows.

On August 16, 1924, an act of the Georgia General Assembly abolished death by hanging and substituted death by electrocution. Electrocutions were then to be held at one location.

The first electric chair was installed at the Georgia State Prison in Milledgeville, Georgia, in 1924 where 162 death sentences were carried out. The electric chair remained at the Milledgeville facility until January 1, 1938. It was then moved to the new Georgia State Prison in Reidsville, Georgia. A total of 256 executions took place in Reidsville with the last execution occurring on October 16, 1964. In 1964 the U.S. Supreme Court suspended all executions in the United States that allowed persons convicted of certain crimes, such as rape, to be executed. At this time twenty-one states had mandatory death for murder. Georgia did not.

The Georgia General Assembly passed a new death sentence law that went into effect on March 28, 1973. On July 2, 1976, the U. S. Supreme Court upheld the new death penalty in Georgia as constitutional.

In June, 1980 the electric chair was moved to the Georgia Diagnostic and Classification Prison in Jackson, Ga. A new chair was constructed. This facility was used until May 1, 2000.

On October 5, 2001, the Georgia Supreme Court ruled that the electric chair was unconstitutional and was cruel and unusual punishment. Lethal injection became the legal method of execution for all inmates under the death sentence. The Board of Pardons and Paroles continues to have authority to grant a commutation to life or give a pardon to any inmate on death row.

Regarding the character of Judge Hawkins, a number of anecdotes illustrate well his personality and his conduct on the judicial bench.

Most judges spent much time in community activities, especially Judge Hawkins, as he was well known on the circuit, especially in the Marietta area. This article is similar to many such stories originating in the press.

The Marietta Journal
February 6, 1936

It must be great to have as many friends as Judge Harold Hawkins. Yesterday when the news reached Marietta that the judge had been injured in an auto accident en route to Cumming in company with Grady Vandiviere, everybody got busy with the telephone to see what they could find out.

The telephone company put on extra operators and then couldn't handle the calls. The Journal was besieged with calls to find out how bad the injuries were and where the judge was and where they could get in touch with him.

It was the big news of the day. The birth of the Dionne quintuplets or the Italo-Ethiopian war news held no such place in the sun, locally speaking, as the news that Judge Hawkins had been injured in an auto wreck.

The judge is at least able to smile this morning at the Marietta Hospital where he is holding public reception to his many friends and admirers, and that isn't all. The nurses are sending out SOS calls for more vases to hold the flowers that are coming in to the Judge; the telegrams are pouring in and they do say that his wife is standing close by, as many of the visits are from members of the fair sex.

Jimmy Carmichael was one of the first to wire and to this effect: "Haven't time to stand in line tonight to see you. Harvey Carpenter says nurses are admitting only Baptists tonight, so that lets me out. By the way, I don't want to hear of you making eyes with any of the nurses. I claim that privilege since I'm single.

The Marietta Journal
Marietta, GA. May 17, 1937

Marietta Shop Talk
By Earl Watson

If I am guilty of contempt of court, here's where I start running right now.

I am seeking a mandatory injunction against that charming gentleman, JUDGE J. HAROLD HAWKINS, to forbid him ever referring to his decidedly distinguished features as "this ugly mug of mine" again.

The judge did that again the other night after addressing the meeting of city mail carriers of North Georgia. You could hear the good ladies buzz in positive amazement as our esteemed jurist made this self-effacing remark.

The lady next to me tittered, sotto voice: "It's no such thing. He's down right distinguished looking."

Now, Judge, I may rate a bench warrant on this one. But here goes.

You have all the distinction of appearance of Al (I'll take a walk) Smith, and you have got something that he has not got.

While you squirm in what must be tougher on your innate modesty than any legal business you ever digested, I add: You have a twinkle in your eye that gives you more personal charm than the Smith boy ever dreamed of.

So if that bailiff starts out looking for me tonight, I too am "taking a walk."

Yep, Ole "Lese Majeste" they used to call us down by the city incinerator.

And hereby a general demurrer is filed to your statement, Judge, that most people expect a jurist to "be a big,
robust somebody." I seem to remember that Mr. Justice
Louis Brandeis is not a heavy weight.

Judge Hawkins recalled an incident that occurred in his office
shortly after his appointment.

A hard-bitten fellow called by and sweeping the admittedly
light but wiry form of our eminent jurist with a skepti-
cal eye wondered with ill-concealed doubt: "Are you the
- - the - -Judge?" Still with that infectious twinkle of the
eye, Judge Hawkins admitted his identity. The astounded
fellow gaped. "Well, all I can say is, if I had been sent out
with orders to shoot the judge, you would have been entirely safe!

CHARTER SIX

SMYRNA RACE RIOT

There was a disheartening incident on Monday, October 17, 1938, that attracted national and international attention by the press.

On Saturday October 16, 1938, an African American, 31 year- old Willie Drew Russell, a construction worker, was suspected of killing George Camp, a farmer, and the farmer's 26 -year- old daughter, Mrs. Christine Camp Pauls. He was also suspected of beating the 9 year- old son of Mrs. Pauls to the extent that he was unconscious for 18-24 hours. Upon regaining consciousness, Cecil, Mrs. Pauls' son, pain- fully made his way to a neighbor to obtain help. He later provided all the details to the police.

Russell was arrested by Cobb County Sheriff E. M. Legg and taken to a prison in Atlanta in order to question him and to remove him from the area for safe keeping. While incarcerated in Atlanta at the Fulton Tower, he confessed to the crime of killing the two victims while intoxicated, but did not remember beating the son. After the confession he was transferred to the new Tattnall Prison in South Georgia.

On the night of Monday October 17, 1938, a mob estimated to be 500 or more formed in Smyrna and began searching the area for Wil- lie Russell. When he was not found, they began ruthlessly attacking blacks anywhere they were found in the area.

The outnumbered police of Smyrna quickly called the State High- way Patrol and the Cobb County Sheriff's department. Adjutant Gen- eral John E. Stoddard, of the Georgia State Patrol, came with state troopers and broke up the human barricade with clubs and tear gas. Stoddard was actively engaged in the fray. The crowd quickly scat- tered and state police advanced into town. The streets were ordered cleared and all gatherings prohibited until the population cooled. State and local police reported that no one was injured in the clash with patrolmen and none were arrested.

This mob, with typical mob mentality, began breaking into homes, smashing windows, pulling Negroes off streetcars, from automobiles and wherever found in the streets, and abusing them. Twenty or more houses were damaged and a two-room, two-story, grammar school was burned. The mob then emptied the section where the victims of the violence lived and blocked off the highway to Atlanta, preventing the return of any Negroes to the city.

The next morning, Tuesday, October 18, 1938, Judge Harold Hawkins called a meeting of the county authorities and learned that no arrests had been made and heard details of the riot from Smyrna Police Chief, C. T. White, and Sheriff E. M. Legg. They all requested assistance. During the meeting Judge Hawkins called Governor E. D. Rivers and demanded that arrests be made by all state officers and that on Tuesday night a National Guard detachment be sent to Smyrna for protection.

Cobb County authorities then moved swiftly and sternly to punish participants in the disorders. There was an investigation regarding the burning of the school. On Tuesday afternoon Sheriff E. M. Legg of Cobb County, who investigated the disturbance, arrested eleven young men, ranging in age from 20 to 26 years, and lodged them in the Cobb County jail; later another 17 were arrested by the state and county officials. Bond was set at $2,500.00. The amount of $2,500.00 in 1938, in the middle of the Great Depression, is equivalent to $35,576.00 in 2006 dollars. Sheriff Legg said other arrests would come later. The Smyrna Police Chief, C. T. White, said the school was burned during the night by unidentified white youths after the mob broke up into small groups.

The Marietta Journal
Tuesday October 18, 1938

Anti-Negro Demonstration Follows Confession

State and county police patrolled the Smyrna vicinity today to prevent a recurrence of anti-Negro demonstrations which followed a Negro's confession to beating to death a farmer and his daughter.

At least 15 Negroes were beaten or stoned and a Negro schoolhouse house was burned last night by a mob estimated to contain 500 farmers, mill hands and a few women. Members of the mob stopped the Atlanta-Marietta trolley and walked down the aisle, flailing Negro passengers with sticks.

They threatened to march to Atlanta, 12 miles away, where the alleged killer, Willie Russell, was lodged in Fulton Tower, the impregnable county jail. The tower guard was doubled.

The mob, however, lacked leadership and was easily broken up by state and county police enlisted by Thurmond White, night police chief in Smyrna.

Capt. B. W. Seabrook of the Atlanta police said Russell, 31, confessed that he had bludgeoned to death with an axe handle George Washington Camp, 66, and Mrs. Christine Pauls, Camp's 26 year-old daughter. The Negro also beat into unconsciousness Mrs. Pauls' 9 year-old son, Cecil.

Cecil lay unconscious from the time of the attack, Saturday night until early Monday. He regained his senses then and crawled to a neighbor's house and told of the slaying, naming Russell, a one-time hand on the Camp farm, as the perpetrator.

Deputies arrested Russell working on a road project in Atlanta and took him to Fulton Tower where he confessed last night. In the confession, the Negro said he had been drinking and had gone to see Camp about a $5.00 debt. Camp threatened him, he said, and struck him with a cane.

Russell declared he then seized the axe handle and struck the farmer several times on the head. Then he went into the farmhouse and when Mrs. Pauls jumped up, startled, he hit her on the head, too. He did not remember striking the boy.

First word of the slaying was brought by the boy, who recovering somewhat from his injuries, managed to crawl to the farm home of Mrs. T. R. Morgan, and tell the story.

Young Paul's story of the crime fixed it as having been staged between 11 o'clock and midnight last Saturday. He said the Negro, whom he and his family knew well, came to the small farmhouse, in a lonely setting off the Cooper Lake Road, and inquired for Paul's grandfather.

"It seemed that Willie was in some kind of trouble," the story of the boy disclosed. "He wanted grandfather to help him out. They walked off together and in a few minutes I heard a scream."

The boy said he revived some time during the night and started to the home of Mrs. T. R. Morgan, their nearest neighbor, but his strength failed and he lost consciousness again until about 6 a.m. Monday and was finally able to reach his neighbor's house.

Cobb County officers arrested the Negro while working on a construction job in Groves Park, near Hapeville. The arresting party included Deputy Sheriffs Lee Strickland, Emmett Marler, Dewey Gable and J. F. Hicks. After the arrest the foursome took the Negro to the Atlanta office of Capt. Seabrook and in three hours gained the confession that he had killed with an axe handle the aged pensioner and his young daughter.

Cobb County Times
Wednesday October 19, 1938

Camp family Plea For No Violence

The following statement was handed the *Times* by Judge J. H. Hawkins:

We, the undersigned children, brothers and sisters and members of the family of Mr. George Camp and Mrs. Christine Camp Pauls, who were recently killed by violence on the part of one Willie Russell, desire to make an appeal to the public generally to refrain from any show of violence, or the arousing of any excitement, in connection with this unfortunate occurrence.

It is our will and sincere desire that the matter be handled by the courts in an orderly manner, that justice may be done and the good name and reputation of our county be preserved. We respectfully request that all of our friends and acquaintances lend their influence to this end.

(Signed) H. E. Camp, C. E. Camp, J. R. Camp, Woodrow Camp, J. N. Camp, Mrs. V. R. Dyson, V. R. Dyson, C. R. Camp, Mrs. D. D. Cowart

Cobb County Times
Marietta, Georgia
October 20, 1938

While languishing in the Cobb County jail Thursday, 17 of the 20 men and boys held in connection with the mob demonstration at Smyrna Monday and Tuesday nights were interviewed by a Times' reporter.

Each of the entire group, whose ages range generally from 17 to 30, strongly denied taking any part in the uprising which grew out of the slaying of an aged farmer...

Several said they were not even in Smyrna at the time.

Cobb deputies and police told a different story, however. Deputy Emmett Marler described many of the group as "ring leaders in the riot." The deputy said prior to the demonstration he had heard several of the "boys" discussing acts of violence which they had proposed to do and were later actually carried out, and had warned them not to put into effect their plans.

Most of the once "brave" men are visibly shaken by their predicament as they stand huddled together in the two cells which hold them. There is fear in each one's eyes—but still they stoutly deny the charges against them.

The youngest suspect, Reid Cranford, of Oakdale, 17, said his greatest fear was that his elder brother might be admitted into the jail "where he could get at him" for being connected with the affair. The Oakdale youth claimed "not guilty" with the rest.

Warrants have been issued for the arrest of more than 90 in all in connection with the rioting, according to Deputy George McMillan, who said that other warrants are being taken out and other persons seized as fast as names are turned in.

A force of deputies, county officers and bailiffs are aiding in rounding up the suspects spreading a countywide net—acting on their own information, tips and rumors as to likely participants to the disturbance.

Deputy McMillan expressed the belief that more than 20 persons will be "picked up" during the next few days.

Records in the sheriff's office list the suspects, formally charged with malicious mischief."...

Cobb County Times
Marietta, Georgia
Thursday October 20, 1938

'YOU YELLOW RATS ---'
In the lingo of the Mob, 'If The Shoe Fits, Wear It'
AN EDITORIAL

For once in its history The Times feels disinclined—in fact, downright ashamed—to print all the news . . . . But in keeping with a 22 year-old policy of frankness and independence your county newspaper presents today full summaries of the events of this week, as shameful as they are.

Briefly what has happened at Smyrna is that a gang of young hoodlums—rats, mobsters, thugs or whatever you wish to call them—for two days violated about every fundamental right that American citizens have . . . . .

The Declaration of Independence says that "all men are created free and equal." We wonder how the innocent white men and Negroes who were mauled and mistreated by the mob feel about this phrase in the Declaration.

The American constitution says that private property is sacred. We wonder how the white men and women whose houses and autos were damaged to the extent of several thousand dollars feel about the sanctity of their property.

There are certain personal rights, privileges and protection to which all private citizens are entitled. We wonder how the white tourists feel about being stopped, intimidated and searched by the mob.

And about now, it's time for one of you cowardly hoodlums, Mr. Mob, to yell, "Oh, yeah. Well, we're going to drive the Negroes out of Cobb County. To hell with your paper." (That is, of course, if you Mobsters can read and think, which is extremely doubtful?)

Well, Mr. Mob, it's your time to get few plain facts through your thick skulls:

1. The Cobb County Times is posting $100—a hundred iron men, to you—for the conviction of the yellow rats who were responsible for the burning of Bethel schoolhouse and the rioting in Smyrna Tuesday night.

2. Commissioner Charles M. Head, of Cobb County is planking down $200 for the same purpose . . . and there may be more from other sources.

3. This newspaper represents the good people of Cobb County who stand for law and order in Cobb County and will proceed to vigorously advocate in every possible manner the arrest and trial of every person who played any part in the shameful rioting.

And now, Mr. Mob, let's get down to cases.

The intelligent people of Cobb County (and you'd be surprised how many there are, Mr. Mob ...you ignorant fool) are still wondering if you really thought you were hurting the Negroes? Fool that you are, you probably thought so.

Let's see if you did.

There's the case of Claude T. Osborn, life long resident of Smyrna. A white man mind you. Mr. Osborn has 14 tenant houses. You, Mr. Mob damaged 11 of them to the extent of, let's say, $500 just to be conservative. Did that hurt the Negroes?

There's the case of P. C. Ragsdale, of Acworth, a White truck driver who was painfully cut on the arm and mauled when you, Mr. Mob, stopped his truck to beat a Negro passenger. The Negroes escaped with much lesser injuries.

There's the case of two aged white women tourists whose car was stopped, the window glasses smashed and the door snatched off. Did that hurt the Negroes? (Two elderly ladies with a Negro chauffer)

By now, Mr. Mobster, you probably have your tongue in your cheek and you leer and sneer, "Well, anyhow we burned their old schoolhouse Monday night. That'll hurt 'em I reckon."

That statement just proves what an unmitigated idiot and moron you are, Mr. Mob. Whose schoolhouse was it? It belonged to the Cobb County Board of Education! This board, in case you and your crazy companions didn't know it, is composed of White men. Whose loss was it? The taxpayers who paid for it and who must rebuild it. And you are not a taxpayer!

We come to a point now, Mr. Mob, that you wouldn't grasp, but the thinking residents of Cobb County grasp it, in fact are already seeing its effects.

The riots Monday and Tuesday hurt business in Smyrna and Marietta this week. Cobb County received some of the worst advertising possible—all over America the decent people are wondering about what kind of civilization we have down here.

They don't know that you, Mr. Mob were a small, criminal minority composed of non-taxpayers, nor residents and just plain non-entities. They don't know that the good citizens of the county—at least 34,700 of the 35,000 inhabitants—were not of the same ilk you were . . . that they think of you in just the same terms we are writing of you.

The Atlanta papers were polite in their handling of the story . . . but not so in the St. Louis, the New York, the San Francisco, the Chicago papers. Their headlines screamed in huge black type—"Race Riot in Smyrna, Georgia—Mob Mauls Negroes. . . ." Ask one Marietta merchant how he felt Tuesday morning when he read the papers in St. Louis where he had gone quite as usual to buy a stock of goods. What could he tell those St. Louis friends of his?

Oh, yes, Mr. Mobster, Cobb County is for justice. And, so help us, we'll see that you get justice. We aren't worried about black Willie Russell. He'll get justice. The law makes full provision for criminals like Willie and—God have mercy on his soul—Willie will pay the penalty without any prodding of the part of the newspaper. . . . But courts, Mr. Mobster, will take care of you, too.

Lynching is already one of the rarest crimes in this nation and sooner or later mob violence will be an impossibility, a thing of the past, in Cobb County, in Georgia, The South and the nation.

If these persons are guilty of the acts of which they are accused, the upstanding citizens of Cobb County want them to be tried and, if they are convicted, they should be sentenced by the courts to the penalties provided by law.

If they are innocent, free them and clear their names. For once and for all, the law abiding citizens of Cobb County want to demonstrate to the people of these United States that Cobb County justice is a sacred thing and that the badge of law and order is a "Badge of Honor."

The reporting about the riot from other sections of the country was researched and a few headlines are included below.

Nevada State Journal, "Negro Attack-Slayer Is Threatened by Mob"
Oshkosh, Wisconsin, "Georgia Negro Baiter Sentenced."
Lincoln, Nebraska, "Mob Action, Smyrna, Georgia"
Port Arthur, Texas, "Stone Blacks"

Each report had a brief description of the disturbance.

Cobb County Times
Marietta, Georgia
November 10, 1938

Judge Asks Jury Probe Of 3 Incidents

Judge J. Harold Hawkins in charging the November term of grand jury of Cobb Superior Court Monday, called for careful investigations into three "major occurrences" during recent weeks in Cobb County.

These included, (1) Murders of an aged man and his 26 year-old daughter on October 16, (2) Disturbances and violent conduct in and around Smyrna on the nights of October 17 and 18, (3) Recent death of a young Marietta citizen, Bill Ward.

The jurist declared "all these matters should receive your careful consideration," citing that no other body has as much power as the grand jury when it comes to enforcement of the law.

In reference to the Smyrna demonstrations, Judge Hawkins said, "So far as I have learned, no person was seriously injured, but there was damage to private property, unlawful detention and assault on innocent persons." The Smyrna disorders followed the murders of ...

"This outbreak is regrettable from any standpoint you may choose to take." Judge Hawkins told the jury. "It has cast a reflection upon the good citizens of the county that will be difficult to overcome for sometime to come."

"If any evidence discloses who was guilty, they should be indicted by the grand jury."

The Marietta Journal
Thursday, November 17, 1938

SMYRNA RIOTS THRASHED, 17 INDICTED

SOLICITOR IS PREPARED TO TRY ACCUSED

Riotous Counts Follow Two Days
Inquiry Into Racial Outbreaks

Seventeen Smyrna and Fair Oaks men were under indictment today for rioting and disturbing the peace in connection with racial demonstrations which followed a Negro's confession to slaying an elder farmer and his daughter on October 17.

Eleven bills were returned today adding to the six returned last night after a two-day inquiry into the anti-Negro outbreaks.

Indicted by the Cobb County grand jury last night were Broughton Teem, Henry Martin, Buck Miller, M. D. Lewis, Paul Hensley and Robert Hughes.

Today's bills called for blanket charges against nine others... They were accused of being violent, riotous and charged with preventing state patrolmen from summoning aid during the night of the second incident.

C.N. Padgett, Senator Mulkey and Milt McClarty were also named today in separate bills charging disturbance of the peace and being riotous and tumultuous and using profane language.

More than forty witnesses including ten state patrol-men, deputies and Smyrna peace officers, charged the seventeen were leaders of violence which included beating and stoning Negroes, damaging their homes and firing a Negro school.

The outbreaks occurred after Willie Russell, Smyrna farm hand, confessed...

Solicitor Grady Vandiviere, who worked with jurymen on the two outbreaks, said today he was ready to bring the group to the stand for trial as soon as officers were ready. The entire group is under bond.

Teem is charged with boarding a street car at Fair Oaks stop about midnight of October 18, demanding delivery of Negro passengers. Henry Martin, a companion was charged with carrying a shotgun over his arm.

Miller is charged with chasing an unidentified Negro down the street "carrying an object resembling a butcher knife" Lewis is charged with "malicious mischief rioting." Hensley faced drunken charges and Hughes of attempted intimidation and threats against two Negroes in separate bills.

Investigation of the disturbance was the third major item probed by the grand jury last week. Jurors spent more than two days on the unexplained shooting of W. A. Ward, Marietta salesman. Indictment and conviction of Russell followed the jury inquiry into the axe handle deaths of the two Smyrna farm residents.

Jury Clerk Merritt Lyon announced the jury will likely be in session...

Cobb County Times
November 17, 1938

Cobb Negro Sentenced To Die
For Axe-Handle Slaying

Willie Drew Russell, 31 year-old Negro construction worker, was lodged in an undisclosed jail Thursday, facing death by electrocution on December 9, 1938, in connection with the axe-handle slaying of Mrs. Christine Camp Pauls, daughter of George W. Camp, aged Cobb farmer who was also allegedly slain by Russell on the night of October 16.

A Cobb Superior Court jury found Russell guilty of the murder charge Monday after less than an hour's deliberation. Judge J. H. Hawkins passed sentence and set the date of execution immediately.

Only the case involving the killing of Mrs. Pauls was heard by the court.

In an un-sworn statement from the stand, Russell admitted being drunk at the time, and said, "I must have been crazy."

"When I went over there, I was drinking pretty heavy—but I must have been crazy or something." He stated. "If I had known I had done it, I wouldn't have gone back to my job, but would have tried to get away," the Negro added.

Judge Hawkins warned several times during the trial that no disturbance of any kind would be tolerated, and asked for perfect order. The crowd of spectators, which filled the court room to overflowing, remained quiet throughout the proceedings.

Chief witness for the prosecution was Cecil Pauls, nine-year old son of the slain woman who reiterated the story he had told officers concerning the dual slayings of his mother and grandfather at their two-room farm home, three miles west of Smyrna in a secluded spot off Cooper Lake Road.

The boy said Russell, whom the family knew, came to their house after the family had retired for the night, and called his grandfather outside for a talk. He testified Russell returned shortly without his grandfather, whom the Negro said had gone to a neighbor's house.

Later, the boy said, Russell struck his mother over the head with an ax handle, and then hit him twice, knocking him into insensibility.

The boy told of remaining in a semi-conscious condition for almost 18 hours and then recovering sufficiently to stagger to a neighbor's house to tell of the brutal killings.

Several other witnesses appeared for the prosecution including: W. P. West, Smyrna blacksmith who testified he sold the axe handle which was found near the scene, to Russell; Hubert Head, of Smyrna, former employer of Russell; Dr. W. H. Perkinson, who testified there was no evidence of a criminal attack upon the body of Mrs. Pauls; John H. Terry, of Smyrna; Deputies Lee Strickland and Emmett Marler, investigation officers; Speare Stone and Robert Baldwin, both of near Smyrna.

Captain B. W. Seabrook, of the Atlanta police department, testified Russell had voluntarily, "without force or intimidation," signed a statement confessing the two murders.

Captain Seabrook stated the Negro said he got into an argument with the elder man over a small debt and struck him, and when the woman attempted to interfere, he struck her also.

No witnesses were presented by the defense.

Neither prosecution nor defense struck a single juror, both agreeing on the first twelve names called. L. H. Atherton, Marietta druggist, served as jury foreman.

In his closing statement to jury, Guy Roberts, defense attorney, pointed out he had been appointed by the court to represent Russell, and had tried to perform the duty "fairly and honestly."

"We have done what we could to bring out any discrepancies in the case, if any, and to present only the facts." Mr. Roberts said. He added he was convinced "the boy was telling the truth" and that the evidence given had coincided substantially on the main points.

His associate, Gordon Combs, made a similar statement.

Solicitor H. G. Vandiviere asked the death penalty for Russell, and stated, "The defendant has received a fair and impartial trial."

On November 19, 1938, the disposition of the indictments for those who were arrested and indicted were considered by Solicitor Grady Vandiviere. As it turned out, only one of the 19 indicted was sentenced or resolved. Buck Miller, about 33, pleaded guilty and Judge Harold Hawkins imposed the sentence of one year in prison for "Chasing Negroes and leading other in the chase." All the others indicted failed to appear in court and forfeited their bond of $1,000.

Judge Hawkins said he might ask the grand jury to review the others in the January term of the court.

A bond of $1,000 in 1938 is equivalent to $14,226 in 2006 dollars. If all proceeded as the law requires today, when a security bail is forfeited, the amount of the bonds would have been deposited in the general fund of the county to defray administrative costs.

It seems to me extremely problematic to arrest members of a mob for prosecution. By arresting dozens it must also be difficult to assign an indisputable charge compatible with their gross behavior and to provide convincing evidence to a jury. The charges used were, malicious mischief, malicious mischief rioting, carrying a shotgun over one's arm, being violent, being riotous and disturbance of the peace, being tumultuous and using profane language. One charge was preventing state patrolmen from using the phone when a rioter climbed a telephone pole and cut the phone wire. The most serious seems to be beating and stoning Negroes, damaging their homes and firing a Negro school. On Monday after the mob was broken up by the state patrolmen and county authorities the gang dispersed into small groups making it nearly impossible to identify the guilty. This is when the school was torched.

Great Depression, Mobsters and Hawkins Hits Ex'es

In the early years of Judge Hawkins' judgeship, crime was not considered the number one national problem, but it was near the top of priorities on people's minds. Because of the collapse of the stock market in late 1929, the economy was obviously the first priority; "Bank Holidays," rampant unemployment, and the Great Depression were destroying the very souls of millions of unemployed and dismayed citizens in the nation. In 1931 Al Capone was tried, found guilty of tax evasion, and sentenced to serve time in the Atlanta Federal Penitentiary. In the early thirties names like John Dillinger, Baby Face Nelson, Machine Gun Kelley, and Pretty Boy Floyd were frequently reported in the newspapers and discussed around pot belly stoves at the local market. Most of the big name gangsters were apprehended or killed in the early 1930s, inspiring special news clips in movie theatres and newspaper headlines. These events were taking place locally and nationally during the early years of Judge Hawkins's sitting on the bench of the Blue Ridge Circuit.

The Eighteenth Amendment was ratified January 16, 1919, and was repealed by the Twenty-first Amendment on December 5, 1933. However, during the life of the Amendment crime was rampant in the nation and organized crime flourished. Locally, whiskey related crimes were perpetrated by petty criminals and well known citizens. Businesses were regularly closed down, and many of those guilty were indicted and tried in the already busy courts. Stills were used by the mountain folks to concoct often deadly bootleg whiskey. Car radiators were frequently used to distill the whiskey, resulting in some lead mixing in the finished product.

Nationally, it was reported that many prohibition agents bought country homes, town houses, real estate, and luxury automobiles on salaries averaging less than $3000 a year. Stories abound that it was not unusual in larger cities for policemen, on salaries of less than $4000 annually, to have up to $200,000 in their bank accounts.

Even after the repeal of the Eighteenth Amendment, authorizing legal sales of whiskey, bootleggers and the sale of illegal whiskey continued. It was a most lucrative enterprise for organized crime and petty criminals, as well as some officials in all branches of the government throughout the nation. The courts, both nationally and locally, were burdened with trials. In the six counties of the Blue Ridge Circuit, Judge Hawkins devoted much time in trying cases of this kind.

Sadly, criminals were able to buy pardons in order to void their conviction. Sometimes even before the trial was convened, preemptive pardons were issued by the sitting governor. Apparently the nature and gravity of the crime were not a consideration in the granting of many pardons. We are fortunate that in the extreme majority of judges, governors, police, and other public officials were people of integrity and carried out their responsibilities honorably.

Roy Barnes grew up in south Cobb County and was a good friend and neighbor of Harold Glore, Justice Hawkins' legal assistance. He has often expressed his respect and admiration for Judge Hawkins. When Governor Barnes was asked why he chose to enter the legal profession, he said that his relationship with Harold Glore and Judge Hawkins was a major influence in making his decision.

Governor Roy Barnes, a friend and successful governor of Georgia, enjoyed telling stories about the good old days in his native south Cobb County, Georgia. A well-read, award-winning, and one of Georgia's top columnists, Bill Shipp, includes the following story in an article he wrote in 1999 entitled, "Barnes Set to Make New Waves."

> "Governor Barnes recalls the time Superior Court Judge Harold Hawkins, a "dry," sentenced a well-known North Georgia bootlegger to prison, only to have the defendant present the jurist at the moment of sentencing with a preemptive pardon signed by governor of that day."

In reality, this makes a great story; there is no doubt it would be enjoyed by the Judge today because he had a wonderful sense of humor, not to mention the ability to laugh at events in which he was involved.

On the other hand, Judge Hawkins learned early the fundamental principles and importance of character that would guide him during his life. Throughout his career, he was courageously outspoken in his conviction that all public officials and especially members of the legal profession should be adamant that equal justice be provided to each and all who come before the courts.

In 1946 an article in the *Marietta Daily Journal* reveals one major concern expressed by the Judge regarding equal justice under the law and integrity of the judicial system. It involves pardons and misdeeds of public officials, even in the highest office of the state. The text of Judge Hawkins' speech is below:

The Marietta Daily Journal
July 7, 1946

Hawkins Hits Ex'es in Saturday Speech

Marietta Judge Reminds Officers of Gene's Pardon for Peek Murderer

Judge J. H. Hawkins, of the Blue Ridge Circuit, broke his 15-year political silence Saturday to come out for Jimmie Carmichael in a statewide broadcast from Brunswick, where the Marietta gubernatorial candidate was making an address. Hawkins called on the judiciary and law enforcement officers to join him in supporting the Marietta attorney, who has the endorsement of Governor Ellis Arnall. The Marietta judge attacked former Governors E. D. Rivers and Gene Talmadge.

"Talmadge and Rivers did more to destroy the courts and to set aside the verdicts of courts than all the lawless elements of Georgia combined," Hawkins declared.

To back up his statement pertaining to Talmadge, Hawkins briefly reviewed the famous Peek Murder trial. He emphasized that less than two years after the Cobb Superior Court had convicted Bill Chappell, of Carrollton, of the murder of Mr. And Mrs. Ed Peek, Talmadge granted him a full pardon.

Text of Judge Hawkins 1946 speech follows:

For the past fifteen and a half years, I have studiously avoided taking any active part in any political campaign in Georgia, for the reason that I have always felt that the judiciary should stay out of politics as much as possible.

But now, with two men running for the office of Governor of this state, who have heretofore, while occupying that office, done more to destroy the courts, and to set aside and nullify the verdicts of juries, and the sentences and judgments of the courts, than all of the lawless elements of Georgia combined, I feel that not only the members of the judiciary, but every other law enforcement officer and law-abiding citizen should stand up and speak out in favor of good government and honest government.

I feel that they should help in every legitimate way to uphold law and justice in the State, and to perpetuate in the minds of the people of this nation the good name and fair reputation which the State has regained during the recent administration of its affairs.

There are many issues presented by the records of these two former Governors which might be reviewed and discussed, but I shall confine myself to the things which I know most about, and which, to my mind, most directly affect the future welfare of the people of our State—and that is, the indiscriminate granting of pardons by these two former Governors, whereby verdicts of juries and sentences of the court, which were reached in a lawful and orderly manner, were flouted and rendered worthless by the abuse of the pardoning power vested in them as the servants of the people.

As to former Governor Rivers, he has, in some of his addresses, admitted that he pardoned one of the most notorious bootleggers in my home county, but he did not tell you that he pardoned him twice within 24 hours.

He now claims that he did this as the result of a trade with the man whom I am now supporting for Governor, in order to obtain his support of some legislative program.
In the first place, I do not believe that Jimmie Carmichael would make a trade whereby he surrendered any conviction he might have had as to the proper legislative program for our State, in order to secure a benefit for one of his clients; and I say this because of the fact that I have known Jimmie Carmichael since he was a school-boy, and I know his honesty and his character.

In the second place, if one who has been entrusted by the people of the State to manage its affairs, and who has sworn to uphold and defend the laws and Constitution of the State of Georgia and of the United States, if he would so far forget his responsibility as to make a trade to defeat law and justice, and the orderly processes of the courts, in order to gain a political aim, then he is wholly unfit and unqualified to hold this high office, and wholly lacking in that fundamental and necessary attribute or character, respect for the law.

But that is not the only pardon which Rivers granted in my circuit that outraged law and justice. In one of the mountain counties, three men were convicted of willfully and maliciously dynamiting, blowing up and destroying the property of another in the dead hours of the night.

After their conviction and sentence by the court, they were released on bond pending a motion for a new trial. A motion for a new trial was presented in their behalf, which was overruled, and they then presented a writ of error to the Appellate Court, but this was never filed or prosecuted.

At the next succeeding term of the court, these defendants failed to appear, and their bonds were forfeited. Some three or four weeks thereafter, while these men were fugitives from justice, and before having served a single day of the sentence imposed upon them, they were granted full and complete pardons by the then Governor Rivers, and they were turned back on society to pursue their lawless and nefarious activities—and these pardons were dated back prior to the bond forfeiture, so as to relieve them of even that penalty.

Former Governor Talmadge stands in no better position. Many of you probably recall reading of one of the most brutal murder cases ever occurring in the State of Georgia.

Early one morning the dead bodies of Mr. and Mrs. Peek were found in a deep railroad cut in Cobb County. It appeared that the automobile in which the bodies were found had been saturated with gasoline and driven off the highway into this deep railroad cut.

The ignition was left on, with the apparent purpose of causing the automobile to catch fire and destroy both it and the bodies therein contained—or else having it run over by a train, and thus demolished and destroyed. In the providence of God, neither of these things occurred and the bodies were discovered.

The police officers of Cobb County spent a year or more ferreting out sufficient evidence to present the matter to the grand jury.

The evidence developed that these two people were strangled and beaten to death by a man (Bill Chappell, of Carroll County) who was involved in fraudulent transactions concerning the management of the affairs of the county, by which he was employed as an armed guard in the penitentiary.

He not only participated in the actual killing of these two people, but as an armed guard over two of the inmates of the penitentiary, he compelled them to aid and assist him in this brutal murder.

After Cobb County had spent thousands of dollars trying this case, and the jury had convicted the defendant, and he was sentenced to life imprisonment in the penitentiary, Governor Talmadge pardoned him within less that two years from that date, and he is now a free man. Thus the Governor of Georgia again flouted and nullified the orderly processes of the courts.

Not only this, but former Governor Talmadge is now promising daily, that if elected to this high office, he will not only defy the courts of Georgia, but even the Supreme Court of the United States—the final safeguard of the lives, the liberties, and the properties of the citizens of the United States.

He claims to be a lawyer, and if he is any lawyer at all, he knows that this cannot be done. He also knows that there will be no mixing of the races in the schools of Georgia, by telling them that unless he is elected Governor, this will be done. Claiming to be a lawyer, he should know that the recently adopted Constitution of this state is the supreme law of the state, and that it provides: "Separate schools shall be provided for the white and colored races."

These are some of the reasons I cannot support, and am now opposed to the election of either of these two former Governors.

The speech was made by Judge Hawkins in Brunswick in support of gubernatorial candidate James Carmichael. What might have been his entire motives and why the atypical departure from his guiding principles of avoiding politics?

Without knowing Judge Hawkins well, it is possible that one may wonder if the speech, in which he criticized pardons of convicted criminals by Governor Rivers and Governor Gene Talmadge, was simply politically motivated. I believe otherwise.

As I review the speech, it is apparent the sense of Judge Hawkins was that disorder in our legal system regarding abuse of gubernatorial privileges had never been worse. Recalling his speech, he said, "I feel that not only the members of the judiciary, but every other law enforcement officer and law-abiding citizen should stand up and speak out in favor of good government and honest government." He was concerned that citizens might lose the basic civic trust necessary to preserve the rule of law. The speech itself remains sensible, legally legitimate, and logically defensible.

First, there is a preponderance of evidence to conclude his was the voice of a dedicated and honorable judge in his passion to support the Constitution and equal justice under the law, as well as an attempt to restore honor and integrity to the judicial system in Georgia by eliminating the abuses of gubernatorial privileges.

Second, as to Governor Rivers, consider that during his last year as governor a federal grand jury indicted four members of his administration for conspiracy to defraud the state. After he left office, a Fulton County Grand Jury indicted Rivers, his son, and seventeen other members of his administration. Only two of those indicted were found guilty. Governor Rivers during his two terms gave a total of 1,897 pardons; twenty-two were to convicted murderers.

Third, as to Governor Gene Talmadge, he was never indicted, as was Governor Rivers, but the Atlanta newspapers were replete with stories regarding his pardons. Rivers' pardons were considerably fewer than the 3,083 pardons granted by Governor Gene Talmadge during one term.

We know the convicted murderer Bill Chappell's sentence was nullified by a pardon from Governor Gene Talmadge. The facts as outlined in Judge Hawkins's speech are a matter of record and well documented.

As Rivers left office in 1940, there was a story relative to the pardons scandal. The story goes that a man accidentally bumped into Governor Rivers on an elevator. The man said, "Pardon me." Governor Rivers replied, "See my executive secretary on the second floor."

CHARTER EIGHT

PEEK MURDERS AND TRIALS

Here I present in more detail the Peek murder investigation and trial, referred to earlier in the statewide speech made by Judge Harold Hawkins in Brunswick during the 1946 governor's race.

In June 1938 the automobile and the bodies of Mr. and Mrs. Peek were soaked with kerosene and pushed over the bank at the railroad bridge near Bankhead Highway a few miles from Austell. The Atlanta and Marietta newspapers covered the trial in much detail from June 1938 through most of 1940. A limited version of the many accounts of the crime and trial of Bill Chappell is as follows:

The newspapers referred to the "mystery murders" for months before evidence was adequate to unravel the mystery. A rope around the neck of Mrs. J. Ed Peek was powerful evidence as the State Patrol was able to positively identify the rope used and where it was purchased. Later in June a number of clues, a missing slipper, the well rope, kerosene, a witness who talked to Mr. Peek and four men the night of the murder, and other clues were beginning to be unearthed, which ultimately helped investigators to slowly put together a case.

Mr. and Mrs. J. Ed Peek, Jr. lived in Atlanta where Mr. Peek was employed selling equipment to county governments including Carroll County. Commissioner Hamp Chappell admitted talking to Mr. Peek the day of the murder about a debt Carroll County owed to Mr. Peek's employer. Mr. Peek had been selling equipment to Carroll County for many years and apparently had been friends with Commissioner Hamp Chappell and his son Bill Chappell. Young Bill Chappell, as a deputy warden, had purchasing authority for Carroll County prison camp. The grand jury of Carroll County was looking into allegations of misapplication of county purchasing funds about the time of the murder.

It was reported in the news that Bill Chappell, in talking with Helen Peek, daughter of Mr. Peek, said Mr. Peek knew too much about his affairs.

The Peek trial, described as sensational and better than a dime murder mystery, had as the principal officers of the court, agencies and officials as listed below:

Superior Court Judge Harold Hawkins was the trial judge.

Other officers of the court in this well publicized trial included Grady Vandiviere, Solicitor of the Blue Ridge Circuit. He tried cases in all counties of the circuit.

Judge Hawkins

Attorneys L. M. Blair and James Carmichael were both from Marietta. Carmichael was attorney for the defense in collaboration with Willis Smith of Carrollton. Blair was hired by Mrs. J. E. Coursey of College Park to assist the prosecution. She was the mother of the deceased Mrs. Peek. Blair and Carmichael were both well-known attorneys in Marietta. A few years later, Jimmy Carmichael would be the opponent of Governor Gene Talmadge and Governor E. Rivers in the 1946 gubernatorial election. L.M. Blair was appointed by Judge Hawkins to defend George Goumos in the murder trial discussed earlier. Bill Chappell was well represented in this trial.

Grady Vandiviere

Lead investigator Deputy Sheriff George McMillan was assisted by Deputy Sheriffs Emmett Marler, Dewey Gable and Sheriff E. M. Legg.

Other officers of the court, assisting defense attorney Willis Smith, were Judge John Wood and B. F. Boykin.

Several outside entities were involved including the Fulton County Police, the Georgia State Patrol, and the Carroll County Police.

James Carmichael

L. M. Blair

The investigation began when the bodies were found in the railroad cut known as the Mahaffey Cut at the intersection of the Bankhead Highway and the Austell-Marietta Road. From, June 20, 1938, the investigation continued until the trial in July 19, 1940.

George McMillan

Excerpts from the first of many newspapers reports are below:

The Marietta Journal
June 21, 1938

Discussing the last conversation with parents she (Miss Helen Peek) said "They told me they were en route to Carrollton on a business trip. Mother had been traveling with father since their marriage at Jonesboro three months ago. They cut through to Austell and I can't believe anything else except they were killed in the plunge off the road."

The car, a standard four-door sedan Chevrolet, apparently struck on its nose. In its hurtle, it came to a standstill on the opposite side of the tracks from where it originally hit.

A Montezuma, Georgia, theater program was found in the rear seat of the car as well as a pool of blood. The two bodies were several feet apart, the woman's body, with the rope around her neck, lying along the railway roadbed. The man's body was lying about fifteen feet away.

The investigation continued more than a year before Cobb County investigators could get sufficient evidence to present the case to the grand jury. Clues and leads most often produced one dead end after another.

At one point the investigators, Deputy Sheriff George McMillan, the lead investigator, and county policeman E. C. Ward, said the case had been dropped because of lack of cooperation by the state penal board that denied a request for the transfer of prisoners. In brief, this was regarding the permanent transfer of prisoners, two of whom it was thought assisted in the crime, to Cobb County from the Carroll County prison farm for interrogation. Bill Chappell was deputy warden for this prison farm.

Marietta Daily Journal
June 22, 1938

Cobb County officers had enlisted the services of Fulton County police and private Atlanta, Georgia detectives overnight in determining the source of a length of rope which was found knotted about Mrs. J. Ed. Peek's neck when she was discovered with her husband early yesterday morning at the bottom of a 70 foot railway cut under circumstances indicating murder and suicide or double murder.

Excerpts from an article in the *Marietta Daily Journal* report comments of Mr. A. O. Blalock, state penal board chairman.

Marietta Daily Journal
July 17, 1938

The state prison board, while desirous of avoiding any movement which would cast suspicion on any county official advises that in the event any convict from one county camp should give evidence which would result in the indictment or conviction of an official of that county, the convict could naturally be transferred so that they would no longer be under the jurisdiction of the officials about whom the testimony was given.

In the present instance, the prison board feels that to order the permanent transfer of the prisoners in question would directly reflect on the county officials and the warden from which they would be transferred, and until the prisoners give such testimony as to make it necessary for their permanent transfer, it would not be wise to grant this request.

In addition to his bowling alley business, Bill Chappell was employed at the prison in Carroll County as an armed guard and deputy warden. He was the son of Hamp Chappell, Commissioner of Roads and Revenue for Carroll County. Governor Rivers, being aware of the statewide publicity of this trial, became involved and offered his support, even to supplying reward money of $200.00 for the arrest and conviction of the guilty party or parties.

Marietta Daily Journal
July 20, 1938

SILENCE SHROUDS PROBE OF CONVICTS

Subpoena Issued to Miss Helen Peek

A grand jury, which has its desk clear of bills and other county matters, was ready this afternoon to launch their investigation of the slayings of J. Ed Peek, Jr. and his 33-year-old wife of three months.

Solicitor Grady Vandiviere who will likely handle investigation of five Carroll County convicts shifted to the Marietta jail in strictest secrecy Monday night, remained silent on jury development. Jurors would not indicate whether the Peek evidence will reach them during the afternoon, after having announced their desk was free from bills which court officials had turned over to them Tuesday afternoon and early this evening...

In addition to the five Carroll County prisoners, it is learned a sixth subpoena had been issued to Miss Helen Peek, 19-year-old daughter of the slain Atlantans, who at the time of her parents death was employed here as manager of the local bowling alley. She appeared before the coroner's inquest which was held the day her parent's bodies were found sprawled beside their machine in deep Mahaffey cut, three miles northeast of Austell, Georgia on the Marietta Highway.

Officers did not know why the five convicts were transferred here and held incommunicado in the county jail. Their transfer, it was learned, was made on an order reported to have been issued by Governor Rivers at the request of Solicitor Vandiviere. The transfer of the Carroll convicts to the Cobb scene was made following a court order issued by Superior Court Judge J. Harold Hawkins.

Dr. W. H. Perkinson assisted the coroner to examine the bodies.

Marietta Daily Journal
July 28, 1938

Coroner John R. Williams is bringing to a close his jury inquest in view of the fact that authorities have been unable to uncover new evidence to explain how Mr. and Mrs. J. Ed Peek, Jr., came to their deaths last June 21 when their battered bodies were found sprawled beside their wrecked automobile in a railroad ravine.

Another article in the *Marietta Daily Journal* this same day reported:

A report that J. Edward Peek, who with his 33-year-old second wife was found dead in the deep Mahaffey cut, was seen talking to four men in a dark sedan at the spot a few miles from where their bodies were discovered, was studied today as officers went into the second week of the most baffling Cobb County case.

L. J. Gibbs, storekeeper and mill operator in Carroll County, told Deputy Sheriff George McMillan he spotted the foursome in a parked automobile some two miles west of the railroad ravine near the intersection of the Bankhead highway and the Marietta-Austell road.

The new witness who claims to have delivered the latest development said he recognized only Peek whom he knew well among the group.

As the crime was committed in Cobb County, the Peek trial described in Judge Hawkins' speech was held at the courthouse in Marietta. The investigation covered Cobb County, Carroll County, and Fulton County.

The Marietta Journal
April 14, 1940

Bill Chappell Waits His Trial

Bill Chappell, son of Carroll County Commissioner Hamp Chappell, and a prominent figure in the probe of the mysterious railroad-gulch deaths of Mr. and Mrs. J. Ed. Peek, Atlanta couple, near Austell last year was slated to face trial in Carroll Superior Court Tuesday on charges of embezzling approximately $50.00 in groceries from the county prison camp.

According to Carrollton press notices Chappell, operator of the Marietta Bowling Alleys, was indicted by a grand jury in Carroll County last fall.

Alec Tregone, in covering the Peek murder trial, recounts below the charge given by Judge Harold Hawkins to the jury for the June term of the Grand Jury.

The Marietta Journal
April 17, 1940

By Alec Tregone

Responsibility of grand jurors, often referred as the custodians of American civilization, featured a charge Monday by Superior Court Judge Harold Hawkins in opening the April session of Cobb Superior Court.

Quoting a recent statement delivered in a city court charge in Augusta by Judge Gordon W. Chambers, the local jurist informed his 23-man inquisitorial body that in being selected for jury service "you have been elevated to the peerage of democracy."

He spoke of the relationship of court officials, peace officers and lawyers with the grand jury, and called their duty "one deserving of the consecrated dedication of a conscientious concentration of their abilities and the just impulse of their honor."

He laid special emphasis on the importance of serving as a grand and trial juror, declaring that in either capacity, just as Judge Chambers of Augusta had said, "you are a shield of protection against false accusers, transitory passions and prejudices and determiners of truth revealing the character of our country as a land of the free and home of the brave."

Jury service is a responsible and necessary service he repeated, because you jurors "are the preservers of liberty that walks with progress and restrains only libertine license to insure its own freedom."

The American peerage also serves as the protectors of all legal rights of society, citizenship and the state, as well as serving as guarantors of justice constitutional and statutory, exactly, evenly and universally applied, he charged.

Discussing further the "gentlemen of the jury," Judge Hawkins quoted additional passages of the Richmond County jurist who said:

"You are custodians of American civilization, for without law there can be no civilization, without truth and independence there can be no courts.

"The only title of nobility recognized by America's loyal house is the peerage of the jury box where trial by peers determines the truth of issues between the state and its citizens.

"This title carries no feudal privilege or materialistic value, however, it merits the accolade of achievement—the accomplishment of the aristocracy of service.

"This high honor carries only the title as a word of address or as an adjective of description. "Gentlemen of the Jury"

Judge Hawkins ...

The Marietta Journal
May 27, 1940

Chappell Attorneys Expect to Move
For Early Release During Afternoon

Carrollton Youth, Three
Others in Jail Pending
New Peek Case Probe

By Alec Tregone

Carrollton attorneys were expected here this afternoon to plan an early release for Bill Chappell, 24 year-old son of Com. and Mrs. Hamp Chappell of Carroll County, who with three others is held here in the revived investigation into the brutal slaying two years ago of Mr. and Mrs. J. Ed Peek, of Atlanta.

When Willis Smith, chief defense counsel for Chappell, left here Saturday in company with his clients' father and a counsel associate, B. F. Boykin, he told reporters that he expects to return to Marietta Monday for a conference with Sheriff George McMillan on releasing young Chappell from custody.

Chappell had been confined in the county jail on a blanket charge of murder in connection with the new probe since Friday night when Deputies Lee Strickland and Dewey Gable arrested him in Carrollton.

Since Solicitor Grady Vandiviere at his home in Canton has said that he will resist any move to free Chappell on bond, it was believed his attorneys would center their move on a commitment hearing plea before Justice E. T. Lance. This was neither confirmed nor denied by Attorneys Smith and Boykin while here Saturday.

Three other men, listed by Sheriff McMillan as Louis Turner, Carroll County convict who allegedly made a confession in the Peek slaying; Jason Clark, lifetime prisoner convicted on another charge and John Holsombach, aged inmate of Carroll County Alms House have been in custody since Friday night on the same questioning.

Turner and Clark were among the five who were questioned during the 1938 investigations of the sensational rail road cut case.

Sheriff McMillan remain tight-lipped on new evidence which revived investigation in the double slaying, declaring he had no explanation to make concerning his arrest nor the case which it was learned, has been under probe for several days before Chappell's sudden seizure.

Com. Lon Sullivan, of the state highway patrol, said he understood new evidence involved a statement of a Carroll County convict who alleges he was with young Chappell on the night of the murder.

Questioned about the convict's story Commissioner Chappell said, "It's just some convict who wants to get out of the gang."

In reply to the confession of Turner, Attorney Smith said he had obtained affidavits from one of Turner's former fellow prisoners to the effect that Turner did not leave the prison barracks the night of the Peek's murder.

On the other hand Solicitor Vandiviere said, we have convincing evidence to refute such affidavits. "We have corroborative evidence to show that Turner did leave the prison camp that night."

He added further he is not planning a special session of the grand jury to consider the revived investigation.

Among week-end visitors to Chappell's jail cell here were his brunette sister, Miss Dorothy Chappell, in training at Grady Hospital and friend, listed by officers as Esthera Hudson, daughter of Meriwether County's school superintendent.

The Peek case, which has all the mysterious implications of a dime thriller, opened at 5:30 a.m. the morning of June 25, 1938, when Hugh Brewer, 21 and his brother, Frank Morris Brewer, 17, who live near the railroad bridge, found the bodies.

The elder brother told investigators that he was coming home about 1 a.m. from driving a produce truck, that he saw a car with its lights blinking on and off, parked near the wooden railroad bridge over the deep cut. Later, he related he heard a car turn around in front of his home and a few minutes thereafter he heard a crash of metal and glass.

This crash, investigators believed, occurred when the Peek car went off the precipice.

The Brewer brothers found both Peek and his wife thrown clear of their smashed car. Their clothing was soaked both with blood and kerosene, and the ignition of their motor was turned on when they were discovered. This led officers to believe they were killed, and their car run over the embankment in the hope that the machine would catch fire, and destroy evidence of the slaying.

Both bodies were badly bruised, and around the neck of Mrs. Peek was a new plow line more that five feet long. Physicians later said she died from strangulation.

Bill Chappell figured early in the case when he testified before a coroner's jury that he saw the Peeks at a roadhouse near Villa Rica about 2 p.m. the day before the murder.

Chappell at that time owned a bowling alley at Marietta, and Miss Helen Peek, 18-year-old daughter of Mr. Peek, managed it for him.

Miss Peek testified the day of the discovery of her father's and stepmother's bodies that Peek often had threatened suicide since his marriage three months before, but she had always believed he was "just teasing."

The Marietta Journal
July 12, 1940

PEEK CASE IS SURE TO FACE JURY

Topped by the investigation of three murder cases, one of which is the sensational and unsolved Peek mystery, a busy session occupies the Cobb County grand jury when it convenes Monday morning at 9 o'clock.

Just what day the jury are expected to study the arrest of Bill Chappell, 24 year old son of Carroll County commissioner, Hamp Chappell, and five others, in connection with the brutal slaying of Mr. and Mrs. J. Ed Peek two years ago, is not known—the case will be considered during the early part of the week.

The Marietta Journal
July 17, 1940

Peek Investigation Will Not
Go Before Jury Till Thursday

Investigation into the deaths of Mr. and Mrs. J. Ed Peek, of Atlanta, described as the storybook mystery of the century, will be delayed another day, it appeared this afternoon.

The grand jury remained busy with a stack of bills Solicitor General Grady Vandiviere sent before it this morning, sufficient to keep jurors busy throughout this afternoon session.

Sheriff George McMillan also delayed issuance of subpoenas in Carroll County for witnesses to appear here when the two year old Peek trial is opened ...

The Marietta Journal
July 17, 1940

Plea From Woman to Locate
Guard Adds To Mystery Probe

Husband Disappeared From Carroll Convict Camp
About Time of Chappell Arrest, Ill Wife Writes

The Atlanta Journal Tuesday reported receipt of a letter from a desperately ill Carrollton woman seeking aid in locating her missing husband, Carroll County convict guard, who disappeared from home "for no apparent reason" about the same time four men were arrested in connection with the renewed Peek deaths investigation. Mrs. S. J. Campbell of Route 3, Carrollton, wrote the Atlanta paper that her husband disappeared almost simultaneously with the recent arrest of four men in connection with the double slaying of Mr. and Mrs. J. Ed Peek, of Atlanta, near Austell two years ago this coming Friday.

In Marietta, Sheriff George McMillan disclosed that a second guard has been reported to him to have disappeared from the camp, under similar circumstances as the disappearance of Campbell.

"I would like to talk with Campbell about the Peek case, and I have had many letters from people in Carroll County pointing out the strange circumstances of his disappearance. There is also a former guard at the prison camp who disappeared about the same time. "I'd like to talk with both of them" the Sheriff added ...

The Marietta Journal
July 19, 1940

Four To Face Trial For Peek Slayings
Trial Set July 29

EXTRA JURY FOR TRIALS SEEN HERE

Bill Chappell, (left) 24-year-old son of Carroll County Commissioner W. Hamp Chappell and three others indicted for murder in the deaths of J. Ed Peek and his wife two years ago, may be tried by a new jury when their case is called July 29, court officials intimated Friday.

Trial date for the foursome, each billed on two counts of murder by the Cobb County grand jury after a five-hour examination of witnesses, has been set for July 29.

Superior Court Judge J. Harold Hawkins is the person who decides whether next week's criminal jury will be returned for the murder cases the third week. The judge told inquisitors he did not know at present what action would be taken in the selection of a jury, but would know early next week, in time to draw new jury panels should they be needed.

The two general indictments returned shortly after 4 o'clock yesterday charged that Peek was beaten to death with a claw-hammer and that Mrs. Peek was garroted with a cotton rope.

Indicted with Chappell were Jason Clark and Lewis Turner, convicts, and John Holsombach, inmate of the Carroll County almshouse. Turner, one of the indicted was among six witnesses called to the jury probe.

Solicitor General Grady Vandiviere, who said Friday he will be assisted by two good lawyers in Sheriff McMillan and county policeman, Elmer Ward, stated he would be prepared to try the foursome together or sever the group. Should the defense decide to separate trials, the Solicitor would then call the Chappell first, he said ...

The Marietta Journal
July 23, 1940

197 Defense Witnesses Summoned by Chappell's Counsel For Trial Here

CHARACTER WITNESSES TO NUMBER OVER 100

City and county officials at Carrollton, prominent judge, educators, lawyers, business and professional men and farmers are among 197 defense witnesses who will be summoned for the Peek case next week, it was disclosed here today.

Subpoenas were issued by court clerk John T. LeCroy late Monday and will be presented during the week, it was learned.

Listed as defense witnesses are more than 100 character witnesses, including Mayor Stewart Martin, of Carrollton; Mrs. H. M. Tyus, sister of Former Governor Eugene Talmadge; Joe McGibboney, Carroll County superintendent of schools; O. Spence, postmaster and brother of Warden Charley Spence; W. R. Robinson, city court judge; J. J. Reese, former judge of the city court; Robert Tisinger, former city attorney of Carrollton; Tom Roberson, clerk of the Carroll County Court, Matt Griffin, Carroll County ordinary; J. H. Burson, Carroll County tax collector; Grady

Baker, member of Carrollton city board of education; Rev W. C. Hammond, Rev. Joe Loyton.

Drs. C. C. Fitts, W. B. Hansard, W. W. Aderholt, Jeff Brock, H. L. Barker, and Jim Webb, former Carroll County Sheriff.

Philip Almon, county commissioner of Heard County and Charlie Bledsoe Sheriff of Heard County, are among witnesses outside of Carroll County who will be summoned.

Members of Commissioner Hamp Chappell's family, whose son is among the four accused for the murder of Mr. and Mrs. J. Ed Peek two years ago last June 21, will also be called by defense counsel. They are Mrs. Carrie Chappell, mother of the accused; Clay Chappell, Mrs. R. J. Chappell, Mrs. Lula Pullins.

Court officials pointed out that they have no record of the number of character witnesses in the group they issued Monday, but believed well over 100 were character witnesses entirely...

The Marietta Journal
July 26, 1940

Witnesses Say Lawyers Will Prove
Innocence of Commissioner's Son

State Announces Miss Helen Peek
Will Appear At Trial As Witness For Them

Witnesses who have been subpoenaed by the defense indicated Friday defense counsel in the sensational Peek case which opens Monday in Cobb Superior Court, were ready to show that Bill Chappell, of Carrollton, one of four under indictment here for the murders of Mr. and Mrs. J. Ed Peek two years ago, is innocent of the bizarre slayings.

From these witnesses, some of whom will appear here as character witnesses, *The Journal* learned Friday, it was presumed attorneys for Chappell were prepared to prove an alibi, show that Turner and Clark, implicated by the state in the double slayings, were locked during the period of the murder in their Carroll County jail cells, and prove good character for Chappell.

Two other developments were made known last night by Sheriff George McMillan, on whom Solicitor Grady Vandiviere will depend largely in the prosecution of the four cases next week;

1. Appearance of the 20-year-old Helen Peek, daughter of the slain couple, as witness for the state.

2. And subpoenas for eight to fifteen additional state witnesses to be added to the previous 30.

Court officials indicated that most of Monday morning will be confined to selection of a 12-man jury from 75 new jurors drawn Wednesday night by Superior Court Judge Harold Hawkins.

Miss Peek served as cashier of a Marietta bowling alley which young Chappell operated during the month of the murders, but since has been employed in an Atlanta Insurance office.

At one time officers have said, the two had been keeping company constantly and were intimate friends.

The Marietta Journal
July 29, 1940

FIRST LIST EXHAUSTED MORE DRAWN
TRIAL INTERRUPTED 3 TIMES DURING DAY

Complete List of Veniremen Expected
By Night from 16 New Names

Delayed twice because of the absence of three state witnesses, trial of Bill Chappell, 24, of Carrollton charged with three others with the murder of Mr. and Mrs. J. Ed Peek, got underway at 1:20 this afternoon.

At 2:15 o'clock when the list of jurors exhausted, only ten had been chosen by the defense and state.

First of the ten jurors draw were …

The presiding judge then adjourned court until 4 o'clock in order that 16 additional names be drawn from the jury box. The jury was expected to be completed by night.

Because the state asked for a severance, Chappell will be tried first for the death of Mr. Peek, Atlanta road equipment salesman who with his wife was found badly battered beside their wrecked automobile in deep Mahaffey's cut, three miles northeast of Austell, on the morning of June 21, 1938.

Just before proceeding with selection of the jury Judge John S. Wood of Canton, one of the five defense attorneys, questioned the state's authority for the presence of L. M. Blair, who told the court he was employed to assist Prosecutor Grady Vandiviere by Mrs. J. E. Coursey, of College Park, mother of the deceased Mrs. Peek.

The prosecution consented to go to trial this afternoon despite a three hour delay during the morning because three "important" state witnesses were not present to answer the roll call at the outset of the trial. After two of the three missing witnesses were accounted for, prosecution attorneys declared they would be ready to proceed but asked their right be reserved to delay trial because of the absent of the third "important" witness listed as Mrs. Ollie Pressley of Newnan, Georgia.

A wire from her later disclosed she was ill at her home and could not be present for today's' session.

Another panel …

The Marietta Journal
July 30, 1940

Sheriff McMillan Meets Chappell
At Railroad Bridge, He Testifies

TELLS COURT OF
INCIDENTS AT CUT SCENE

CRIME ESTABLISHED BY STATE WITNESS

Mayes Ward Testifies Blunt
Instrument Used on Peeks

By Alec Tregone

Sheriff George McMillan testified in Cobb Superior Court today that he saw the defendant, Bill Chappell, on trial here for the death of J. Ed Peek, at the scene where his body and that of his wife were discovered at 11 o'clock on the same morning.

The sheriff testified that on his second visit to Mahaffey's cut he saw Miss Helen Peek, 20 year-old daughter of the slain couple, and at that time a steady companion of the defendant, jump out of the sheriff's automobile and enter the machine of Chappell, who with a companion had approached the scene.

Miss Peek was expected to take the stand with other state witnesses Wednesday after Superior Court Judge Harold Hawkins recessed court at noon today to allow a member of the defense counsel to meet a previous scheduled appointment.

Earlier in the morning the state apparently established corpus deliciti statements from a mortician and undertaker that wounds on the two deceased persons could have produced death.

Capt. J. H. Lott of the state highway patrol, the only other witness to testify during today's proceedings, said he observed blood spots as far as a quarter of a mile from the scene where the two bodies were found and that splotches of blood were observed at internals of 30-60 feet.

The sheriff, pressed by special attorney L. M. Blair for details of his second visit to the railroad cut in company with Mrs. Mayes Ward and Miss Peek, said, "We got out of the car, viewed the scene and about that instance, Miss Peek said, 'there's Bill'. She got out of my car and entered Chappell's car that had just driven up with another companion from the Austell side of the bridge."

Continuing his testimony the Sheriff said, "The Chappell car then drove toward Marietta at a speed of 60-65 miles an hour. I asked Esmer Ward to follow them and it was not until we met at the Ward Funeral Home that I saw Chappell again."

During cross examination Willis Smith, chief defense attorney, asked McMillan if he had told all he knew concerning the case, which the sheriff asserted, "I'm familiar with all the developments, but can't say whether or not I have told all I know.

Other cross examination questions to McMillan included that he confirm his multiple interviews with Lewis Turner, Carroll County convict at the time of the murders, and others that the defense charged, have been brought here for questioning, he admitted having requested the transfer of Turner from Tattnall prison on May 18 of this year but denied that he went to Tattnall prison to interview several of the convicts from the Carroll camp.

Early in his testimony, Sheriff McMillan said he found a spot of blood on the left rear door of the Peek automobile badly strewn beside the railroad track in the 51 foot ravine, in addition to blood on the floor board of the automobile.

He further testified that the back seat of the Peek auto was found lying some 8 feet away from the car. Corroborating the state patrolman's testimony the sheriff declared blood was found along the roadway on the Marietta side of the bridge.

Today's proceedings came to an abrupt end shortly before 12: o'clock. Counsel Judge John N. Wood of the defense had a previous scheduled appointment and asked a recess. Superior Court Judge Hawkins recessed court until 8 o'clock in the morning to grant him the request.

Mayes Ward, Marietta mortician was first of the state witnesses, remaining on the stand for more than 55 minutes. Following him was Dr. W. H. Perkinson, first doctor called to view the bodies after they were taken to the Mayes Ward Funeral Home.

The physician swore that death could have been produced by the car going off the road, but declared in answer to a prosecution question: "It could not have strangled Mrs. Peek in the fall."

Blue-eyed Helen Peek was expected to be the central figure among witnesses called for Wednesday's proceedings. Her attitude toward Chappell, whom she served as cashier while he operated a bowling alley here, has been an angle closely watched by followers of the case.

For the second consecutive day, Cobb Superior Court was jammed with spectators, in addition to the many state and defense witnesses who were perched inside rooms and along the rear hallway.

Under direct examination by attorney Blair, Mayes Ward declared that the heads of both Peeks had been battered with some heavy instrument, which he said might have been a hammer. He also related that a rope was discovered about the neck of Mrs. Peek, knotted so tightly that it had left a severe burn.

Under cross examination, Mr. Ward admitted that he could not be sure the crash of the car could have caused all the injuries, although it was his opinion they could have.

In seeking to show that the blood which had dripped from the automobile could not have shed before the wreck took place, Mr. Ward testified he observed some blood had dripped from the Peek automobile.

Jurors drawn for the case...

Court had been recessed a third time before the 12th juror had been accepted by the defense Monday. During the course of jury selection, the defense had struck 19 of 20 strikes, while the state used all of their strikes. Sixteen jurors declared themselves opposed to capital punishment. Sixteen additional Veniremen were drawn from the jury box by court officials after the original list of 75 had been exhausted because of excuses, disqualifications and strikes.

The Marietta Journal
July 31 1940

Peek Case Described
By Convict Lewis Turner

Witness Testifies Defendant Said
"That Old Man Ought to Be Bumped Off"

In a lengthy detailed confession, Lewis Turner, one of the defendants on trial in Cobb superior court for the murder of Mr. J. Ed Peek and Mrs. J. Ed Peek, two years ago, described how he maneuvered and participated in the slaying of the deceased.

Testifying to questions of Solicitor General Vandiviere, the convict-witness told how the defendant's father, county commissioner W. Hamp Chappell, attempted to send Turner out of Georgia on numerous occasions, one of which was a contemplated trip "across the waters".

Turner said the Peeks were killed on a lonely road in southwest Cobb County, Mr. Peek dying from a machine hammer blow on the head and Mrs. Peek from a head blow and strangulation.

During the entire questioning, Solicitor Vandiviere said he could and would corroborate every fact given during future questioning.

At the height of the questioning A. H. Stringer, of Carrollton, was arrested and jailed on an attachment for contempt of court. Solicitor Vandiviere notified Deputy Sheriff Dewey Gable, the arresting officer, that Stringer was transmitting information from the proceedings to defense witnesses on the outside.

Turner testified that Bill Chappell, Jason Clark and John Holsombach, all defendants, participated in the double murder and later drove to Mahaffey's cut where the Peeks were dropped in their kerosene-soaked clothes to the railroad tracks, 51 feet below. The witness also swore that Bill Chappell, Alvin Pitts, Villa Rica Textile worker and Hugh Jason, an associate of Chappell at Carrollton left Carroll County for an extensive trip through Georgia and Florida remaining there until "papa gave the signal to return" after everything appeared quiet.

It was several months later, he testified further, that Bill's father sent me to Birmingham and suggested a trip "across the waters".

Turner swore that it was during the time he was in the Carrollton County prison camp that he first met the Peeks and in Bill's camp office that he first observed any serious threat upon the life of the road machinery salesman.

He said he heard them arguing in Bill's camp office one day but stepped out of his office immediately, Turner went on. Bill then turned to me and said "That old man ought to be bumped off".

Asked to describe events from that occasion to the time the bodies of the Peeks were found on the early morning of June 21, 1938, at the railroad cut, northeast of Austell, Turner swore:

"I made a trip to Atlanta two days later with Bill as driver and went out to Grady Hospital. Also went to Mr. Peek's home, in Atlanta. When we found Mr. Peek out, we came to Marietta with Bill's sister, Miss Dorothy, driving the car. In Marietta, Bill conversed with Miss Helen Peek, cashier at Bill's bowling alley, and then we three left for Carrollton.

"We went to my house in Carrolton on our return and Bill and Dorothy took me to camp a short time later because I was too drunk.

"On the morning of June 20, I was working at Mr. Chappell's home when Bill asked me to prepare some kerosene. Bill told me then we might have a party that night.

"I saw him shortly afterwards, but it was not until later in the night that we all gathered for the party. The Peeks were to meet us in front of the courthouse in town. I left the camp in Bill's car with Bill and Jason Clark, who at the time was cook at the camp. When we arrived at the courthouse Bill told me to drive his car and that he was to drive the Peeks four-door machine.

"We first went to Pullins Fish Camp, stayed there an hour, and from there went to "Shine Morgan's", big bootlegger, and Bill gave us more whiskey.

"From there we went to Mr. Hamp's house. "Bill went in the house and as soon as he came out we all left. Coming through Villa Rica, we stopped near a church and stopped for more drinks. We followed this with a short visit at the "Dip", and from there went to Bolton.

It was at Bolton that the witness testified young Chappell and the Peeks went inside a roadhouse for something to eat.

Leaving Bolton, Turner swore that they crossed the Chattahoochee River on the Bankhead highway and turned right on the first dirt road passed the bridge.

"That was a rough dirt road and it was about 1½ miles from the highway that we stopped for more drinks."

Asked what surroundings he remembered at the spot where they stopped the witness said, "There was a house pretty high on the hill."

Turner testified further: "Bill got out, Mrs. Peek got out. Then I went to their car. In order, Jason and I took more drinks. Mr. Peek was drunk already and told Bill he wanted to go home after Bill insisted on more drinks."

"It was here," Turner said, "that Jason Clark hit Peek on the head with a machine hammer. Clark opened the door and Peek fell out. Mrs. Peek, coming from around the car then screamed, 'Oh! Lord, help me.'" "Bill had grabbed her."

The witness said it was then that young Chappell ordered, "Hell, help me put that man in that auto." Holsombach, the other person on the trip, according to Turner's testimony, put the rope around Mrs. Peek's head. "She had been strangled down."

Turner testified that Bill had assisted Holsombach as he had "one hand on the rope."

The witness then described events during their drive from the "lonely dirt road" to the railroad cut.

Turner testified he had orders to follow his car and not allow any car to get between them on their drive along the Bankhead highway.

Before making their turn at the Marietta-Austell intersection, Turner went on, both cars were stopped and Bill gave us orders about stopping the car at the signal of light blinks. "I drove one car alone," he said.

During the course of the drive to the Mahaffee cut, Turner told of having met a car whose driver was ordered to proceed down the highway and later of meeting a man walking along the Austell-Marietta road near the overhead bridge.

He testified that he was not at the bridge when the Peek machine crashed in the ravine below but could hear the thunder of the crash.

Bill came back to the car and demanded, the witness said, "slide over and let me under this damn car."

Describing the trip back to Carrollton Turner said, "We detoured through Austell and Villa Rica and went straight to the camp.

"Bill couldn't find the key and it was necessary that he call Charley Spence, the warden, to let us in.

"We then had orders to burn clothes which we had on because they were sprinkled with blood-stains. Jason's clothing had the most blood."

The day following the killing, Turner added, "Bill came to me for a talk and told me I was going to Florida because things were getting hot in Cobb County."

Hugh Johnson, an associate of Bill's, Alvin Pitts, textile worker of Villa Rica and a former convict at Carrollton, made the trip according to Turners testimony.

"The defendant's father," Turner went on, "carried me to Columbus once and gave me $149.00 to leave the country, but after thinking it over, I returned by bus to Atlanta."

The witness said he first told the story of the killings to A. L. Hutchins, captain of the state highway patrol at the Dallas, Ga. camp, in May of this year.

Under cross-examination late Wednesday, Lewis Turner testified that he was sent to the state asylum on two different occasions, one time for a period of three weeks and the second time for 12 days. Questioned about his commitments to the state institution he testified that he had been drinking heavily and officers were apparently seeking to correct this habit.

It also became known during cross-examination that the defendant's father was supporting Turner's family at the time the convict was stationed at the Dallas camp, but this support was withdrawn as soon as Cobb County authorities brought him to Marietta in connection with the Peek case.

Before closing proceedings Wednesday, the state presented testimony from seven telephone operators, to substantiate Turner's statement earlier in the day that telephone calls had been made from various Georgia cities and Florida points while the grand jury was probing the double slaying.

The solicitor introduced into evidence toll tickets for calls recorded on July 21, July 23, July 24, July 26 July 27 and July 30 to Mr. Hamp Chappell at Carrollton.

The courtroom was full. Judge Harold Hawkins is seen on the bench while the defense attorney is questioning Helen Peek, daughter of Mr. Peek.

Special Collections & Archives, Georgia State University Library

83

The Marietta Journal
August 1, 1940

Helen Peek Describes Transactions
Between Her Father and Bill Chappell

Efforts To Persuade Her To Sign
Numerous Papers Are Described

State Seeks To Establish Motive of Killing
on Dealings Between Salesman and Defendant

By Alec Tregone

A conversation between Bill Chappell on trial this week for the death of J. Ed Peek, and Miss Helen Peek, his one-time companion and a daughter of the deceased man, in which Bill allegedly told her, "I have made all my money with your father and I wouldn't have anything happen to him" was described in Cobb Superior Court today.

The blue-eyed pretty daughter of the Atlantan for whose deaths four persons are under murder indictments, said under direct examination: "Bill said to me the first time I was ever with him 'your dad has helped me make all my money and he knows enough to take all my money and all my daddy's money and that he did not know what he would do.'"

Asked by prosecuting attorney L. M. Blair what he then said, Miss Peek testified she asked Bill "what are you going to do, are going to kill him?" Miss Peek said he replied, "oh no, nothing like that."

She swore that she was too young to take the conversation seriously, as she was only 18 years then and was still attending high school in Atlanta.

The witness also testified that she had never known her father and Bill to have been crossed, and that she considered the Chappell's, Bill, his sister, his mother and father, her family's best friends.

"Daddy always called on the Chappells when we ever needed money or during any emergency," Miss Peek continued, "So when I was first told of my father's death, I immediately called for Bill at Carrollton."

Miss Peek further testified that she since had been persuaded by Willis Smith, Chief defense attorney for Chappell, to sign a paper to the effect that the Chappells had never given her father any commission on his sales to the county.

Peek was a salesman and had transacted much business with the defendant's father, W. Hamp Chappell, Carroll County Commissioner. It was here that the state sought to establish a motive for the double slayings.

Miss Peek insisted she thought of Bill as a brother and the Chappells had been nice to her before and after the bodies of her family were found.

"Before the funeral on Thursday", Miss Peek went on, "Mr. Smith came to me to sign a paper to the effect that no fees had been given my father in his transactions with Carroll County and that no groceries were delivered us."

She also testified that they (Mr. Smith and Mr. Chappell) told me to swear before the Carroll County grand jury that Bill had never brought groceries to dad and that he never received a fee.

"I was lying" when I swore that, she added. Bill was facing the grand jury there on an embezzlement charge, she said. Other papers which Mr. Smith and Mr. Chappell persuaded me to sign were signed, the witness continued.

Miss Peek was attractively gowned while sitting on the witness stand during the morning and afternoon. She was dressed in a neatly pressed brown and white striped dress and a white turban. Her entrance into the courthouse at 10:45 re-freshened the eyes of the packed audience which had managed to get seats for the fourth day's session.

Several times during cross examination she appeared emphatic responding to attorney Smith's questions.

Continuing her testimony Miss Peek said an intermediary, a Mr. Jones, came to her insurance company office in Atlanta where she had been employed since May 1939 to tell her Mr. Smith and Mr. Chappell wanted to talk with her.

"Mr. Chappell came and conversed with me." she said, "and told me that Bill had sent me some money." After I questioned, "why should Bill be sending me money." Mr. Chappell replied, according to Miss Peek, "that's right, you don't need money." Other efforts of Bill and family to confer with her since March, 1939 were described by Miss Peek. She swore that only that day at 3 o'clock in the afternoon "Mr. Jones" came to her office but she refused to meet the callers.

Once during the morning session, Superior Court Judge Hawkins warned the audience (highly charged) against disorderly conduct and instructed his deputies to take anyone disorderly to the jail until he was ready to see them.

Earlier in the morning the state sought to show how efforts had been made by Hamp Chappell and the defendant to hide witnesses during the grand jury investigation of the double murders.

Alvin Pitts, 42, material witness who has been held incommunicado in the Cobb jail in connection with the deaths was the first witness to take the stand Thursday. He said he was a member of the party on the trip to South Georgia and Florida financed by the defendant.

Pitts told the jury that he heard Bill Chappell tell Lewis Turner, the convict, "if they bill us, we will catch a ship to Mexico and let Hugh take the car back." Hugh Johnson, whom he referred, was one of the four men making the trip with Turner and Chappell.

During the alleged hide-out trip, according to Pitts, young Chappell kept the foursome furnished with liquor and paid lodging expenses while spending the night at tourist camps.

He corroborated Turners statement Wednesday that young Chappell frequently called his father by long distance "to see if they had billed us or not."

At Carrollton, on their return trip, Pitts said, the older Chappell told Pitts that he could come home, but that Turner was being sought.

Pitts asserted that the county commissioner had been helping him and his family since the murder with money and grocery orders.

Under cross examination, Pitts admitted he had served five sentences, most of which were for auto thefts.

W. S. Gilland, of Villa Rica, appeared on the stand in an attempt by the state to corroborate Wednesday's testimony by Turner that a man was motioned to proceed while two cars were parked on the Bankhead highway, between Austell and Atlanta, Georgia.

Gilland testified he saw two cars parked alongside the highway and that a man stepped out as he slowed down and motioned him to proceed.

Gordon Reeves, who lives near the railroad cut where the Peeks' bodies were found, said he saw two cars going toward Marietta turn around and park near the cut.

The Marietta Journal
August 2, 1940

TURNER STORY ATTACKED BY DEFENSE WITNESSES CALLED TO DISCREDIT TESTIMONY PRESENTED BY TURNER

"Tall, Dark, Handsome Man" Reported Seen with Peeks at Bolton Inn Night Before Deaths

John Holsombach, 68-year-old former inmate of the Carrollton County alms house this afternoon completely denied Lewis Turner's story of the death of Mr. and Mrs. J. Ed Peek. A few minutes later, Jason Clark denied any participation in the double murders.

By Alec Tregone

Five witnesses were brought to the stand by counsel for William Chappell, on trial alone this week for the murder of J. E. Peek, Atlanta road machinery salesman, as they attempted to establish the young defendant was not in company with the Peeks when they visited Riverview Inn and Pullins Fish Camp during an alleged spree of visits the night before their bodies were found.

Three waitresses then employed at the Bolton roadhouse, and a garage mechanic, who incidentally was called to the wreck scene near Austell on June 21, 1938 when the Peeks dead bodies were discovered, agreed on the stand the Peeks had joined a "mysterious couple" at the river tavern, but gave conflicting testimony as to whether they arrived together.

Mrs. Marie Bond, proprietor of the Inn, Althea Bond, her daughter, and Bonnie Parker, a waitress all described the man a tall dark complexioned handsome man with much grace in his dances. They were all vague at describing the woman, but swore she was medium height and not plump, as the slain Mrs. Peek.

Eugene Ashmore of Douglas County, corroborated defense testimony of Thursday "that Chappell had not visited Pullins fish camp during the alleged round of visits."

H. B. Aldridge, operator of the "Dip," Douglas County roadhouse which Lewis Turner, chief state witness, swore Wednesday that he, Chappell and his party had visited there on night of June 20 declared the slain couple visited the establishment with the defendant on that afternoon, but not on that evening.

Defense attorneys said they were prepared to call Jason Clark, one of the four defendants charged with the double murder to the stand later in the day. Clark, a life term murderer, was accused by Turner as the one who killed Peek with hammer blow on the head at the time the entire party stopped on a lonely road near the Chattahoochee river bridge to continue their drinking.

Since mid-afternoon Thursday when the state rested its case, defense counsel has vigorously sought to discredit the story of the state's star witness Lewis Turner.

Mrs. Bond, now of Hapeville, said the Peeks came to her place of business between 7:30 and 8 o'clock on June 20, and that she greeted them before going out for a short trip.

"I came to Marietta the next day at the request of Fulton County police to identify the bodies of the Peeks as the couple who were reported in my establishment the night before" she went on.

Continuing her testimony, she said, "I drove up about 10 o'clock after my trip to Atlanta and they (the Peeks and an unidentified couple) were leaving as I was walking into my place." Asked if she noticed any strange attitude on Peek that he might go out and slay his wife? Mrs. Bond said, "No."

Turner earlier had testified that the Peeks and the defendant visited the Bolton Inn for something to eat just before leaving for Cobb County and the scene of the alleged crimes.

Mrs. Bond also asserted that she attended the Peek funeral on the Thursday following their death at the request of Fulton County police for the purpose of identifying the "couple" who were reported with the Peeks that night. She said she did not see them.

One of the waitresses at the Inn, Miss Bonnie Parker, native of Jasper, Ga., and now a belle of Akron, Ohio, also testified she saw the Peeks come in alone and that later another couple entered, recognized the Peeks and seemed surprised to see then.

"The man was all of six feet tall and handsome. Can't recall the girl companion, she asserted to answer to cross examination questions. She said Mr. Peek appeared nervous but there was no indication that Peek would slay his wife as quarreled by the special prosecutor.

Herbert Harris, Fulton County mechanic and brother of the operator of "The Speedway", at Bolton, said he was in the Riverview Inn when the Peeks came in and was certain young Chappell was not with the Peeks nor visited the establishment at any period the Peeks were there from 8 until 10'oclock. At this point, the defense sought to show Peek may have died from indigestion, prosecuting attorney sarcastically whispered.

Harris testified at length concerning the position of Mr. Peek's body in the 51 foot ravine, during which questioning he replied that he did notice bloodstains on the floor board of the car front.

Miss Parker inserted a bit of humor in Friday's proceedings when she agreed with State's attorney L. M. Blair that "most women do notice only the men when they meet a couple." She previously had described the "mysterious man" as "tall and the most graceful dancer I have ever seen."

During her testimony, Miss Bond, waitress daughter of the then Inn proprietor, detailed for the jury the meals the Peeks ordered, asserting, they were served cantaloupe, fish and beer.

Other defense witnesses this morning were Alvin Pitts, a states material witness, Judge W. R. Robinson, Carrollton City Court Judge who declared he would not believe Turner on oath and Tom Robertson, Carroll County clerk of court, who also testified he wouldn't believe Turner's testimony on oath.

The Marietta Journal
August 5, 1940

Father of Defendant Denies Any
Irregular Deals With Deceased

Merle F. Edgeworth Lumber Dealer,
Received $26,691 in Business
Last Two Years, State Charges

By Alec Tregone

In a deep serious voice 22-year-old William Chappell, told a Cobb County jury this afternoon he did not kill Mr. and Mrs. J. Ed Peek.

"Gentlemen of the jury, before God, I did not kill Mr. and Mrs. J. Ed Peek." He opened his two and one-half minute statement, his words carefully put and his stance one of deep intensity." He continued:

"Gentlemen of the jury, I am not guilty of the crime with which I am charged. I did not kill Mr. and Mrs. Peek, and I knew nothing of their deaths until the following morning when Miss Helen Peek called me and told me her father and step-mother had been found dead."

He said: "the Peeks were my good friends, and I had absolutely nothing against either of them. I would not have killed the Peeks or anyone else if I had the best cause in the world."

Referring to Miss Helen Peek's testimony that he was worried because Mr. Peek knew enough on him and his father to get every cent we've made, the defendant said: "The statements of Helen Peek are untrue. The statements she attributed to me are false, and I never heard of them until she took the stand in this trial. I don't know why she would turn and swear something that is not true unless she was influenced."

He said the Florida trip in July 1939, was true. "I went to Florida to hunt some convicts, and I carried Alvin Pitts and Lewis Turner with me because they said they could locate the escapes. I never ran or tried to hide from any officers or courts."

At this point, he paused a moment to emphasize: "Before God, I am innocent."

Shortly after two o'clock, Mrs. Hamp Chappell, mother of the accused defendant, told the jury her son was at home on the night of June 20. A sister of Bill, Dorothy Chappell, testified she had never ridden in a car with her brother and convict Lewis Turner, as claimed by the state in Turner's statement last week.

The state opened its rebuttal shortly before 3 o'clock. Miss Martha Chappell, 18-year-old brunette sister of the defendant, constantly answered "I don't know", or "I don't remember", to state's questions, Did you see any one come to your home on June 20? –Did you see Charley Spence talk with Bill at 10 or 10:30 on that night? –Did you see Merle F. Edgeworth come to see Bill that night?"

Earlier in the morning Merle Edgeworth, 43, hefty lumber dealer of Whitesburg, Ga., in Carroll County, declared during direct questioning that he visited the Chappell home on June 20 and talked with Bill Chappell concerning a lumber order which he had already received, but which he didn't know whether or not the order had been delivered.

Under cross-examination the state produced figures from a memorandum charging Edgeworth had received $26,691.92 from Carroll County for lumber since July 2. Before that time, the state charged, Edgeworth had not received an order.

The defense later made arrangements to return official figures and warrants paid Mr. Edgeworth by the county during business dealings before and after July 2, by a representative in Hamp Chappell's office.

Edgeworth testified he stopped at the Chappell home about 11 o'clock on his return from Alabama and conferred with Bill on a lumber order which had been given him previously. He said he remained there 20 to 30 minutes, having talked with Bill on the front porch of the Chappell home.

Charging that Edgeworth had received his first check ($49) from Carroll County on July 2, 1938, Solicitor Vandiviere produced further figures to show that Edgeworth received $384 from the county in his second transaction and since July 2, has received a total of $26,691.

"Business picked up considerably since the Peeks murder," commented Vandiviere here. The defense objected and the question was passed.

Edgewood further testified Carroll County had been his principal business in recent years and that the county had repaired a number of bridges as well as constructed some under a WPA program.

How much lumber have you sold Carroll County since June 1940, queried Vandiviere a minute later. Using his memorandum figures the solicitor charged Edgeworth received another $100 from Carroll County on June 1, 1940.

A brother of Edgeworth, fishing camp operator in Carroll County since 1930, testified he had never seen young Chappell and Lewis Turner, one of the four defendants jointly indicted for the double slaying, at his fishing camp together.

Listed as Will Edgeworth, the witness contradicted Turner's earlier story that he (Turner) and Chappell visited the river camp together.

The defense called Mrs. Faye Sessions, Florida sister of the defendant, to swear her brother and Hugh Johnson, Bill's Carrollton friend, visited in her home during the trip through South Georgia with Lewis Turner, the convict, and Alvin Pitts, Villa Rica textile worker.

The defendant's rotund father and commissioner of Carroll County, W. Hamp Chappell, told a superior court jury this morning that he had never received or split commissions on sales of equipment and supplies to Carroll County.

During a lengthy cross-examination by the state, the witness declared he never knew of any county property being taken from the camp, or did he ever give anyone authority to do so. "I took Bill, off the county payroll after he was indicted by the Carroll County grand jury", he answered to questions concerning his son's employment at the Carroll convict camp.

Discussing the state's intimation that Peek split his commission with Commissioner Chappell in transactions between the two, the elder Chappell said he never at anytime gave Peek a warrant in his name and never at any time gave him by check or draft a commission for any transactions.

He said he had purchased convict camp supplies from Peek, but never any road machinery. "I've always paid the firm Peek represented and never paid Peek personally," he testified further.

Mr. Chappell admitted he first sought Counsel advice after his son had been accused for the Peeks' murder and after Cobb County authorities had asked transfer of certain convicts in the Carroll County camp.

Asked if he knew his son was making a frolic out of the Florida trip in July 1938, the witness said the object of the trip was to return two escaped convicts back to Carroll County.

"Lewis Turner told me he would catch two loose convicts if I would allow him to go with Bill on his trip to Florida," the commissioner added.

"And you didn't care whether Bill was making a frolic out of that trip and you don't now, added the prosecuting attorney. "Absolutely not," the witness replied.

He said he promised Turner $25.00 as reward on each of the prisoners he would catch and that Hugh Johnson's expenses were his own.

Only when the state's attorney was questioning the elder Chappell regarding Lewis Turner's trip with Bill to Atlanta did he ever seem confused. He testified Lewis would go to Atlanta to pick out special paint which was used at the camp since Turner was familiar with paint mixtures. Turner was classed as a trusty at the convict camp while a prisoner and often was used on paint jobs.

Mr. Chappell swore that he had not heard of county supplies being taken from the camp until a grand jury in Carroll County was probing his son's activities.

The first alibi witness, Charley Spence, political friend of Chappell and warden of the Carroll County prison camp, took the stand just before the week end adjournment Saturday and swore that he visited the Chappell home about 10 or 10:30 o'clock the night the Peeks met their deaths. He testified he went to accompany him to Florida the following day to bring back an escaped convict.

He declared he did not ring the door bell of the Chappell home, but opened the door and called. The elder Chappell appeared at the door and invited him in. The warden further declared he found young Chappell asleep in his room and that, although he turned a flashlight on young Chappell, he did not awaken him.

Under cross examination, the warden admitted to a state's attorney it was approximately 22 days after that night before the prisoner was brought to Carroll County from Florida.

Spence's testimony was brought as an attack on the testimony of Turner, the convict, who with Jason Clark and John Holsonbeck, are co-defendants for the double murders. Turner had testified that Bill Chappell came to the prison on that night and took him (Turner) and Clark on the "murder party."

The suicide theory was inserted into the trial early Saturday when a defense witness, Ed Goble, of Oglethorpe, Ga. selling county supplies for a Whitehall Street firm, testified that on the Sunday afternoon (about dark dusk) before the Peeks' bodies were found Mr. Peek had remarked to him, "I might as well end it all if I can't get the money" in reply to being refused a $50.00 loan, he had asked of Goble.

While the defense has under subpoena enough witnesses to carry on the trial for several days, a spokesman indicated today that the defendant may be called to the stand before Tuesday. The state was expected to assume some time with rebuttal testimony. Young Chappell is on trial for ...

The Marietta Journal
August 6, 1940

JURY TO GET PEEK CASE DURING DAY

Vandiviere Apologizes For Not Naming Hamp Chappell Co-Defendant

Arguments Have Featured Tuesday's Trial, Carmichael says Turner's Testimony Impeached

By Alec Tregone

Solicitor general Grady Vandiviere today startled a packed courthouse auditorium when he told a jury in the opening state argument in the Peek case that "I owe an apology to the people of Cobb County for the fact that Hamp Chappell is not a co-defendant in the killing of Mr. and Mrs. J. Ed Peek. Those remarks coming toward the close of his charge followed his general resume of events which he said led to the murder of J. Ed Peek on the night of June 20.

Defense attorney James V. Carmichael immediately motioned the court for a jury recess after which he charged there was no evidence to show Mr. Chappell, commissioner of roads and revenues in Carroll County, had any part in this, and asked for mistrial.

The jury was recessed and Superior Judge J. Harold Hawkins overruled the defense motion but instructed the jury upon their return to disregard the argument regarding the defendant's father.

Rapping the character witnesses which the defense brought forth to testify in the 8-day trial, Solicitor Vandiviere declared "there is not a person who testified for the defense that is not a relative of Bill Chappell, an employee of Carroll County, a relative of employees of Carroll County, or a criminal." with but two exceptions.

The exceptions, as he listed them, were Mrs. Ella Brumbelow, of Atlanta, and witnesses who were brought by the defense to testify to oath testimony of Lewis Turner, the state's star witness.

First of the defense counsel to face the jury was James V. Carmichael who declared "Lewis Turner's testimony was impeached by the defense by every method the court code allows." And he listed the four methods:

1. Generally bad character.   2. Contradictory statements.   3. Disapproving the facts to which Turner testified, and   4. Proving Turner had been convicted for moral turpitude.

The case was expected to reach the jury before nightfall, Judge Hawkins expecting to charge the jury about 5 o'clock. The presiding judge notified court officials he would be available as late as midnight should a verdict be returned by that hour.

As second speaker for the defense and third orator to face the jury, Willis Smith, immediately jumped on solicitor Vandiviere in a vigorous manner. "This is the most unscrupulous, the most unfair attack ever made upon counsel in a courthouse," he told the jury.

"It is only done to prejudice you against me, and I would not reply except that otherwise I should be unfaithful to my client."

He clarified a statement made last week during cross examination of Alvin Pitts, a state's witness, when he (Smith) said "and you can tell those folks to go to hell" as referring to officers, who he explained, had been hounding Pitts for information regarding the Peeks' death.

Other remarks directed against the chief counsel, from Carrollton, were included in Vandiviere's argument.

"You may be a Mussolini or a Stalin in Carroll County, but in Cobb County where people breathe free air and dispense justice, you are just another citizen."

Attacking further Mr. Smith, the Solicitor said, "If there ever was a Dr. Jekyll and a Mister Hyde, it was Mr. Smith. He changed his personality so often."

Mayor L. M. Blair, employed by Mrs. J. E. Coursey, of Atlanta, to aid the prosecution, will wind up arguments after the last of the defense orators, Judge John Wood of Canton.

In a brief un-sworn statement, Monday the accused son of commissioner Chappell made a general denial of confession testimony of Lewis Turner, former convict, who said he was with Chappell and two other men on the night Peek and his wife were killed, and that Chappell played a leading part in the tragedy.

Referring to Helen Peek, pretty daughter of Peek, he declared:

"I do not know why she should come here and tell something that is not true unless she had been advised."

Miss Peek, a star prosecution witness, was formerly employed by young Chappell as manager of his Marietta Bowling alley.

She was called to the stand after the defense rested to cast doubt on a statement by Carroll County Warden Charles Spence. Spence said he had visited Chappell late on that night of the slaying, had seen him at home, and told him to leave town the next day in order to return a convict from Florida.

The girl declared that Chappell had told her several hours before that he was to make the trip, although Spence had said it was not planned until later in the day.

Before resting from its rebuttal evidence early Tuesday, the state recalled to the stand the defendant's father who was asked to identify a number of counties warrants made payable to Merie Edgeworth, the Carroll County lumberman. This evidence was introduced by the state to show that $27,692 was spent by Carroll County for lumber since the time the Peeks were found dead, and a total of $1,418 from the time Chappell took office as commissioner to June 20.

Another rebuttal witness for the state was Miss Sara Stephenson, of Huntsville, Ala., a friend of Mrs. Peek, who was visiting at the Peek home in Atlanta at the time of the Peek deaths. She told of going to Carrollton with the Peeks on June 15, five days before the Peeks died.

Earlier in the testimony, two defense witnesses, attendants at one time of a service station between Atlanta and Carrollton, had told of the Peeks and Miss Stephenson having come by their station on the afternoon of June 20. Miss Stephenson declared she was not with the Peeks on that day in her testimony.

Capt. A. L. Hutchins, of the State Highway Patrol, Sheriff George McMillan, John Holsombach, one of the four indicted defendants, county policeman Esmer Ward and the Solicitor himself, appeared as rebuttal state witnesses before adjournment Monday afternoon.

The financial angles of the trial which hinted at graft, included prosecution assertions that one defense witness, Merie Edgeworth, had sold the county $27,692 worth of lumber since the double slaying; that Peek had made a commission of $1,717 on the sale of a tractor to Commissioner Chappell and that Wiley Garrett, a defense investigator, had been paid $3,000 by Carroll County and has frequently been made chief of the Carrollton police.

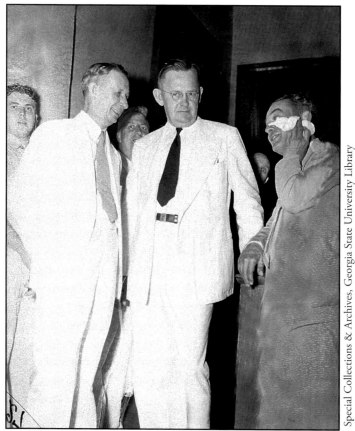

Special Collections & Archives, Georgia State University Library

Those waiting on the Verdict are Judge Hawkins on left in white suit; Willis Smith, lead attorney for Bill Chappell; and Grady Vandiviere, Solicitor General of the Blue Ridge Circuit on the extreme right.

Marietta Daily Journal
August 7, 1940

CHAPPELL FOUND GUILTY, IS GIVEN LIFE

Mercy Of Court Asked In Trial Jury Verdict
Defense Asks New Trial

By Alec Tregone

Twenty-two year old William Chappell (left) was sentenced by Superior Judge J. Harold Hawkins to life imprisonment today after a trial jury found him guilty for the murder of J. Ed Peek, Atlanta salesman. The jury recommended the mercy of the court to be given him.

Immediately afterwards the defense filed motion for a new trial and Judge Hawkins granted them a hearing to be held in Marietta on Oct. 26.

The defendant showed little if any emotion when the Solicitor read the jury's verdict to the court. Members of his family, his mother and father, sisters and brothers, appeared tired as they occupied an entire row of seats in the 68-year-old courthouse auditorium, to hear the verdict and sentence.

"I feel justice has been done and the state is satisfied with the jury's verdict," commented Solicitor Grady Vandiviere after receiving the verdict.

Willis Smith chief counsel for the defense told newsmen he was confident young Chappell will be granted a new trial. Chappell was seated between his mother and father, commissioner of Roads and Revenues of Carroll County, when jury foreman W. W. Weeks gave the verdict to the court.

Asked if he wanted to make a statement, the defendant stood between attorneys Smith and James V. Carmichael and without hesitancy replied, "I don't think so."

Although indicted for both the deaths of Peek and his wife, Chappell was on trial only for the death of Peek. Solicitor Vandiviere said he expects to go into the indictments against Jason Clark, Lewis Turner and John Holsombach, at the November term of court.

The foursome were jointly indicted in two general murder bills by a grand jury last month.

Before returning their verdict shortly before noon today the trial jury had been brought to the courtroom for further instructions on suggestion of foreman Weeks. Instructions as to "what constitutes a reasonable doubt and the meaning of mercy of the court" were given them fifteen minutes before they returned with their verdict.

The jury had been out since 6:15 last night. They deliberated on the case until 10:30 when they left the jury rooms to go to their lodging quarters for the night.

A large crowd had been seated in the auditorium when the verdict was returned. The auditorium was half filled at 10:30 last night when court clerk announced jurors had closed deliberations and had returned to their quarters for the night.

The Peeks were found beside their automobile in deep Mahaffey's cut southwest of Marietta on the Austell Road June 21, 1938.

State witnesses testified they were killed on a lonely road just off the Bankhead highway and then bodies placed in their car and run off into the 51-foot ravine during a spree of drinking for which Chappell was accused of planning.

The star state witness' story was denied by the others, all of whom are under indictment for the killings.

Chappell's defense attempted to show that he was asleep at the time of the murders, which operators of several roadhouses Turner said the party had visited, denied that they had seen Chappell or the other men on that night.

Implications of county graft were raised by the prosecution in presenting evidence which purported to show that Peek and Commissioner Chappell had a working agreement that a witness for the defense was given large county contracts following the murders and that Peek had several times taken county material away from the convict camp where young Chappell was a guard.

The Marietta Journal
August 7, 1940

Bill Chappell, 22-year-old son of Carroll County Commissioner Hamp Chappell, was sentenced to life imprisonment Wednesday after a Cobb County jury at Marietta had returned a verdict of guilty with recommendations for mercy in connection with the slaying of Mr. and Mrs. J. Ed Peek on the night of June 20, 1938...

Attorney Smith, back in Carrollton early Wednesday afternoon and showing signs of fatigue after the strenuous eight days of the sensational trial, expressed disappointment and surprise at the verdict.

Young Chappell, whose self-composure and nonchalance was apparent throughout the investigation and trial, was accompanied from the defense table by Attorney Willis Smith and James Carmichael to hear Judge Hawkins pass sentence.

For the first time since being implicated in the crime more than two years ago, Chappell's face paled, but not an eye blinked nor a muscle twitched as he heard his fate pronounced in the half-filled court room where he had been accused by a convict of participating in the murders.

Marked by sensationalism and shrouded in mystery, the dramatic trial had attracted widespread attention and speculation...

The jury retired to deliberate at 6:05 P. M. Tuesday and after recessing one hour for dinner, returned to closed quarters where it remained, until 10:20 Tuesday night. Discussion of the case by the jury was resumed early Wednesday morning, and at 11:30 the foreman called for Judge Hawkins to repeat the law's interpretation of 'a reasonable doubt.' Five minutes later Forman Weeks announced that the jury had reached a verdict...

Solicitor H. Grady Vandiviere, Solicitor General of the Blue Ridge Circuit, and who directed the prosecution, said Wednesday that the state was satisfied with the outcome of the trial, and felt 'that justice has been done."

Now that the trial was over and Judge Hawkins had sentenced the defendant, you might think the incident would be complete. However, there are several more court proceedings to follow in this tragedy that would create much outside interest.

Solicitor Grady Vandiviere said he would prosecute the other three defendants in the November term of the grand jury. Bill Chappell would now have to be tried for the death of Mrs. J. Ed Peek. Following is a sampling of front-page stories in November 1940.

The Marietta Journal
November 8, 1940

Court Recesses Friday Until Monday;
Chappell Case Set For Thursday

Grand Jury Returns 101 True Bills

Superior court recessed this afternoon until Monday when first of a large number of criminals cases are called by Solicitor Grady Vandiviere for review ...

Solicitor Grady Vandiviere said this afternoon he hopes to secure a jury for Bill Chappell's trial for the death of Mrs. J. Ed Peek by Thursday of next week. He said practically the same witnesses as summoned during the first Peek case trial in July will be called by the state.

Previous commitments indicated that the Peek case would continue for four or five days and that Jason Clark would be called before the end of the third week of court.

Clark was returned here Wednesday night from Tattnall prison for this trial next week after the state penal board authorized the transfer. He, Lewis Turner and John Holsombach are under indictment for the Peek deaths.

Counsel for Chappell following his conviction filed motion for a new trial and the hearing on the motion recently was postponed until November 30. This however will in no way interfere with the second trial.

The Marietta Journal
November 13, 1940

Chappell's Second Murder Case Called

Willis Smith, chief counsel for Bill Chappell, this afternoon motioned Superior Court Judge J. H. Hawkins for a change of venue in Chappell's second murder trial set for this afternoon. The attorney asked the change of venue on the grounds that Chappell would not get a fair trial in Cobb County and that if acquitted might be subject to personal violence.

Second trial of Bill Chappell, son of Carroll County commissioner, W. Hamp Chappell, for murder in connection with the deaths for Mr. and Mrs. J. Ed Peek, opened in Cobb Superior Court this afternoon. The Grand Jury indicated at the recess that they will close investigation for the quarter during the day.

Chappell was convicted and sentence to life in July for ...

Solicitor Grady Vandiviere of the Blue Ridge Circuit, who will again be assisted by Mayor L. M. Blair in prosecution of the Chappell case, said he has new evidence for the second case and has summoned several new witnesses to testify.

Chief defense counsel, Willis Smith of Carrollton, disclosed the employment of Gordon Gann and Claude M. Hicks local lawyers to the defense staff. The trial has been set for 1 o'clock.

Much negotiation was going on between the officers of the court, especially between the defense and prosecution. Apparently a plan was agreed upon.

The Marietta Journal
November 14, 1940

Consent Verdicts Taken, Ending Peek Trials

DEFENDANTS SECOND CASE DISCARDED
Grand Jury Probing Charge of Fraud's Affidavits
in Wednesday's Plea

By Alec Tregone
The final chapter to the 29 months old Peek case was written this morning after:

1. Jason Clark and John Holsombach, two of the four defendants under double murder indictments, were sentenced to life imprisonment after consent guilty verdicts with mercy recommendations were taken by state and defense counsel.

2. Lewis Turner, a state's witness in the July trial and the third of the foursome, was sentenced to a 1-3 years prison term as an accessory to the fact.

3. Bill Chappell's motion for a new trial of the July hearing was withdrawn by defense counsel.

4. Prosecuting attorneys nol-prossed second murder charged against Chappell, Clark, Holsombach and Turner.

Today's lightning-like movements followed withdrawal of defense motion for a change in venue, petitioned by chief defense attorney Willis Smith after the case was opened in Superior court yesterday afternoon. Defense attorneys agreed to withdraw their change in venue petition after prosecuting attorneys broke down defense efforts to show that a number of affidavits were procured falsely in supporting a contention that Bill Chappell could not get a fair trial here during his second hearing.

Solicitor Grady Vandiviere called grand jurors back in session Thursday morning to investigate fraud affidavits which prosecuting attorneys under cross examination established had been maneuvered by a Marietta agent for defense counsel.

The affidavits were submitted by attorney Smith on a claim that "inflammatory" articles written about the case made a fair trial in Cobb County impossible. In backing up his contention, he also submitted affidavits signed by two citizens of Carroll County.

Signers of the allegedly fraud affidavits were ordered to report this morning for grand jury hearing and it was believed that many were called as witnesses in the grand jury investigations during the day.

One highlight of Wednesday afternoon's proceeding was the withdrawal of James V. Carmichael, Claude M. Hicks and Judge John S. Wood from the defense staff. Counsel would not elaborate as to their sudden withdrawal.

Recently I had an interesting meeting with Alec Tregone, the author of most of the articles relating the many fascinating events surrounding the murder of Mr. and Mrs. J. Ed Peek. Attorney Don Smith, a long time friend, invited me to a meeting at which Alec was to be present and we had an interesting conversation. Alec said he thoroughly enjoyed covering the trial and that several non-local reporters made it big covering this sensational trial. He mentioned one who had gone to a large city newspaper and then on to the *Saturday Evening Post*.

His superior reporting of this case presents an excellent history of the trial and the participants.

The above Peek trial has been presented here in more detail in order that you might comprehend that in spite of the massive amount of time and thousands of dollars incurred by the people of the State of Georgia, Cobb County courts, and other counties involved, it was all for naught. Gov. Eugene Talmadge pardoned Bill Chappell in less than two years from the date of the trial, flouting and nullifying the orderly process of the court. It was just one of numerous pardons granted to murderers in the state of Georgia during this period

In order to put this case to rest, *The Marietta Journal* was reporting in November 20, 1940, that Lewis Turner was being questioned by Carroll County Jurors, "The Chappell Regime Investigation."

The Marietta Journal
November 22, 1940

Carroll Jurors Urge Check On County Funds

CARROLLTON, Georgia. A Carroll County grand jury empanelled 45 days ago Wednesday night crystallized its study of the administration of Roads and Revenues Commissioner Hamp Chappell with the recommendation that a "disinterested party" be appointed to check all incoming and outgoing supplies at the prison farm...

During the time of the investigation and trial, 1938 into 1940, there were many headlines competing for front-page space resulting from the stunning events taking place in the world. The investigation and trial occurred as Hitler was acquiring absolute power in Germany, Chamberlain of Great Britain was futilely working for peace in Europe and on September 3, 1939, Europe exploded into what would become World War II. Newspapers reports confirm that courts presided over by Judge Hawkins were occupied with record numbers of trials immediately before and after the Peek trial, several for murder.

CHAPTER NINE

GRAND JURY AND EQUAL JUSTICE

About four years after the Peek trial, in 1944, Judge Hawkins again demonstrated his allegiance to equal justice and fairness. The incident was covered by a local Marietta paper as follows:

The Cobb County Times
November 16, 1944

Judge Hawkins Scores Grand Jury
For Gambling Indictment Action

Wellons Says "No Bills" Based On Evidence, Facts, Information

JUDGE J. H. Hawkins, of the Cobb Superior Court, heavily scored the Grand Jury this morning for failing to return true bills against Eli Garrison and seven others arrested on that night of September 23 and charged with gambling. The Judge asked the jury to include in its presentments advice and counsel as to how they wanted the gambling laws enforced.

The Grand Jury, in presentments returned just before noon today, ignored the Judge's "recharge." In his remarks to the grand jurors this morning, Judge Hawkins referred to the Pledge to the Flag, to the Constitution of the United States, and to the State Constitution, as those documents refer to equal justice and impartial administration of the law.

He stated that two Cobb Countians who were arrested in the Garrison affair came to him and said that they would like to enter pleas of guilty. He said further that after that, there were other citizens of Cobb County arrested for gambling who came up and did file pleas of guilty. These men were fined $100 each by the court. He added that quite a number of the colored race had been charged with the offense of gambling and had pleaded and paid fines.

Then he said 'If some of our citizens are to escape prosecution for an offense of that sort and others are to pay the penalty for it, then we do not have equal protection under the law, and I am unable to carry out my oath to deal fairly and impartially with the rich and the poor and do equal justice among all citizens.'

If you gentlemen feel that the gambling laws should not be enforced, then I feel in your presentments you should recommend that they be repealed. As I stated I have no desire except to treat every citizen the same. If some of the people who are guilty of a violation of the law are not to be punished, then I have to feel that others guilty of the same offense should not be punished.

If it were within my power I would feel like we should revoke the sentences which I imposed upon those citizens who pleaded guilty and who were arrested along about the same time that these other men were arrested. But that term of court having expired, I do not have the power to refund the fines.

I am calling these matters to your attention and would appreciate your counsel and advice about it, whether we are to enforce the gambling laws against all our citizens or not to try to enforce them. I would appreciate an expression in your presentments about it.'

Frank Wellons, Forman of the Grand Jury, at the conclusion of his official service, made this statement: 'I have no comment to make with reference to the Judge calling the Grand Jury back into the general court room or to any statement made by him during the course of his charge. Insofar as the bills of indictment referred to by His Honor are concerned, they were given every consideration by the members of the Grand Jury and the Jury's action in connection with those bills were based upon evidence, facts and other information submitted.'

After considering the evidence against Mr. Garrison and seven other prominent Cobb Countians, the Grand Jury yesterday returned no-bill on the charges that they were gambling in the Garrison ranch house. The men were arrested that night of Sept. 23 following a raid by officers of the Sheriff's department. Warrants charging gambling had been issued against Garrison, Gene Matlock, L. P. Burton, L. P. Barrett, C. E. Howard, Howard Dunn, S. Read and Will Latimer.

CHAPTER TEN

1946 GOVERNORS CONTROVERSY

In the 1946 Democratic primary the candidates included Eugene Talmadge, Eurith D. Rivers, and James V Carmichael. Because there were few Republicans to oppose the winner, the winner of this primary would be the governor of Georgia. Eurith Rivers had assisted the current Governor, Ellis Arnall, when Arnall won the governorship. Rivers assumed that Arnall would support him in the 1946 race, but Arnall supported Carmichael. Rivers decided to run anyway and split the vote, but he only received a little over 69,000 popular votes. Carmichael won the popular vote but fell far short of having enough county unit votes.

Georgia voters were almost entirely Democratic during the first half of the twentieth century. Elections were usually decided at the primary rather than in the general election.

Because of the county unit system, established in 1917, candidates were more interested in the county vote than in winning the popular vote, so they did more campaigning in the rural counties. Just as an example, in 1960 the three smallest counties with a population of 6,980 had a unit vote that equaled the unit vote of Fulton County (Atlanta), which had a population of 556,320. There were 410 unit votes in the 159 counties, requiring 206 unit votes to win.

Federal Judge Griffin Bell in Atlanta, President Carter's Attorney General in 1976, headed a judicial panel that ruled in April 1962 that the county unit system was indeed invalid in its present form and must be redesigned before the September primary of that year. The panel ruled that every vote must be given equal weight regardless of where in the state a voter lived.

Since Judge Hawkins was so outspoken during the 1946 election regarding Governor Rivers and Governor Eugene Talmadge, it may be appropriate to mention briefly the worldwide attention this election received. The following information is a summary of many articles and sources I researched to present a better understanding of the events that ensued following the death of Governor Gene Talmadge.

To understand the personalities in this astonishing story, keep in mind the following:

Governor Eugene Talmadge served two terms from 1933 – 1937. The two terms of Governor Eurith D. Rivers were from 1937 – 1941. The last time Governor Eugene Talmadge served as governor was from 1941 – 1943. Ellis G. Arnall, the current governor at the time, served for two terms from 1943 – 1947.

I recall well the 1946 election. It was a wild and truculent campaign. Since Jimmy Carmichael was a local candidate many friends worked for Carmichael. The Klu Klux Klan played a significant role in the campaign and had no qualms about intimidating any group of voters. Without restriction, randomly all across the state fiery crosses were burned.

Stetson Kennedy fearlessly joined the Klan in order to expose them, and his exciting Georgia experiences were related in his book, *I Rode with the Ku Klux Klan*. In this book he described the 1946 election for the Governor of Georgia. With his kind permission I quote:

> Talmadge was elected Governor of Georgia after a whirlwind campaign of Klan terror aimed at keeping Negroes from going to the polls. On the eve of the election, fiery crosses had flamed on courthouse lawns all over Georgia. Notices signed "KKK" were tacked on to Negro churches, warning, "The first Nigger who votes in Georgia will be a dead one." Other warnings were sent to Negroes through the U.S. mails, and others were dropped from airplanes over Negro neighborhoods.
>
> On Election Day, thousands of Negroes awoke to find miniature coffins on their doorsteps. My union friend Charlie Pike led his locals, white and Negro alike, to march to the polls and vote as a body. And though many thousands of Negroes defied the Klan and voted for the first time, in the end the forces of hate carried the day, Talmadge was elected, and the liberal supported by Governor Arnall was defeated.

Incidentally, the liberal candidate, Jimmie Carmichael, carried Cobb County. On another note, Herman Talmadge, son of Governor Gene Talmadge, lost Cobb County and Marietta in the gubernatorial race two years later although generally he was loved and supported by many Georgians, especially in the rural areas.

Dr. Scott E. Buchanan, at Columbus State University, wrote an article entitled *"Georgia's Three Governors Controversy."* I have selected several excerpts for the summary. This interesting article can easily be found on the Internet via a search engine using the article's name.

> In 1947 one of the most bizarre incidents took place in the history of U.S. state politics. Eugene Talmadge had been elected governor of Georgia for the fourth time in November 1946. The problem arose when "ole Gene" died of cirrhosis of the liver on 21 December 1946 before he had been inaugurated governor. The controversy that followed quickly evolved into a constitutional crisis.

Additional summaries of reports on this election, including Dr. Buchanan's, follows and will further explain the events heard around the world. The gubernatorial race of the century for governor, or more precisely, governors, of Georgia occurred in 1946.

Eugene Talmadge was elected for the fourth time. It was known that he was gravely ill. Clever politicians and followers of Talmadge, being aware of the health of Gene, started a write-in campaign for Herman Talmadge, his son. Georgia law stated that the Georgia General Assembly would elect a governor from the next two candidates "then in life" if the winner of the general election died before taking office.

Before 1945, since Georgia had no lieutenant governor before this time, this ploy would have been constitutional. The 1945 Georgia Constitution created the office of Lieutenant Governor to succeed governors should they die while in office. The lieutenant governor is also the constitutionally mandated president of the Georgia Senate. Before 1945 state senators chose the president of the senate, who then became the governor if a vacancy occurred in that office. Several times in the nineteenth century, governors died and were replaced by the president of the senate.

Georgia lieutenant governors, unlike candidates for vice president of the United States, do not run on a ticket system. Instead of being chosen as the running mate of a gubernatorial nominee, candidates running for lieutenant governor stand for election independently. Thus the state's two highest elected officials may view each other as political opponents. This occurred in 2002 when Governor Sonny Purdue, a Republican, was elected governor and Mark Taylor, a Democrat, was elected Lieutenant Governor.

In 1946, M. E. Thompson, not a Talmadge fan, was elected Georgia's first lieutenant governor.

Many wondered if a write-in candidate was feasible under the constitution. Since no Republican candidate was in the election, the write-in proponents believed that Herman would become governor if Gene died. At the same time the outgoing governor, Ellis Arnold, a supporter of Jimmy Carmichael and Gene Talmadge's opponent, refused to relinquish the office of governor until the Georgia Supreme Court heard the case. Herman Talmadge, Ellis Arnold, and M. E. Thompson maintained their claim to governorship until the Georgia Assembly convened in January 1947.

The General Assembly, which was overwhelmingly in support of the Talmadge forces, moved to disregard the new Constitution. The General Assembly decided that M.E. Thompson, the Lieutenant Governor elect, was not the governor since neither Thompson nor Talmadge had been sworn in when Gene met his demise. In the attempt to thwart the Talmadge forces, the Thompson camp is said to have begun serving drinks laced with knockout drops to pro-Talmadge legislators. After the unconscious legislators were revived, the General Assembly moved to choose the next governor from the next two candidates receiving votes.

It was quickly discovered, however, that young Herman had actually placed third among write-in votes. The General Assembly quickly pressed for an adjournment to regroup.

Finally, it was resolved when it was "discovered" that when the election was held in 1946 a set of ballots from Telfair County, Talmadge's home county, had gone "uncounted." The ballots were rushed to Atlanta to be counted. Upon arrival of the Telfair ballots, the write-in ballots placed Herman Talmadge into the top two of candidates receiving votes behind his late father.

It was later discovered by investigative reporters that all of the Telfair ballots were written in the same handwriting. The voters had also cast their ballots in alphabetical order, and some of the voters resided in local Telfair County cemeteries. Herman Talmadge denied any knowledge of these dead voters. *The Atlanta Journal Constitution* reporter, George Goodwin, confirmed that some of the alleged Telfair County write-in voters for Talmadge were dead; others who were alive, and whom Goodwin interviewed, said they had not voted.

George E. Goodwin won the 1948 Pulitzer Prize in Journalism for Distinguished Local Reporting. (*Vote Fraud in Telfair County, Georgia.*)

There was major concern regarding violence around the state and at the capitol. The National Guard supported Talmadge; the State Guard had not been disbanded by 1946 and it supported Governor Arnall. Thankfully, no violence erupted during this crisis. Herman Talmadge was sworn in as governor at 2 a.m. on January 15, 1947.

Stating that Talmadge was a "pretender" to the governorship, the outgoing governor, Ellis Arnall, refused to relinquish the office. Talmadge left the governor's office and ordered the adjutant general, Marvin Griffin, to see to it that Ellis Arnall got back safely to his home in Newnan, about 40 miles south of Atlanta. Griffin was then instructed to change the locks on the doors of the Governor's office at which point Talmadge would take control. Talmadge's orders were followed, and he took control of the governor's office later that morning.

Arnall returned to the Capitol late on the morning of January 15, 1947, and when he tried to go into the governor's office, he was told that he could wait to see Governor Talmadge just like any other citizen.

Fuming at the turn of events, Arnall took control of the information booth at the front door of the Capitol building. From here, Arnall would continue to claim that he was still governor. When a pro-Talmadge legislator dropped a firecracker into the information booth, Arnall then moved to his nearby law office, although rumors circulated that Arnall had commandeered the men's restroom as his office. The firecracker was loud enough that a reporter called his editor that an assassination attempt had occurred. Arnall resigned three days latter in favor of M. E. Thompson.

Upon the "resignation" of Arnall, Lieutenant Governor Thompson then claimed to be the acting governor. Some of the other state department heads began to choose sides between Talmadge and Thompson. The Attorney General refused to bond Talmadge's choice for State Revenue Commissioner, and the State Treasurer refused to honor any spending request from Talmadge. Not knowing which man was the legitimate governor, the Secretary of State even began sitting on and sleeping with the state seal, which was needed by the governor to make certain documents legal.

On January 21, 1947, Talmadge proposed that he and Thompson resign and re-run the election, allowing voters to decide among the two. Thompson quickly refused to do this, but he did file a motion before the Georgia Supreme Court. Herman Talmadge was governor at this point for 67 days, from January 14, 1947, to March 18, 1947.

The controversy was settled in March 1947 when the Georgia Supreme Court overturned two lower court rulings and decided that M. E. Thompson was the Acting Governor. The court ruled that a special election be held in 1948 to decide the remainder of the term ending in 1950. Talmadge abided by the Court ruling and gave up the governorship to Thompson. *The Atlanta Journal* asked: "Is this Georgia or South America?" *Newsweek* said the mix-up was "so fantastic that it makes the historic gyrations of the Balkans seem sedately sober in contrast."

It is said that Herman Talmadge burst on the scene in 1947, a revolver tucked under his belt as he claimed the governorship in a legendary power struggle after the death of his father.

In 1948 Herman Talmadge won the governorship with 312 to 98 unit votes and 357,865 to 312,035 popular votes.

Herman Talmadge was governor until January 1955. He was elected to the U. S. Senate and served from January 1957 until 1981. In 1980, he ran again for the Senate and narrowly lost the election to Mack Mattingly, the first Republican elected to the Senate from Georgia since Reconstruction. This was the end of the "Talmadge Dynasty" as well as the end of only one political party in Georgia. Herman Talmadge had gone from notoriety as a defiant segregationist to a nationally respected Senator as a member of the Senate Watergate Committee, and then to humiliation by the actions of the U.S. Senate Ethics Committee in a campaign fund-raising scandal. His years in the Senate were advantageous for Georgia.

Notwithstanding their occasional ethical lapses, Governor Herman Talmadge and Governor E. Rivers obtained legislation that was beneficial to Georgia. Rivers was able to get legislation passed that had been blocked by Eugene Talmadge: legislation providing for the national rural electrification program, the expansion of the state's public health services, and the reorganization of Georgia's Department of Welfare.

The philosophy of Eugene Talmadge is said to have been "each man for himself" and "self-help." This was not so different from that of President Herbert Hoover who felt that relief should be left to the private sector and the individual.

Gene Talmadge was outspoken and vigorous in opposition to Franklin Roosevelt's entire New Deal including the CCC, WPA, and NYA. He also opposed Georgia's participation in the Social Security benefits and all other programs of the Social Security Act.

It is reported that Eugene Talmadge told a department head that the best way to handle individuals on relief would be to "line them up against a wall and give them a dose of castor oil." Eugene Talmadge apparently was unable to see or feel the tears and pain of the people in the midst of the Great Depression.

The opposition of Gene Talmadge to the New Deal and the Roosevelt administration eventually caused Harry Hopkins, in April 1935, to federalize Georgia's relief program. Georgia was one of only three states with this dubious distinction. Harry Hopkins was the Federal Administrator of Relief Programs for the Roosevelt administration, and a close friend to the President and his wife Eleanor.

During Governor E. Rivers' administration, the Georgia Legislature passed legislation that would qualify Georgia for several programs. It allowed Georgia to cooperate with federal agencies, thereby to receive federal funds providing relief for the people of Georgia from the misery of the Great Depression. This occurred in 1935 when Judge Hawkins had served four years of his 18 years on the Blue Ridge Circuit.

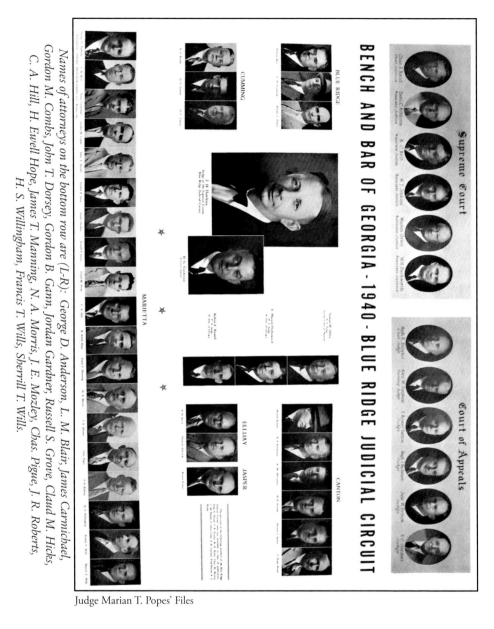

Judge Marian T. Popes' Files

The portraits of the following members of the Blue Ridge Judicial Circuit were not
available at the time of publication:
John S. Wood, J. P. Fowler, R. E. Kirby, Chas. M. Brown, C. M. Dobbs, J. Glenn Giles,
T. E. Latimer, Fred Morris and S. J. Welsh.

CHAPTER ELEVEN

Levity In Speeches

Old Cobb County Courthouse on the square in 1943, Marietta, Ga.

When court convened in Cobb County, Judge Hawkins held court in this old Cobb County Courthouse from 1931 until his election to the Supreme Court in 1948. In 1864 Federal soldiers burned the previous courthouse and much of the contents. The building was built in 1873 and served well until its demise in 1966 to allow for construction of a new courthouse.

One event of personal import occurred in 1948, when I went into the courthouse, (previous page) to see Judge Hawkins. I saw him in the hall and asked if I might see him a minute. He replied that he was just going back into the courtroom. I said I would be glad to come back, that I wanted to discuss Ann. He said, "Wait just a minute," went into the courtroom and returned. Apparently he had put the court proceedings on hold while I asked to marry his daughter, Ann. This thoughtful man listened to me and then, speaking in his soft, gentle voice, explained why he knew it would be a wonderful relationship. So far, it has lasted over fifty-seven years. The little room we briefly occupied was the small shaded room (window) on the left side of the second floor.

Ann Hawkins

During the time Judge Hawkins was on the bench of the Superior Court of the Blue Ridge Circuit and later on the high court, he was asked to speak to many organizations. This was customary for any Judge of Superior Court of Georgia. For one reason the judge of the Superior Court is one of the most powerful positions in a county while the Supreme Court is the court of last resort of appeal in the state. Most judges are most willing to speak at appropriate gatherings.

In his speeches he always included some form of levity. Frequently in my research I found outlines of speeches or other communication that included a note about the subject of a humorous story as a reminder to him. Unfortunately the stories were not recorded in full, as I know it would have been good reading. I have found a couple of stories in his records that he apparently used in his many speaking engagements.

The stories were usually used to emphasize a point in his speech. The Judge was undaunted at hearing jokes, which were not flattering to him.

When Judge Hawkins was to speak at a statewide meeting the following story was told during the speech:

Years ago when Judge Hawkins was presiding in Fannin County, a fellow had been indicted for having a little liquor, and was being tried. The sheriff had raided his home and found nineteen pints of whiskey, with the defendant there in the room.

In his statement to the jury he said: 'You know I was about 45 years old; I got married, and we were expecting our first baby. The Doctor over there in Mineral Bluff told me to get some liquor for the occasion, but I didn't know exactly how much you needed for such an occasion like that. And, too, I had been so nervous for about nine months that I couldn't stand it. I decided to get the liquor, just like the Doctor prescribed, and I went out there and got a ten-gallon keg and put it up in the back seat of my car and started home with it, when I met the Sheriff. He took my liquor away from me and made a case against me. Now, that is just exactly the truth about the matter.'

Following the conclusion of the trial Judge Hawkins charged the jury, and said: 'Now gentlemen, you have heard the testimony here of your Sheriff about how this happened. Of course, if you believe your Sheriff, you ought to convict this man. You have heard the defendant's explanation of the affair. Now, if you believe the defendant, you likewise ought to convict him; now go out and make a verdict.'

After being out all day, Judge Hawkins got hold of a bailiff and inquired if he knew what the trouble was with the jury. The bailiff replied, 'Well, Judge, they have split eleven and one. One man on the jury wants to turn him loose. I heard one fellow say, 'Now wait a minute, you believe our Sheriff, don't you?' He said, 'No, I know him, I wouldn't believe him on oath any time.' He said, 'Well you know the defendant?' He said 'You would believe him, wouldn't you?' He said 'No sir, I wouldn't believe him either.' He said 'Well, you know our Judge," he said 'You would believe him wouldn't you?' He said, 'Hell no; he don't know any law.' "

Another amusing story utilized in a speech involved Judge Patterson, who was from Forsyth County as was Judge Hawkins who was born in Forsyth County and also lived the early part of his life there. While he served as Judge of the Superior Courts of the Blue Ridge Circuit, he appointed Harold Hawkins as his Court Reporter. The following is the opening section of a speech made by Judge Hawkins at the Georgia Bar Association. Judge Hawkins said:

> Ever since I have been a member of the Association and at every meeting I have attended, I have heard the complaint by those present that the Association had not been able to enlist the country lawyer; that the charge was frequently made that the Association was being run by the city lawyers, and that this idea should be corrected, and the country lawyer enrolled and enlisted.
>
> My information is that when this same discussion arose in the executive committee meeting when it met to prepare a program, my good friend, and a member of the Bar of the Blue Ridge Circuit, Hon. William Butt, suggested that in order to forever refute and end the unwarranted charge that the lawyers from the cities were seeking to monopolize the Association, they ask me to appear on the program, and there by conclusively demonstrate that the country lawyer would have a place in the Association.
>
> When asked by some of the other members of the committee as to just how country I was, my information is that he related a little incident that happened some several years ago.
>
> We have one member of the Bar of our Circuit, who, to put it mildly, is rather eccentric, and always takes any adverse ruling by the court as a personal affront. At that time the Judge of our circuit was Honorable H. L. Patterson, who was a resident of Forsyth County, and in which county I was born. Judge Patterson, a mighty good man and an able lawyer, was advanced in years, wore a beard and was not one of the handsomest men I ever saw, and was frequently referred to as "Snacks Patterson." One day after he made some ruling against this lawyer to whom I referred, the lawyer went out on the streets and was unburdening himself in something like these words:

Things have come to a pretty pass when Old Man Snacks Patterson and Harold Hawkins, two men raised over in Forsyth County, twenty miles from a railroad, who never heard a train whistle blow until they were grown, and where the hoot-owls holler in the day time, comes down into an enlightened community and take charge of Cobb Superior Court. Why, Old Man Snacks ought to be driving a canvas-covered, ox-drawn apple wagon, peddling apples, and Harold Hawkins running along behind with two rocks in his hands keeping the wagon tires knocked on.

As such things sometimes will, this statement got back to Judge Patterson, and the next time this particular lawyer was over in Forsyth County strenuously objecting, and arguing his objection after the court had already ruled upon it, Judge Patterson reached up and got hold of his whiskers, and said, 'Sit down Colonel, Harold Hawkins and I are running this apple wagon.'

Judge Tom Candler of the Supreme Court of Georgia being introduced by Judge Hawkins:

When Judge Candler was with his granddaughter while waiting to see the dentist to fix some store-bought teeth his granddaughter asked him, 'Grandpa, were you in the ark with Noah?' He said, 'Why, no I wasn't in the ark with Noah.' 'Well, how come you didn't get drowned?' she said.

At Judge Hawkins' first appearance as a speaker to the Bar Association he was somewhat reluctant as what to choose as a subject. He noted that, although honored to be invited, he was a little depressed about this responsibility and that it reminded him of a friend of Bob Troutman who was having bouts of depression.

"It seems this man frequently became despondent, felt that he was confronted by insurmountable obstacles, that his last friends had deserted him, and he would worry until he would almost blow his top. He visited a psychiatrist, and was advised that when in that condition he should go away out in the orchard, get out under an apple tree, and commune with nature and his maker, and he would, in that way, get relief. Not long thereafter he felt one of these spells coming on and he went out and sat down under the tree. About that time a large bird lit in the tree above him. Looking around, he took out his handkerchief and brushing off his shoulder, said: 'Lord, this is what I am talking about. The birds sing for everybody else."

CHAPTER TWELVE

Excerpts From Selected Speeches

The speeches of Judge Hawkins are one of the best indicators of his philosophy. They provide us with some understanding and feeling about Judge Hawkins. In order to provide a better insight into this good man, I have located a few of his speeches and will include very short excerpts from some of them.

Following are a few excerpts highlighting subjects used in speeches made by Judge Hawkins at various times during his tenure as a jurist:

Legal and Citizens Responsibilities
1952

We find the United States of America cast in a role of leadership more powerful and important that was ever before, either by fate or chance, thrust upon any nation. The attendant responsibilities of this hour are trying the fabric of our national strength. The legal profession is largely the architect, guardian, and sponsor of that organized government which reflects more than anything else our way of life. We must ever be mindful of the fact that the legal profession is a living, integral part of what America is, with a definite goal to assume the great responsibility of fostering and preserving the highest order of civilization yet known to history.

There is much governmental extravagance and waste, calling for higher and higher taxes, to the extent that they are becoming burdensome and oppressive. Much abuse has been heaped upon our President, upon Congress and upon the Judiciary. It may be each branch of our government deserves some part of this criticism, and is partly responsible for the condition in which we find ourselves, but I call attention to the fact, as pointed out in the decision of our Supreme Court in Plumb v. Christie, 103 GA. 686: "In all independent states and nations absolute power rests somewhere. In this country it is neither lodged with the executive nor the legislative nor the judicial branches of the government, nor with all combined; but sovereignty rests with the people of the several states."

If the President has been wasteful and extravagant, it is because Congress by its appropriations has permitted him to be so, and if the Courts have upheld such extravagance and waste, it is because we live under a constitutional government, established by the sovereign people and under written laws passed by the legislative branch of government whose members are elected by the people, and the Courts can enforce only such rights as our laws protect, and remedy such wrongs as they redress.

If the people want to stop waste and extravagance it is within their power to do so by ceasing to make so many demands for the furnishing of service and supplying of benefits by the government. I think is rather inconsistent for us, as American citizens, to criticize and deplore waste and extravagance on the one hand, and on the other to boast of the vast sums of federal funds we have obtained for the carrying out of some of our pet projects.

Return to Fundamental Beliefs of Our Forefathers
February 3, 1953

In recent years many theories have been advanced by the deep thinkers of our times as to the possible fate of our nation, and indeed of the world, if men continue to live in the present state of confusion, strain and uncertainty. All agree that somewhere we seem to have lost the way and that we must find ourselves and set a course if we are to survive.

We, as citizens of this country, need to return to the fundamental beliefs of our forefathers:

In the supreme worth of the individual and in his right to life, liberty, and the pursuit of happiness:

That every right implies a responsibility; every opportunity an obligation; every possession, a duty:

That the law was made for man and not man for the law; that government is the servant of the people and not their master:

In the dignity of labor, whether with head or hand; that the world owes no man a living, but that it owes every man an opportunity to make a living:

That thrift is essential to well-ordered living and that economy is a sound requisite of a sound financial structure, whether in government, business, or personal affairs:

That truth and justice are fundamental to an enduring social order:

In the sacredness of promise, that a man's word should be as good as his bond; that character—not wealth or power or position—is of supreme worth.

That the rendering of a useful service is the common duty of mankind and that only in the purifying fire of sacrifice is the dross of selfishness consumed and the greatness of the human soul set free:

In an all-wise and all-loving God, and that the individual's high fulfillment, greatest happiness, and widest usefulness are to be found in living in harmony with His will:

That love is the greatest thing in the world; that it alone can overcome hate; that right can and will triumph over might:

If we return to these fundamental beliefs, we will preserve this Nation and avoid disaster.

𝔐𝔞𝔯𝔦𝔢𝔱𝔱𝔞 𝔇𝔞𝔦𝔩𝔶 𝔍𝔬𝔲𝔯𝔫𝔞𝔩

June 25, 1953

Certain Acts Endanger Rights of The People

The rights and liberties of many of our citizens have been restricted because of two legislative acts of Congress, which strain provisions of The Constitution. Judge Hawkins warned that wage and hour laws and Fair Trade acts are close to "creeping socialism" but pointed out that power still lies in the hands of the people.

He said wage and hour acts at present apply only to minimum wages and maximum hours, but he warned that, if valid for that purpose, they would also be valid to fix maximum wages and minimum hours.

Referring to the right of eminent domain, as exercised by the various governmental subdivisions, he pointed out that the right of the government to take property for the public welfare is being used to take the individual's property for devotion to private purposes. Under the Marxist theory, essential to the establishment of a communist government, is the destruction of the right to private ownership of property.

Since sovereignty rest with the people of the several States, it behooves each and every one of us to take a vital interest in our government.

The ultimate source of legislative power is traceable to the people; and, in their sovereign capacity, they have a right to frame laws for their government, and for the regulation of human conduct on all matters over which exclusive power has not by them been delegated to the federal government.

Acting in their organized capacity, and under the forms of existing laws, they can rend asunder all bonds that are thrown as restraint around individual action, unbridle liberty, and make license as free as the winds of heaven and as wild as the waves of the sea.

They can, on the other hand, so frame their organic and statute law as to place upon their own necks a yoke as galling as ever serf carried under the edict of a despot.

The Georgia Constitution
1957

Judge Hawkins addressed the Marietta Rotary Club in 1957 stating that the Georgia Constitution was treated too lightly. A state constitution is designed to be a permanent, certain and fixed document, binding on the courts, and basic protection for all the people. He said the Georgia Constitution was rewritten and adopted in 1945, only 12 years ago, already has been amended 168 times and 15 more amendments are pending to be voted on in 1958.

Only 19 of the amendments have been of general nature, applying to the people of the whole state. All the remainders have been local amendments, applying to certain counties or political subdivisions. Thus, rather than a constitution applying to all the people, it now has been chopped up to the point that it means one thing in one county and another somewhere else.

Amendment of the constitution is treated the same as a local bill, and this basic document has little more standing that a statute. It no longer is a supreme law of and for the whole state.

Judge Hawkins' Files

Justice J. Hawkins at a community meeting with Lockheed Aircraft Corporation Executive Officer Carl Kotchian, who was later president of the company. Circa 1955.

CHAPTER THIRTEEN

CIRCUMSTANCES DURING JUDGESHIP AND RUN FOR SUPREME COURT

During the eighteen years Judge Hawkins served as Judge of the Superior Court on the Blue Ridge Circuit, many significant events reshaped the world's paradigm. These events no doubt affected the process of the judicial system. Primary among these events are The Great Depression, Franklin Roosevelt's New Deal, the creation of Social Security of 1935, the Wagner Act of 1935 (allowing unions), Prohibition, and the Declaration of War in 1941 when the United States entered World War II.

Throughout the 1940s transformation of Cobb County, was just beginning. The Bell Bomber Plant manufactured many B-29 long-range bombers for use during WW II. The B-29 was used to deliver the first atomic bomb on the cities of Hiroshima and Nagasaki, Japan, August 6, 1945.

Bill Kinney Collection

President Truman authorized the first use of the new weapon to end World War II. He no doubt had on his mind that the death count of young American soldiers killed in the action was approaching 400,000. The use of the bomb eliminated the need for men, home from Europe and in route for the invasion of Japan, and many thousands of others to leave the European Theater of Operation and participate in the invasion of Japan.

The advent of Bell, and later Lockheed, which took over the plant, changed the culture and lifestyle of Marietta. All of these events contributed to the court systems being overloaded and Judge Hawkins' chairmanship of the Marietta Board of Education being considerably more complicated.

The Great Depression reshaped the American dream into a nightmare where basic desires became desperation and hope became despair. Many Americans were even questioning the viability of democracy and capitalism. During the late 1930s and early 1940s while Judge Hawkins' served on the Blue Ridge Circuit, the average American family's annual income had been reduced by 40 percent, from $2300 to $1500. Their greatest hope was survival.

Democracies such as Italy and Germany had fallen to dictatorships, bringing about the Second World War, but most importantly the United States, its Constitution and court systems adhering to the rule of law, survived.

The only Presidents of the 1930s and 1940s were Herbert Hoover, Franklin Delano Roosevelt, and Harry Truman. Much as did Gene Talmadge, President Hoover felt that relief should be left to the private sector and the individual. Hobos, the unemployed, traveled throughout the country by riding in boxcars or anywhere they could hide on freight trains as they sought employment wherever available. Mostly, they would be fed by families living a few blocks from the tracks. Large camps of unemployed workers were referred to as Hoovervilles.

The young people were dancing to big band music, playing card games and board games, as well as listening to *Lum and Abner*, and *Amos and Andy*, with time left to hear, with their parents, the Fireside Chats of President Roosevelt. The younger children were, in the absence of electronics, devoting their time to making carts and scooters out of egg boxes. When they could cut a neighbor's grass for a dime, they could go to a movie.

The United States had been engaged in World War II for about four years when Nazi Germany and Japan surrendered in1945. Because of the War and the production of massive military equipment for the United States and our Allies, the country had overcome the desolation that existed in the 1930s. All of these things took place while the Judge was holding court in the Blue Ridge Circuit; a period no one living at the time would forget. No doubt, beliefs and attitudes of the juries, prosecutors, and those appearing in Judge Hawkins' court were somewhat prejudiced by the conditions discussed above. The United States and world economy were much improved, and there was considerable diminution of world tension. The cold war was just beginning and would last for many years.

The 1948 election was approaching. In 1947 many friends, both local and statewide, encouraged Judge Hawkins to seek the Democratic nomination for election to the Supreme Court of Georgia. Chief Justice Jenkins, for whom he had worked, was retiring from the court early to become a law lecturer at Emory University, thus creating a vacancy.

The Judge began to think seriously about this possibility. In the Blue Ridge Circuit during the eighteen years he presided over the court, he was elected four times without opposition. His entire life had been devoted to the legal profession. He had experience as a court reporter, legal assistant to Appeals Court Judge William Frank Jenkins, private practice for eleven years, and eighteen years as a Superior Court Judge. He was eminently qualified.

In late 1947 the decision was made to enter the race for Associate Justice of the Supreme Court of Georgia. He was encouraged by many friends and associates, and if he were successful in this endeavor he would reach the apex of his career.

The decision to run was no minor decision because a state-wide race for any office necessitated an organization and personal appearances in all 159 counties of the state. As Georgia is a very large state with over 58,000 square miles, this was no small task. It also required contacting and seeking support from as many attorneys and law firms in the state as time and funds would permit.

Attorneys of the Blue Ridge Circuit who unanimously supported Judge Hawkins in the six counties of the Blue Ridge Circuit are listed later. Cobb County was in the Blue Ridge Circuit.

I do so regret that so few names of the committee set up and headed by J. G. Roberts (left) and many other local friends and supporters are not available. I am sure it would be entirely too lengthy to list here. The Judge had a wealth of friends locally and across the state who were eager to support him. It is apparent from correspondence that Robert Troutman and Henry Troutman from Atlanta were very helpful in their support.

In addition to attorney J. G. Roberts and attorney Henry Trout-man, the following friends and associates are known to have contributed to the campaign of Judge Hawkins.

John L. Tye, Jr.	R. B. Troutman	William Butt
J. G. Roberts	James A. Branch	Thomas Branch
McKibben Lane	J. Glenn Giles	Jordan Gardner
Claude J. Hicks	H. C. Schroeder	F. C. Owenby
G. F. Hagood	Benny Kaplan	W. H. Perkinson
O. R. Dobbs	John T. LeCroy	Joe E. Johnson
H. N. DuPre	Guy H. Northcutt	E. T. Lance
C. W. Kiker	E. T. Hudson	A. H. Burtz
A. C. Wheeler	James T. Manning	Dan W. Dobbins
J. Hines Wood	J. N. McEachern	Harry Scoggins
Harold Glore	Mr. &Mrs. Dwight Vaughan	

Campaigns in 1947 were not conducted as they are today. The Judge had no well-funded statewide campaign organization to handle the necessary acquisition of funds or to arrange appointments for speaking engagements and personal appearances. He did have an outstanding local campaign committee, made up of attorneys, friends, and associates.

An article prepared by Charles A Rowson & Associates was circulated by the local campaign committee to newspapers over much of the state. This part of the plan was apparently successful. The Judge expressed this sentiment to Mr. Rawson in a letter following the election.

These important arrangements were accomplished by the Judge, his friend, Attorney Harold Glore, supporting law firms, attorneys, and friends across the state. Many phoned or mailed invitations to advise when the Judge should be in a certain county to speak or to meet with influential officials in the county who wished to support him. As requests were received, Harold Glore and the Judge set the itinerary.

Judge Hawkins' campaign itinerary was thoughtful and well planned. An examination of one of several itineraries reveals that there was a typed itinerary which included the date, town, and contacts to visit in each town. It also set the time to spend at each visit and identified overnight stays. I suppose this type itinerary is common; however, it appears that it was produced with the fastidious approach of the Judge's friend, Harold Glore.

The Judge was overjoyed and grateful for letters received from hundreds of the most prestigious attorneys and law firms in the state who volunteered support. These letters and letters from him expressing his gratitude to these supporters are in the Russell Library at the Athens campus of the University of Georgia. The files also include letters and notes from many prominent businessmen and professionals who wrote him to acknowledge their support. Many of the letters are from firms and supporters across the state that are actively engaged in law practice today but are too numerous to fully be listed in this biography. Even some local bar associations passed resolutions to unanimously support him.

The most notable was a resolution of the Blue Ridge Circuit Bar Association giving unanimous support to Judge Hawkins. In addition, every sheriff, every superior court clerk in the circuit expressed support. These are the people who knew him and his qualities best.

The primary election was to occur on September 8, 1948. At this time those elected in the Democratic Primary were the winners. There were few Republicans in Georgia, and the November general election was primarily for presidential and other national and local candidates. A look at his itinerary reveals the long days and hundreds of miles that were traveled in order to cover the state, as he knew he must. He had a speech or meeting in all 159 counties of the state during the campaign in 1947 and 1948. In many counties there were several appearances.

The race for the Supreme Court of Georgia was also a real challenge for Judge Hawkins because he had been unopposed in four elections to the Superion Court of the Blue Ridge Circuit. It remained his duty to file as a candidate with the appropriate authorities and prepare for the election.

Judge Hawkins' only opponent, Joe Quillian (Below) from Winder, was an honorable man and experienced attorney, but he had no judicial experience. He was the son of a Methodist minister and active in his church and community. Mr. Quillian also was a relative of Senator Richard Russell and had backing from this powerful source. Judge Hawkins would not get much support from the Talmadge machine since two years earlier he was so outspoken about Govorner Gene Talmadge and Govornor Rivers in a speech recorded here earlier.

ELECT

JUDGE J. H. HAWKINS

Marietta, Ga.

Justice of the Supreme Court of Georgia,
to succeed Hon. W. F. Jenkins, retiring.

Democratic Primary, September 8th, 1948.

From newspaper reports I have found, the race was not negative, nor did it include personal attacks. It was a close and hard fought campaign. Though defeated in this campaign, Joe Quillian served on the Supreme Court at a later time.

This campaign brochure, (left) partially reproduced below, was used for the entire campaign. It was six pages and included a history and experience of Judge Hawkins and resolutions from bar associations which supported him. It also included a letter from the law firm of Powell Goldstein, Frazer & Murphy signed by Arthur G. Powell. This letter was typical of hundreds of letters received from lawyers over the state. The letter is reproduced below.

Powell, Goldstein, Frazer & Murphy
Citizens & Southern National Bank Bldg.
Atlanta 3, Georgia
March 16, 1948

Honorable J. Harold Hawkins
Marietta, Georgia

Dear Judge Hawkins:
I have your letter announcing your candidacy for the position on the Supreme Court, from which Chief Justice Jenkins is retiring. I am glad to tender you my unqualified support.

While the names of other friends of mine have been mentioned for this place, yet with me, when it comes to electing a man to the Supreme Court, friendship ceases. I am going to support you, not because you are my friend, but because you are, in my best judgement, the very best available man for the position. Your ability and your experience, the judicial bent of your mind, your demonstrated sense of law and of fairness, your ability to look upon all men high and low with an equal and impartial eye, your fearlessness, and considerations such as these, are my reasons for supporting you, and not merely because you are personally a very fine fellow liked by all who know you.

The Court needs you, and I shall vote for you.

Sincerely yours, Arthur G. Powell.

The suggested letter prepared by Charles A. Rawson & Associates in Atlanta, as mentioned above, is reproduced as follows. It was used with editing as necessary for the location.

A special appeal to the citizens of _____ County for their support was issued this week by the campaign committee for Judge J. H. Hawkins, candidate for the Georgia Supreme Court. "Judge Hawkins' record throughout his 18 years of service as a superior court judge is outstanding for fairness, ability and honesty," said J. G. Roberts, chairman of the committee, "and his home folks in the Blue Ridge circuit, where he is best known and where he has been four times re-elected without opposition, want all the people of Georgia to know about that record before they vote."

The statement pointed out that Judge Hawkins is the only candidate for this Supreme Court post who has had experience as a judge in the lower courts and has served on the Supreme Court in numerous cases. His candidacy has received the unqualified endorsement of every lawyer, every sheriff, and every superior court clerk in the circuit. He is 56 years old, married and has two daughters. He is the son of a Spanish war veteran and the grandson of a Baptist minister who served in the Georgia legislature during the War Between the States. He has served as superintendent of his Sunday School for the past 26 years and as a member of the school board of his city for 14 years. "Judge Hawkins" the statement concluded "will appreciate the support of every voter in Georgia who believes that demonstrated ability on the bench, together with fearless honesty, fairness and public service, are the best qualifications for election to the Supreme Court.

In 1947 the actual campaign began. With letters, phone calls and personal contacts from supporters, an itinerary was beginning to materialize, and in no time the Judge was off on speaking engagements.

Judge Hawkins was an exceptional public speaker and impeccable in expressing himself on any occasion.

With Harold Glore managing the office, the campaign continued to make progress in further introducing Judge Harold Hawkins to citizens across the state.

It seems that members of the legal profession are the group most responsible for the successful election of a judge or justice. I often wonder how many people remember the candidate for Associate Justice of the Supreme Court in any election for which they were not involved. I confess that I would very likely fail this test.

The campaign was active from the first speech in 1947 throughout 1948 until the evening before the primary on September 8, 1948. I have no doubt that many exciting and interesting events occurred during the campaign. Unfortunately, the Grim Reaper has cut a wide swath through those who were present at the time of the election and the only ones who could recall the personal events occurring during the campaign. Few records remain to peruse.

In 1948, before my banking career, I was traveling for Holeproof Hosiery Co. in Marietta. I remember well the long and arduous roads that crisscrossed the largest state east of the Mississippi. Four lane highways were rare, and this meant it took much more time to traverse the state from the beautiful mountains of North Georgia to the towns on the eastern Atlantic coast and on through the plains of South Georgia.

Nevertheless, the commitments were made and the Judge resolutely followed the itinerary. The travel and meetings were demanding. Knowing the Judge and his penchant for enjoying the fellowship of friends and strangers, there was no doubt he enjoyed a genuine pleasure from much of the activities required by the campaign. Many he would long remember.

As September 8, 1948, approached, tensions were high, and it appeared there was no landslide for either candidate. An article appeared in the *Augusta Chronicle* September 4, 1948, entitled "Victory Is Seen For Quillian." It mentioned: "his friends had predicted he would have a comfortable majority when the votes were counted." On the other hand, many newspaper articles and supporters predicted that Judge Hawkins would be the winner. Friendly predictions are not unusual, but the outcome of this race was entirely too close to call.

The voting occurred on schedule, Wednesday, September 8, 1948. Knowing that either way the election turned out, rest was soon to be had, the Judge and his friends and supporters waited for the results. Unfortunately, there was nothing conclusive on election night and probably not much rest.

On Friday, September 10, 1948, in the morning paper:

Atlanta Constitution
September 10, 1948

"Quillian Holds Narrow Lead In Supreme Court Race." The score was 48 county unit votes for Quillian and 40 for Hawkins. Joe Quillian had a narrow lead in the closest of four races for Capitol Posts.

Atlanta Constitution
QUILLIAN HOLDS BARE 4-UNIT MARGIN OVER HAWKINS IN HIGH COURT RACE.

The county unit tally in the Quillian-Hawkins contest with 120 counties reporting was Quillian 161, Hawkins 157. The county unit vote in many counties was so close that 10 votes or less separated the two contestants for the Supreme Court seat previously occupied by Chief Justice W. Frank Jenkins. In Quitman County, Hawkins split the county's unit votes with Quillian, each polling 335 votes. A total of 206 unit votes are needed for victory.

On September 10, 1948 the *Atlanta Journal*, an evening paper, reported with the headline below, excerpts follow:

Atlanta Journal
September 10, 1948

Hawkins Appears Court Race Winner

Judge J. H. Hawkins of Marietta Friday appeared to have won the nomination for a seat on the Supreme Court of Georgia as the home town of Herman Talmadge prepared for the biggest "Talmadge Victory Party" in history.

Judge Hawkins who is judge of the Blue Ridge Circuit Superior court was leading Joe Quillian, Winder attorney, by a county unit vote of 201 to 177. Only 32 unit votes were unreported. Needed to win are 206.

Virtually all earlier returns had kept Quillian in or near the lead.

On Sunday September 12, 1948, finally, with almost complete returns, a story in *The Marietta Daily Journal* included the following article. Excerpts follow:

The Marietta Daily Journal
September 12, 1948

HAWKINS WINS SEAT ON SUPREME COURT
Returns Late on Closest Race in State Democratic Primary

Marietta Judge J. H. Hawkins today was declared victor in the bitterly contested race with Joe Quillian, of Winder, for the Supreme Court seat vacated by retiring Chief Justice W. Frank Jenkins.

Almost complete returns from Georgia's 159 counties showed the Mariettan winner with 213 county unit votes over Quillian's 167. With nearly complete returns announced on all the races in the primary election the Supreme Court race was the only one to hang in the balance beyond Friday morning.

Acting Governor M. E. Thompson named L. C. (Tiny) Groves, former assistant attorney general of Lincolnton, Georgia, to fill the short unexpired tern of Justice Jenkins, as the latter's retirement became effective in September 1948. Grove was to occupy the seat until Hawkins was installed. Meanwhile, the present Supreme Court Justices were slated to meet to elect a new chief justice from among their own number. There was no prediction at the time as to who the choice of the justices would be.

Judge Hawkins, being quoted in the *Atlanta Journal*, made a statement expressing his appreciation for the voters support and pledged "to devote to the performance of the duties of this office every ounce of energy and ability which I possess" and declared his gratefulness for the cooperation he had received during his 18 years as judge of the Blue Ridge circuit.

The official tally and the final results for this race are as follows:

For Associate Justice Supreme Court in the 1948 primary.

	Total Popular Vote	Total Unit Vote
J.H. Hawkins	338,484	217
Joe Quillian	301,532	193

Judge Hawkins was one of very few persons elected to the Supreme Court of Georgia by both county and popular vote without having first been appointed to the position by a Governor. Upon being elected, he became the 57th person to serve on the Supreme Court of Georgia.

The Supreme Court had ruled in 1947 that M. E. Thompson take over as Acting Governor and for Governor Thompson and Herman Talmadge to run in the 1948 election. Other statewide candidates elected on September 8, 1948, included Talmadge's running mate Marvin Griffin, as Lieutenant Governor. Judge Howell Brooke won the race for Judge of the Blue Ridge Circuit to replace Judge Hawkins.

Thompson carried all Marietta boxes by a substantial margin. In the Marietta Negro box, Thompson received 440 votes, Willis 3, Rabun 2 and Talmadge 0. The statewide totals for governor gave Talmadge 357,865 popular votes and 312 unit votes. Thompson received 312,835 popular votes and 98 unit votes. Overall, Talmadge won big in the state and headlines read: "TALMADGE ELECTED BY LANDSLIDE." Herman Talmadge, son of Gene Talmadge, was thirty-four years old and just beginning a long, successful, and colorful career in politics.

On September 11, 1948, when it was obvious that Judge Hawkins had won the election, he received the following telegram.

WESTERN
UNION
1948 SEP 11

AA 19
A. TU002 DL PD=TU ATLANTA GA 11 838A=
JUDGE J H HAWKINS=
    MARIETTA GA=

YOU MUST HAVE WALKED UNDER A LADDER, GOT BEHIND THE EIGHT BALL, HAD A BLACK CAT CROSS YOUR PATH, AND LIGHTED THREE CIGARETTES ON ONE MATCH ON YOUR WAY TO THE POLLS. YOUR THRILLER RACE MADE ME AS NERVOUS AS AN OLD MAID UNDER THE MISTLETOE. HEARTIEST CON-GRATULATIONS=

JOHN F ECHOLS=

An interesting note appeared in the *Savannah Evening Press* regarding the candidate who ran last in the five man gubernatorial race in the Democratic Primary. As part of the story, campaign expenses for candidates were listed. Judge Hawkins reported expenditures of $4,125.00 and contributions of $2,520.00. If this cost for expenses seems small, the facts are that $4,125.00 in 1948 is equivalent to $33,427.90 in today's dollars, calculated using the Consumer Price Index. Considering records indicate that while on the Blue Ridge Circuit Judge Hawkins never received more that $6000 annually and had no supplements from the counties of the Blue Ridge Circuit, this was a substantial amount. Relative campaign expenses today for engaging in statewide elections far exceed the cost of earlier elections.

With the September Democratic Primary a matter of record, the State Democratic Executive committee scheduled a meeting on September 24, 1948, to prepare for the general election to be held in November. This meeting was to nominate Judge J. H. Hawkins, of Marietta to take his post on the State Supreme Court nearly two months ahead of schedule. The committee was to nominate Judge Hawkins for the un-expired term of Chief Justice W. Frank Jenkins.

Letter from U.S. Senator Walter George after the election in 1948.

The post was being filled by L. C. (Tiny) Groves, who was appointed to Justice Jenkins' vacancy by Governor Thompson. Judge Hawkins was nominated for the full term at the recent state primary. The full term would begin January 1949. The committee would put Judge Hawkins on the general election ballot for both the short and full terms. Justice William Jenkins retired before the end of the term. The Judge was unopposed in the general election.

Nationally, the U.S. presidential election of 1948 is best known as one of the greatest political upsets in history, as incumbent President Harry S Truman, against the predictions of contemporary polls and in spite of a three-way split in his own Democratic party, defeated Republican Thomas Dewey. The Democratic Party was split into the Progressive Party, which nominated George Wallace as their candidate, the Dixiecrat Party, which nominated as their candidate

Strom Thurmond, and the old Democratic Party which nominated President Harry Truman. The Republican party nominated Thomas E. Dewey, and he was expected to win easily. Even large newspapers came out the morning after the election with headlines that Dewey was the winner. The Dixiecrat Party desolved shortly after the 1948 election. Georgia voted overwhemly, 243,000 to 76,000, for President Harry Truman in this election. I recall commedian Bob Hope sent a one-word telegram to President Truman; "Unpack."

CHAPTER FOURTEEN

HAROLD GLORE AND EARLY YEARS ON HIGH COURT

Before he became Associate Justice of the Georgia Supreme Court, among the last official acts performed by Judge Hawkins, was one which he enjoyed the most because it involved young people; it was the swearing in of young lawyers, all of whom expected to be great lawyers. Young Fred Bentley, a friend and classmate of mine, was, much later, sworn in by Judge Hawkins a second time so he could practice as an attorney in the Georgia Supreme Court. The initial swearing in does not include privileges of appearing in the Supreme Court or Federal Courts.

Memorable Day

Friday, Sept. 10, was a momentous day, not only for these three young men admitted to the Georgia bar, but also for Judge Harold Hawkins who is seen swearing them in. The judge had just got the word that he was ahead in his race for the State Supreme Court. (Left to right) Judge Hawkins, James B. Sutherlin, Fred D. Bentley, and Thomas E. Camp. *(TIMES photo printed by Fletcher Studio)*

Judge Hawkins' File

This picture and story appeared in the Cobb County Times on September 10, 1948, and it was a memorable day for them all.

After Judge Hawkins had won the election, he called Harold Glore, his long time friend, and explained that the Court had asked him to select his Law Assistant. Judge Hawkins told Glore that even though he would not take office until after the general election he was asked to send his selection of Law Assistant to the Court. Harold Glore responded that he had been out of his office while working on the campaign and had neglected his practice and personal affairs. Harold suggested that he ask someone else. The Judge then asked Harold to come to see him in Marietta the next day, at which time he informed Harold he wanted him to report to the State Capitol the next Monday morning, even if he resigned after he assumed office. I suspect neither anticipated a resignation would occur.

Reluctantly, Monday, September 27, 1948, Harold reported to Associate Justice L. C. Groves, who had been appointed Associate Justice September 10, 1948, by acting Governor M. E. Thompson. Harold Glore was sworn in as Judge Hawkins' Law Assistant at a special called session of the Supreme Court. Glore served faithfully as the one and only Law Assistant for the entire twelve years and one month that Justice Hawkins served on the Court. Harold Glore resigned simultaneously with Judge Hawkins' semi-retirement on December 30, 1960.

Harold Glore was the only law assistant for Justice Hawkins.

Harold Glore was Justice Hawkins' Law Assistant and devoted friend. I know of no friend whom the Judge held in higher esteem. A letter in the files of Harold Glore indicated he and the Judge had plans to open offices in Marietta, and do legal research for law book, publishers. This was one of many plans disrupted by Judge Hawkins' illness.

Judge Hawkins' File

The above picture appeared in the *North Georgia Tribune* in Cherokee County December 3, 1948. Judge Hawkins was administered the oath of office as an Associate Justice of the Supreme Court by Governor Herman Talmadge. Judge Howell Brooke, who was succeeding Judge Hawkins on the Blue Ridge Circuit, took his oath at the same time.

Judge Hawkins was the first citizen of Marietta to serve on the Supreme Court of Georgia. He was the first Cobb County citizen living in Cobb County at the time of his election; however, Justice Samuel Atkinson most likely lived in Cobb County while serving on the Court.

Others from Marietta who have occupied a seat on the Supreme Court are Judge G. Conley Ingram, now Senior Judge for the State of

Georgia. Judge Ingram served on the High Court from 1973-1977. Retired Supreme Court Presiding Justice George T. Smith was elected to the High Court and served from 1981 to 1991. Currently serving on the Supreme Court is Preston Harris Hines who was appointed in 1995. Justice Hines also has served on both the State and Superior Courts of Cobb County.

I have known these gentlemen in one way or another for many years and know well of their sterling characters. Judge Ingram is best known to me, and short of another book there is no way for me to list all his accomplishments.

Also serving on the Supreme Court with connections in Cobb County is Spencer Roane Atkinson who served on the Supreme Court of Georgia from 1894-1897. His grandson, Samuel Carter Atkinson, served on the Supreme Court for 36 years from 1906 until October 1942. Both were in Cobb County for a few years.

Georgia's Appellate Judiciary was written by William Scott Henwood and Judge Braswell D. Deen, Jr. Mr. Henwood, since 1984, has served as Reporter of the Decisions for the Supreme Court and Court of Appeals. I discussed with Mr. Henwood the history of the Supreme Court included in his book. With his permission, you will find this well researched but brief history below. The history was originally prepared by former Chief Justice Bond Almand and updated by Mr. Henwood and Judge Deen. Justice Almand, a good friend of Justice Hawkins, served on the Supreme Court concurrently with Judge Hawkins.

THE SUPREME COURT OF GEORGIA
Prepared by former Chief Justice Bond Almand
HISTORY OF THE COURT

The first three Constitutions of Georgia (1777, 1789, and 1798) made no provision for a supreme court or a court for the correction of errors of trial courts.

Although the Constitution was amended in 1835 so as to authorize the General Assembly to create a "tribunal for the correction of errors of law," consisting of three judges to be elected by the legislature, which would sit at least once a year in five judicial districts to be designated by the legislature and finally determine "each and every case on the docket at the first term after such writ of error brought," all efforts to vitalize this amendment failed until 1845.

The General Assembly on December 10, 1845, enacted a statute creating the Supreme Court. It provided for three judges to be elected by the General Assembly. The ten judicial circuits were divided into five districts, and nine cities were designated in which the Court was required to sit at least once a year. The first session of the Court was held in Talbotton, Georgia, on January 26, 1846. The annual salary of each judge was fixed at $2,500. No provision was made for travel expense of the judges. The act also provided for a clerk, a sheriff, and a court reporter.

It was not until 1863 that the General Assembly made any provision for a chief justice.

The first three justices elected by the General Assembly were Joseph H. Lumpkin, E. A. Nisbet, and Hiram Warner. Lumpkin served as presiding justice from 1846 to 1863, when by legislative act he became chief justice and served as such until his death in 1867.

A constitutional amendment adopted in 1896 added three justices to the Court, and provided for election of the chief justice and the justices by the people. The Constitution of 1945 added a seventh justice.

In 1896, by legislative act pursuant to a Constitutional amendment, the Court was authorized to sit in two divisions for the purpose of hearing and determining cases, and until the late 1930s it sat in two divisions of three justices on each division, with the chief justice presiding over one division and a designated justice presiding over the other.

To qualify for office as a justice, a person must be at least 30 years of age, a citizen in Georgia for three years, and a practicing attorney for seven years.

Until 1936 the work of the Court in the hearing and disposition of cases was divided into two terms a year, March and October. The Court was required to dispose of a case submitted at the March term by the end of the October term. If not disposed of, the judgment of the lower court would be affirmed by operation of law. In 1935 the General Assembly provided for three terms per year, January, April, and September. The requirement that cases be decided by the end of the second term is retained in the 1983 Constitution.

It may be noted that in the history of the Court's operation, no case has ever been affirmed by operation of law because of the court's failure to decide a case by the end of the second term.

OPERATION OF THE COURT

The Court operates under Rules adopted by it for its administration and for the guidance of the bar and litigants.

These Rules are published in the official reports of the Court and printed copies are available upon request to the clerk.

For the purpose of hearing oral argument the Court sits each month, except August and December. The clerk prepares the calendar of cases to be argued or submitted. The cases are assigned in rotation to the justices for preparation of opinions and decisions of the whole Court.

When a justice prepares an opinion, he circulates it for study to the other justices, and after discussion en banc, the opinion is adopted or rejected by a majority of the justices. If a justice is unable to serve, or disqualifies himself, in a particular case, a substitute judge may be designated by the remaining justices to serve.

THE COURT'S JURISDICTION

The 1983 State Constitution provides that the Supreme Court shall be a court of review and shall exercise exclusive appellate jurisdiction in the following cases: (1) all cases involving the construction of a treaty or of the Constitution of the State of Georgia or of the United States and all cases in which the constitutionality of a law, ordinance, or constitutional provision has been drawn in question; and (2) all cases of election contest. The Constitution also provides that unless otherwise provided by law, the Supreme Court shall have appellate jurisdiction of (1) cases involving title to land, (2) all equity cases, (3) all cases involving wills (4) all habeas corpus cases, (5) all cases involving extraordinary remedies, (6) all divorce and alimony cases, (7) all cases certified to it by the Court of Appeals, and (8) all cases in which a sentence of death was imposed or could be imposed. Additionally, the Supreme Court may answer any question of law from any state or federal appellate court and may review by certiorari cases in the Court of Appeals which are of gravity or great public importance.

The Supreme Court has power to make such orders as are necessary in aid of its jurisdiction or to protect or effectuate its judgments.

OFFICERS OF THE COURT

Reporter. The reporter of the published opinions of the Court is appointed by the Supreme Court. He serves as the official reporter of the Supreme Court and Court of Appeals.

Clerk. The clerk is appointed by the Court for a term of six years "unless removed for incapacity, improper conduct or neglect of duties." The duties of the clerk are specified by statute and the Rules of the Court. The clerk has charge of the Court's records and keeps its Minutes.

Law Assistants. The justices are authorized to appoint law assistants to serve at their pleasure. They must be duly qualified attorneys, licensed to practice law in the State, but they are not permitted to practice while employed by the Court. Their duties are to assist the justices in the research and preparation of opinions for decision by the Court.

Judge Hawkins' File

Picture of the Court after Justice Hawkins was first elected to the Supreme Court. Judge Hawkins is on extreme right. Circa 1949

The Chief Justice of the Court, in this picture W. H. Duckworth, sits in the middle with the Presiding Justice to his right. The senior Justice, (most time on the court) sits to the left of the Chief Justice. Newest member sits on the extreme left of the Chief Justice and moves to the extreme right of the Chief Justice when a new Justice comes on the Court.

From left to right: Associate Justice Harold Hawkins, Associate Justice Grady Head, Presiding Justice W. Y Atkinson, Chief Justice W. H. Duckworth, Associate Justice Lee Wyatt, Associate Justice Tom Candler and Associate Justice Bond Almand. March 12, 1950

Pictured above are the Supreme Court Justices after another Justice has come on the Court. Associate Justices sit in order of time served on the court. Justice Hawkins is second from the right. Three new Justices were elected or appointed to the Court since Justice Hawkins was elected to the Court in 1948. Circa 1954

CHAPTER FIFTEEN

LIFE AS A SUPREME COURT JUSTICE

In my humble opinion, Judge Hawkins was one of the few self-made great men of this century. While he was not a high school graduate, among many other accomplishments, he associated with the most learned men in Georgia. His membership in *The Ten Club*, a group of the most prominent and intellectual Georgians, is an amazing example to reinforce my conclusion. In additional to his ability to be comfortable in any situation, his mastery and command of the English language and grammar was beautiful. I often wondered if the beauty of his grammar and writings was acquired not only from his reading law, but also from his faithful study of the Bible.

On July 14, 1948, during the election, retired Chief Justice of the Supreme Court, Justice W. F. Jenkins, invited him to attend a meeting of *The Ten Club*. Later the members of the club invited Judge Hawkins to join, and he accepted. Every member in this club was intellectually endowed. Some of the other members of the club are listed below.

❑ Ralph Emerson McGill: Columnist and Editor of the *Atlanta Constitution*, a major paper in Atlanta.

❑ Hal Stephens Dumas: Executive Vice President of AT&T. At that time AT&T owned Southern Bell and many others.

❑ Arthur James Moore: Bishop of the Methodist Church as well as former minister, teacher and author.

❑ Louie Devotie Newton: Druid Hill Baptist Church Pastor, author and former President of the Southern Baptist Convention.

❑ Raymond Ross Paty: President of the University of Alabama, and later Chancellor of the University system of Georgia.

❑ Arthur Gray Powell: Judge of the Georgia Court of Appeals in Atlanta.

❑ Samuel Hale Sibley: Judge of the Fifth Circuit Court of Appeals in Atlanta, a Federal Court.

- ❏ Goodrich Cook White: President of Emory University and later Chancellor of Emory.
- ❏ Marion L. Brittain: President Emeritus of Georgia Tech in Atlanta.
- ❏ James Ross McCain: President of Agnes Scott College in Decatur.
- ❏ William Frank Jenkins: Chief Justice of the Georgia Supreme Court Emeritus and lecturer at Emory University.

On one occasion, I had the distinct pleasure of my life when Judge Hawkins invited me to attend a meeting of *The Ten Club*, which was to be in his home in Marietta. I attended that day. The paper presented was "Shakespeare's Sonnets; proving by a preponderance of evidence that the sonnets were the words of Nicholas Bretona, a contemporary poet, not Shakespeare." After the presentation a thorough discussion ensued. Judge Hawkins responded with ideas and questions as if he had been a Shakespearian professor in college. At first I felt as if I were a pair of brown shoes in a world of tuxedos; however, in no time gentlemen put me at ease. It seems that when people truly rise in prominence, the more compassionate and personable they can be. I did ask one question and received a very thoughtful response from Justice Jenkins. It was indeed a wonderful experience for me, and one that I will not forget. After the meeting Irene, Judge Hawkins' wife, served lunch with quail, hot biscuits, gravy, and an array of the best vegetables anywhere as only Irene could prepare. The dessert was, of course, Southern Pecan Pie.

Judge Conley Ingram was a friend of Judge Hawkins for many years and was associated with him in several endeavors. In fact, Judge Ingram served on the Supreme Court several years after Judge Hawkins retired. In talking with him I asked if he knew of any special event that he remembers about Judge Hawkins. Judge Ingram responded that he remembers well the incident when the Supreme Court was being remodeled and he presented me with the following information.

Judge Conley Ingram

Joe McTyve collection

As to recalling an event about Judge Hawkins, I especially remember this. There is emblazoned above the bench of the Supreme Court of Georgia in the courtroom a statement in Latin that is carved in marble. 'Fiat Justitia Ruat Caelum.' Translated, it says, 'Let justice be done, though the heavens may fall.' When the courtroom was constructed the Supreme Court members were asked to provide an inscription to be placed in the courtroom. That inscription was provided by Justice Harold Hawkins who suggested it because it was the statement used on the cornerstone of the courthouse in Cobb County. That cornerstone remains on public display outside of the present Cobb Superior Court Building in Marietta. It was saved when the old courthouse was torn down and can be seen today on the cornerstone in Cobb as well as above the bench of the Supreme Court of Georgia, thanks to Judge Harold Hawkins who served as a Superior Court Judge before being elected to the Supreme Court.

The banner including the inscription is used by the Supreme Court on its current website.

The event above is a very appropriate addition to the legacy of Judge Hawkins since justice for all, manifested frequently in this biography, was always uppermost in his mind as he made any kind of decision.

Law Assistant Harold Glore kept notes and records during the time Justice Hawkins was on the court. In his collection of records, he noted the Supreme Court dockted over 4500 cases and that Justice Hawkins prepared 541 written opinions for the Court during the 12 years and one month he served. Justice Hawkins apparently reached the peak of his popularity in 1951. In Volume 208 *Georgia Reports* every decision of the Court he prepared was a full-bench decision. This rarely, if ever, occurred. This meant that all seven Justices concurred in these opinions. He prepared more opinions that were adopted by the Court than any other Justice then on the court. These were published in volumes 204 through 216 in the *Georgia Reports*.

Glore noted that when the Court was not *en banc* (on the bench) Justice Hawkins was always available to the press. While he would not discuss any case pending before the court, he would carefully explain technical legal terms and the meaning of any opinion that was in the Clerk's office for public inspection.

Justice Hawkins was considerate of the press because he was concerned that information printed was accurate and because of his years of good relations with the press. Harold Glore noted that there was only one available copy of each opinion released to the Clerk. This made it impossible for several reporters to read the opinion and copy it. There was no reproduction equipment as today. So Judge Hawkins would have his Law Assistant make extra copies for the press, especially members that had a weekly deadline that was drawing near. When an important decision would be released by the Supreme Court or one that was not understood by reporters, such as a decision that "affirmed in part and reversed in part," after having read the opinion in the Clerk's office, newspaper reporters would rush to the office of Judge Hawkins, for an interpretation. He was always available to the press.

It is my opinion that after he had been there for about four months, Justice Hawkins had an influence on the Court. I have no clear evidence of this; however, I have strong belief that the following story was his idea.

The Atlanta Journal
April 17, 1949

LEARNED JUDGES TO TRY SELVES - - - AT FISHING

There are a number of ardent fishermen on the Georgia Supreme Court, and sometimes they argue their ability to catch fish, instead of arguing law points.

During the first three days of this week the high court justices will match their skills and decide who is the best fisherman on the bench. The scene will be an undisclosed spot on the Georgia coast near Darien.

Chief Justice Henry Duckworth and Associate Justices Lee B. Wyatt, Grady Head, William Y. Atkinson, Tom Candler and J. H. Hawkins will be in the party. Justice R. C. Bell will be the only dissenter. He will be unable to make the trip.

There must have been a gag order because nothing else has been found to answer the implied questions in the report. If Judge Hawkins were to stretch the truth at all, it would have been the size of a fish he caught, exaggerating the splendor of his grandchildren, or reporting his gas mileage to me.

I had the pleasure of talking with many people who knew Judge Hawkins and were kind enough to recall many interesting stories. On March 23, 2006, I had a conversation with Judge Marion Pope, Jr. (below) in Canton. Judge Pope served on the Court of Appeals of Georgia from 1981-2002 and was Chief Judge for 1993 and 1994. He was appointed as Superior Court Judge on the Blue Ridge Circuit on March 24,1967, where he served until moving to the Court of Appeals.

Judge Pope quickly recalled some stories about Judge Hawkins. He said they both were at a meeting, and he asked Judge Hawkins to have a drink with him. Thanking him, Judge Hawkins declined and said he didn't drink. Judge Pope said, "It will be all right, nobody will know," whereupon the Judge said, "The Lord will know." Judge Pope said he would never forget Harold's faith. Of course, many today would call this banal or sanctimonious, but this behavior was embedded in the faith of Judge Hawkins. Mark Twain defines *sanctimonious* as; "Feigning piety or righteousness: a solemn, unsmiling, sanctimonious old iceberg that looked like he was waiting for a vacancy in the Trinity." Obviously, this description was not in the heart or disposition of Judge J. Harold Hawkins.

Judge Pope also recalled the time as a young lawyer when he presented his first case before the Supreme Court. He said it was a fearful time for him. He had spent hours and hours on his presentation to the court. He was well into his case when Chief Justice Duckworth said," All right, Mr. Pope, I have heard enough. He said that he was unnerved until some help came. He remembers that Justice Hawkins said, "I would like to hear more." Judge Duckworth, reversing his first opinion, said, "I think I would like to hear more as well." Judge Pope said, with that contagious smile of his, "After this, I quit shaking in my boots for the first time." Judge Hawkins was always known to have been kind to young attorneys.

Upon leaving, Judge Pope made a comment that I often heard during my research. He said, "Judge Hawkins was the epitome of what a judge should be." I thanked him for the kind comment and he said, not quite irritated, "Well, it's true." Judge Pope has been successful in everything he has done and has served the state and community well in many capacities. He is still very active at this time.

Judge Hawkins was devoted to his legal work, his family and his church; however, he had many other interests that he enjoyed very much. He loved outdoor activities such as hunting quail, wild turkey, and pheasants and fishing, both at sea and upon inland waterways. Part of this enjoyment was the involvement of so many good friends.

Top is a picture of Frisco at work on one of the many hunting trips the Judge and his friends enjoyed. The photo was taken in Camden County in 1935. The other, on the right, is Sport. Both were great friends of the Judge; as a mater of fact, the Judge stayed with Frisco and Sport in the baggage car on train trips.

His hunting partners were many over the years, but frequently he hunted with Dr. Mayes Gober, Shuler Antley, Hines Wood, and many other friends. Depending on the season, usually he would come home from South Georgia with the limit on turkeys or quail. Holi-

days were often a feast of wild birds superbly prepared by Irene with hot biscuits, gravy, and choice of scrumptious desserts.

In 1954 an article was written by Jean Rooney in which she inquired as to the routine followed by Judge Hawkins and his wife Irene. The story reveals some of the activities in which they are involved when the judge is not on the bench. In picture are Irene and David A. Dosser, Jr.

The Atlanta Journal and Constitution
Sunday January 24, 1954

Shop Talk Taboo in Justice's Home
By JEAN ROONEY

One Supreme Court Justice "lays down the law" in his comfortable Southern home in Marietta as well as in the oak—paneled State Capitol courtroom.

He is Justice J. Harold Hawkins, one of Georgia's seven highest magistrates. His lively, brown-eyed wife reports that "the Judge" lays down the law evenings as well as day-times. And she means that her jurist-husband literally lays down his legal problems and leaves them at the office.

"We don't discuss cases at home," explains the trim, Marietta matron, crediting this philosophy with much of their marital success. The Hawkins haven't time, as a matter of fact. They're too busy doing good things around Marietta, the town where Mrs. Hawkins was born and reared and the Justice has lived since childhood.

Marietta's First Baptist Church gets the first fruits of their civic efforts. Justice Hawkins recently retired from 27 years' service as Sunday School Superintendent.

A yard-full of varied colored iris and blue hyacinths will make a show place of her columned, white frame home on Marietta's Church Street in a few weeks.

Though her husband seldom talks shop at home, Mrs. Hawkins understands his work-a-day problems. In the old days when he was a superior court judge of the Blue Ridge Circuit, she never missed one of his "strong trials."

But she now has other things on her mind. She's planning big surprises for when she and the Justice Hawkins celebrate their fortieth wedding anniversary in April.

Judge Hawkins' File

Mentioned in the above story is the last home of the Hawkins family. The Judge moved his family into this more elaborate home on Church Street across from their previous home. Albeit in disrepair, it was purchased from an insurance company for about $9000 in 1930, and he lived in this house until his death in 1961. He and Irene made the home a beautiful place. His wife Irene sold the house a few years after his death. The original price is about right because my father, James H. Dosser, purchased a home in 1939 on Whitlock Ave in Marietta, for about the same amount. The Dosser home is now the Whitlock Inn. I took the above picture in 2002.

CHAPTER SIXTEEN

THE HONORABLE
JUDGE HAWKINS AND SELFLESS SERVICE

In order to note a little more about the character and philosophy of Judge Hawkins, I have included a few typical examples when the Judge was praised or honored privately or publicly. Also included is a review of a few of his contributions to the community covering a prolonged period. I have been intrigued to read the many letters, articles, and comments that were lavished on the Judge over the years of his life. Following are a brief history and just a few of these tender and thoughtful conclusions that I am sure filled his heart with joy.

Cobb County Times
Marietta, Georgia
September 29, 1949

Faithful Servant

Judge J. Harold Hawkins retired Sunday after 27 years as Sunday School Superintendent at the First Baptist Church in Marietta. In those 27 years, which means 1,440 weeks, he was present and on the job 1,296 Sundays.

Very appropriately the Baptist put on a "Hawkins Day" program, in recognition of the good layman.

The *Times* joins with them in that recognition of a remarkable record of service to the church and through the church to the community.

"Faithful" is the word the Rev. George Brown, pastor of the church, used to sum up the Hawkins' years as head of the Sunday School."

If you want to cite to your youngsters a living example of diligence, integrity, achievement, and humility, you can do no better than to point to Judge J. Harold Hawkins.

The community is proud of him.

A. S. Kytle, Treas.   Phone 957   Julian Shannon, Clerk

First Baptist Church
Geo. F. Brown, Pastor
Marietta, Georgia
September 1949

RESOLUTIONS

Whereas, for the past twenty-seven years, Judge J. Harold Hawkins has been the faithful, loyal, active, aggressive, and conscientious Sunday School Superintendent of this, the First Baptist Church of Marietta, Georgia; and

Whereas, during those many years of outstanding leadership in which he gave liberally of his time and most graciously of his talents, the Sunday School grew, developed, and expanded.

Whereas, during that long period of service to mankind and allegiance to God in his consecrated service as a Sunday School Superintendent, many boys and girls, men and women were inspired by his earnest devotion to his duties and were influenced by his sincere application of Christian principles in leadership to lead better, finer Christian lives.

Whereas, his present existing duties as Justice of the Supreme Court of Georgia, coupled with his unselfish personal desire to allow others to assume leadership in the Sunday School, have compelled him to resign as Sunday School Superintendent; now therefore

Be it resolved, and it is hereby resolved by the membership of this Church, duly assembled, that in appreciation of, and in honor of Judge J. Harold Hawkins and his splendid exemplary Christian leadership in this Church, that the Fourth Sunday in September 1949 be set aside as Judge Hawkins Day, and that an appropriate program be planned for this day.

Be it further resolved, as it has already been voted in Church Conference, that Judge Hawkins, because of his splendid service and accumulated wisdom through the years, that he be made Honorary Superintendent of our Sunday School;

Be it also resolved that these Resolutions be spread upon the Minutes of this Church, and that the Church Secretary be instructed to furnish a copy to Judge J. Harold Hawkins and also to the Christian Index our Baptist State paper.

Let us resolve as members of this Church that we shall accept humbly the service rendered by Judge Hawkins in our Sunday School, and that ours shall be a continued faithful service in the Master's Kingdom.

Committee

Scott C. Hutton

Harold Goodwin

Sam Welsch

Citation of Service

Judge and Mrs. J. Harold Hawkins survey the handsome silver tray given the judge by the First Baptist Sunday School in appreciation of 27 years' service as superintendent. Also admiring the tray are the Rev. George Brown (left), pastor and Royce Stephens right), Hawkins' successor as superintendent. (*TIMES photo printed by Fletcher*). (At the right) Rachel Arnold, nine-year-old junior department member, proudly shakes hands with Judge Hawkins at the close of the Hawkins Day program. (*TIMES photo printed by The Sportsman*) For further Hawkins Day coverage see the editorial page, 4-B.

Cobb County Times Photo

On this "Hawkins Day" evening, honoring Judge Hawkins for service to the First Baptist Church his granddaughter, Betsy Ramsey, presented to the Judge a silver tray inscribed with loving and appropriate words for the occasion. This special tray is always displayed in a conspicuous place in their home.

State of Georgia
Supreme Court
Atlanta, Georgia

May 3, 1960

Mr. Justice J. H. Hawkins
Supreme Court of Georgia
State Judicial Building
Atlanta 3, Georgia

Dear Judge:

I regret to see from this morning's paper your announcement not to offer for re-election to the Supreme Court.

Your retirement will be a tremendous loss to the Court and to me especially. As a Justice of the Supreme Court, you have made a most enviable record and one not excelled, in my opinion, by any other person. By my intimate association with you as a consulting-mate, I have witnessed and observed your fine character and your rare ability as a judge.

Since you came on the Supreme Court, you have been motivated in every decision you prepared for the Court, or participated in, only by a desire to uphold the law and to see that justice was properly administered, regardless of whom the parties were. As a lawyer and as a judge, you have made a record which will endure with the ages and which will always be an honor to you and to your family.

By your retirement from the Court, I sustain a great loss. I shall miss you terribly when you leave us.

With Kindest personal regards, I am sincerely,
Yours,
T. S. Candler

James Ross McCain, (President)
Agnes Scott College
Decatur, Georgia
May 4, 1960

Dear Judge:
The news that you will retire gave me a bit of a shock, for
I still think of you as a young man. It does give to me and
to others concern for our highest Georgia court. You have
been such a dependable justice that we all feel that you can
hold the boat steady. There may be others who will keep it
up, but I do not know personally any in whom I have such
complete confidence as in you.

Retirement has been so satisfactory with me that I am sure
that you will enjoy it, and you will find plenty of good
work to do.

With all good wishes for you and Mrs. Hawkins, I am,

Your friend, J. R. McCain.

   The above letters are representative of many letters received by
Judge Hawkins during his life time. Some in response to requesting
support during an election, letters expressing appreciation for his
kind assistance or public service and many others as the result of his
notice of retirement.

Atlanta Constitution
May 3, 1960

Judge Hawkins Served Cause of Justice Well

Associate Justice J. H. Hawkins of the Georgia Supreme
Court has announced he will not be a candidate to succeed
himself at the end of his present term.
   Judge Hawkins has served ably on Georgia's court. He
is one of the reasons why this court has such an excellent
record in the handling of cases and in the wisdom and judicial strength of its decisions.

Many of us forget that we live by law and that the processes of it flow through and from our courts. Unless our
courts are staffed with able men who know the law and
who possess integrity and the will to express it, then law-
lessness will grow as the enemy of society.

In wishing Judge Hawkins long years of contentment
and happiness in retirement, we also express the hope that
his replacement, to be chosen by the people, will match
him in character, ability and dedication.

Judge Hawkins was a pillar of the community and a leader in
civic, financial and religious circles. A partial list of community and
religious activities include his devotion to the Marietta First Baptist Church and his service as Vice President of the Georgia Baptist
Sunday School Convention. He was Chairman of the Cobb County
Chapter of the American Red Cross, and a member of the Board of
Directors of the Northwest District and State Y. M. C. A. of Georgia.

Judge Hawkins accepted invitations that involved youth. An ar-
ticle in the *Atlanta Journal*, December 11, 1952, reports that Justice
Hawkins of the Supreme Court and Judge Howell Brooke of the Blue
Ridge Circuit were participating in a dramatic production, "Christian
Youth on Trial," sponsored by the Hi-Y and Tri-Hi-Y clubs of seven
North Georgia towns. Judge Harold Hawkins presided as the trial
Judge and Judge Howell Brook acted as the prosecuting attorney. The
purpose of the production was to demonstrate the need for young
people to live a life commensurate with their designation as Chris-
tians. The production was repeated in several counties.

Judge Hawkins worked with Baptist organizations locally, statewide, and nationally. To initiate a Baptist Campaign in raising five
million dollars for schools, on April 23, 1941, the Rev. George Brown
and he hosted a meeting for Dr. George W. Truett, world famous Baptist leader and author.

He was a director and President of the Cobb County Federal Sav-
ings and Loan Association in Marietta where he served for many years.
Other members of the Board were J.J. Daniel, Robert L. Osborn, W.
Paul Gresham, Dr. Earl D. Williams, and Harold Glore. A friend, Dan
Worley, was a senior officer of the firm and gave me the names of
those serving on the board of directors.

One of his most important opportunities to assist and guide young
people was his service on the Board of Education for the City of Marietta, Georgia, from 1933 to 1947. This is close to the entire time he

served as Judge of the Blue Ridge Circuit. For the last several years of his tenure, he was President of the Board. As such, he had the dubious distinction of signing my high school diploma. In 1941 an article in the local paper reported on the accomplishments of the school board.

The Marietta Journal
September 12, 1941

When Marietta Schools open their doors at 8:45 o'clock on Monday morning they will begin the year entirely out of the red for the first time in approximately 30 years according to members of the Board of Education who announced this fact with pride especially as it is coincident with the announcement of a number of outstanding improvements in the school system.

According to Judge J. H. Hawkins, chairman of the Board, all fees for resident pupils in High School have been abolished. Extensive improvements have been made in lunch room facilities, new stickers have been installed at the high school and at Waterman Street, and the interiors of all the school building have been calcimined, painted and cleaned up, improvements made on the athletic field and in athletic equipment and other changes made to step up the general standards of the all the schools.

Mr. Guy Northcutt, Chairman of Finances on the Board says that the financial report as of July 1st shows the surplus account in black for the first time in 30 years, and that the Board is going into the new year with a balanced budget which it will strictly maintain and that the Board is endeavoring to give the very best school facilities possible for each dollar of revenue expended. Mr. Northcutt also says that the abolishment of all tuition fees for resident pupils is a goal toward which the board has been striving for some years and this was done just as soon as it showed itself out of debt. (The football stadium was named in honor of Mr. Guy Northcutt who was totally engaged in civic activities)

Changes in curriculum and school administration include two things specifically recommended in the school survey made in the spring by the University Department of Education...

Recent additions to school properties was the purchase of a lot 150 by 309 feet fronting on Lemon Street and adjacent to the colored school properties to enlarge the present school grounds there...

Dr. Sam L. Rambo, house chairman, with the assistance of Mr. Max Pittard, has supervised the extensive improvements on cafeteria facilities, receiving the cooperation of the N.Y.A, the W.P.A. and the P.T.A. to make it possible to serve hot lunches at 5 cents per person and an additional 5 cents for milk.

Approximately 1200 white children and 600 colored children will answer the bell at 8:45 on Monday and begin their studies in what bids fair to be one of the most successful year in the history of Marietta Schools.

The tenure of Judge Hawkins and other members of the board were during a time of massive growth for the school system in Marietta, Georgia. This was mostly due to World War II and the construction of Bell Bomber Plant, which created a large influx of people moving into Cobb County; thus creating massive adjustments in the school system. Another contributing factor was the occupation of Lockheed Aircraft Corp. opening a plant in the vacated Bell Aircraft Corp. building.

Presiding at a Y.M.C.A. meeting in Marietta. First row from (L to R) are Judson Palmer, Ed Covington, Bill Morrison, Judge Hawkins, Dr. Earl Williams and an unknown gentleman. Recognized on the back row are (L to R) #4 Foster Yancey, #5 Sidney Clotfelter, #10 Ewell Hope, #11 Ed Baskin and #12 Frank Golden.

The picture (opposite page) portrays Judge Hawkins conducting a meeting of the Y.M.C.A. in Marietta, Georgia, in the 1950s. Judge Hawkins was a member of the Board of Directors of the state Y.M.C.A. as well as a member and chairman of the local board, being one of two people to show up for the organization of this group.

In another youth activity, he was Chairman of the Court of Honor of the Boy Scouts of America in Cobb County. Below, as reported by the *Marietta Journal* in 1941, is an example of his cooperation and support for this group.

Shown in the picture is Scout Kemp Mabry who had just made Eagle Scout. The award is the highest honor in scouting. Standing are his parents, Mr. and Mrs. Norris Mabry, and Judge J. H. Hawkins, Chairman of the Court of Honor, when the award was made. Also included in the picture is Scoutmaster Sherry Hamilton who is saying in the picture that this is the first time he has ever seen a girl kiss Kemp Mabry, even if the girl was his mother.

In one of many such activities, Judge Hawkins was always willing to do his part. He is involved below in some kind of show in Marietta that required participants just to have fun laughing at each other.

Judge Hawkins' File

Prize winners at this community affair were given as follows: (L-R) Mrs. Paul Sloan, most unique; Judge J. H. Hawkins, most unique man, Mrs. A. V. Cortelyou, tackiest woman, Johnny Walker, tackiest man; Little Miss Betty Blair, tackiest girl and Adrain Whitlock, tackiest boy.

(L-R) Sam Welsch, Dr. Earl Williams, The Judge, James (Jigger) Hancock
and Guy Northcutt. This group was most likely meeting to promote the Boy
Scout Program, although my research has revealed no precise purpose for the
gathering.

(L-R) Judge Hawkins, Judge Sam Sibley and Judge J. J. Daniel a the
opening of the First Baptist Church Library. Circa 1950-1952

Courtesy of Marietta Museum of History Archives.

Courtesy, Georgia Archives, Vanishing Georgia Collection, Cobb 189
(Fletcher Studio)

CHAPTER SEVENTEEN

THE LAST DAYS AND REMEMBRANCES

Judge Hawkins was determined to serve the full term as Justice of the Georgia Supreme Court through 1961 to which he had been elected by the people of Georgia.

Unfortunately, during the last year or two he was not well, but had no specific complaint. He did, however, do all that was assigned to him by the court and continued obligations made for civic activities. He had plans to do many stimulating tasks following his retirement, which included continued devotion to his church and to public affairs.

After announcing his retirement, the Judge accepted a call to head a local commission to make plans for building the new Cobb County courthouse.

Harold Glore said the Judge and he had plans to open an office in Marietta where they would do research for law book publishers. The Harrison Company also had discussed with Judge Hawkins the possibility of preparing a charge book to be used by Superior Court Judges. When considering plans they had made for travel and recreation, he would have been very active.

In November 1960, Judge Hawkins and I were asked to be pallbearers for Howard Northcutt, a relative in Irene's family. Following a ceremony at the First Baptist Church in Marietta, the procession traveled across the square to Citizens Cemetery on Powder Springs Street.

When Mr. Northcutt was removed from the hearse by the pallbearers, the Judge grimaced and it was apparent he was in pain. After the funeral and on the way home, he said he had hurt his back and was having severe back pain. The injury was a symptom and not the cause of his illness. That afternoon he got an appointment to see his doctor, Dr. W. H. Benson. X-rays exposed two broken vertebrae. Over the following days and weeks, he had many tests to diagnose the cause of his vertebrae being so brittle. They were not healing. After several consultations with specialists it was determined that he had multiple myeloma.

Today multiple myeloma, a cancer of the plasma cell, is an incurable but treatable disease. There are therapies that are helping patients live longer, healthier lives. It is heartbreaking that in 1960, in the middle of the twentieth century, no such hope or treatment was available for patients.

Judge Hawkins was treated with the best-known medications of the day and fitted with a brace to support his diseased spine. As soon as the diagnosis was made in late April or early May, the doctors gave no encouragement and little hope. Realizing the disease was irrevocable, Judge Hawkins and Irene spent all one evening, in the hospital room, discussing their apprehensive future. Irene said to Ann and me that they talked, prayed, and cried together for a long time and soon found peace sufficient to face the future. It was obvious they were just as much or more in love that day as any day of their lives.

Early in 1961, a few days after Christmas 1960, it was necessary for the Judge to sleep in a hospital bed that had been moved to his home on Church Street. At that time he was able to be up and around to a small degree, but as a result of the pain, he required much rest. He did welcome visitors and looked forward to seeing his many friends. At first, many came by for short visits.

In March 1961, eager to do anything possible to relieve his mind, I was preparing Judge Hawkins' income tax for him. It was a relatively simple return, and he knew where every document was and when to pull it out of his file. Of course, he was compelled to remain in bed, but this was of no concern for what we were doing.

As I completed the return and prepared it for mailing, our children, David, Jane, and Sue, came over to see him for a brief visit. As the children came into the room, he was almost a different man, kidding and making faces at his grandchildren, and they would show their pleasure with the appropriate smiles and squeals. They loved the Judge and Irene. The Judge and Irene had spent much time sitting with them and at times going on vacation with our family. He also spent time with his other daughter, Jane Ramsey, and her family and when possible went on vacations with them. He was devoted to his grandchildren.

The above incident with the grandchildren reminds me of a time in 1952. Judge Hawkins was introduced by Supreme Court Chief Justice William Duckworth; he was to speak to the Georgia Bar Association meeting in Savannah. Chief Justice Duckworth's comments were, "I could present your speaker and do it sincerely, and do it as I think it ought to be done, that is to say, in my honest, candid opinion, Judge Hawkins is the nearest approach to a perfect gentleman of anybody I ever knew in this life. It is my happy privilege to present to you a great man, a great lawyer, a great judge, and one of the finest baby sitters in Georgia."

Associate Justice J. Harold Hawkins became Associate Justice J. Harold Hawkins Emeritus on December 30, 1960; He entered the hospital on December 31, 1960, and after returning home, for all practical purposes never got out of bed until his premature death on June 8, 1961.

Harold Glore, a long time friend and law assistant to Justice Hawkins, was surely as close to the Judge as any man. As long as Harold Glore lived, he kept the name of Judge Hawkins alive by writing letters to family and friends, with some history of the Judge. On the tenth and twentieth anniversaries of the Judge's death, he wrote more detailed letters.

Judge Hawkins and Glore worked together flawlessly and would have worked together much more except for the Judge's illness. In one of his letters Harold said, "I remained loyal to Judge Hawkins until his death, visiting his sick bed and complying with his every wish." This is absolutely true as Harold often visited the Judge and took dictation for letters and other correspondence for the entire time the Judge was ill. He went to a Georgia Bar Association meeting and reported to the Judge his conversations and greetings from his many friends. He recalled all matters that might be of interest to the Judge. All of these kind considerations were truly a gift of love.

I have several letters written by Harold Glore that have been most valuable in writing this book. One in particular, written on June 15, 1961, to Sheriff L. R. Waddey relates his activities in the last days of Judge Hawkins' life. Sheriff Waddey had been out of town and was anxious to hear about Judge Hawkins. Harold was in a position to prepare press releases and contact the proper reporters, newspapers, and television stations. Judge Hawkins had always been a friend of the press. The letter is factual, informative, and also is representative of his thoughtful support to the family. Thus, it is important coverage of the days prior to Judge Hawkins' death. Personal references in the letter have been omitted.

On Monday, June 5, I went to Marietta and talked with Mrs. Hawkins. She told me that the Judge had a bad weekend, and that Ann had called Jane to come from Charlotte,

N. C. I returned to Marietta on Wednesday, June 7, and Jane told me that Judge Hawkins was much better and she planned to return to Charlotte. She also told me that Judge Hawkins wanted to see me. Judge Hawkins asked me to answer a letter he had received from Mr. John A. Sibley, a fellow member of The Ten Club, and while he did not actually dictate this letter, he told me some things to say. He did dictate a short letter to Bishop Moore.

About 9:00 AM Thursday, June 8, I telephoned Judge Candler and told him that I had visited Judge Hawkins the day before and that he seemed to be resting comfortably. Later, I carried my 16-year-old cousin to Stone Mountain. Judge Hawkins passed away that day, about 12:30 PM or shortly thereafter. I received a message as I entered the Cyclorama at Stone Mountain, Georgia about 2:30 and the attendants said that I had an urgent call. This was when I first heard about the passing of Judge Hawkins.

I immediately proceeded to Marietta, via my home, and after talking to Mrs. Hawkins and Ann, and being told that they had not been able to contact Jane, as she was on her way to Charlotte, I was told to contact the Undertaker. When I reached the undertaking establishment, I was asked for some information for a press release, and was told that *The Cobb County Times* was holding its presses for a front page story, it being a weekly paper. I immediately went to the Editor of the Times and gave him a press release.

I was then told that Mr. Ralph McGill's secretary would be waiting at his office for me to arrive there with a press release, and I immediately proceeded to Atlanta and the *Constitution* office. After giving a press release to the *Constitution* and picking out one of three pictures which they had to use in Friday's paper, I proceeded to White Columns on Peachtree, (WSB) and was permitted to talk with Ray Moore on my arrival there at 6:25 PM. When I asked Ray if he knew that Judge Hawkins was dead, he replied that he did not, and I looked at the clock and said we just have five minutes until the 6:20 PM newscast. He called Don Stewart out of his broadcasting studio and told him. Don turned to his secretary and told her to take the information from me, and write up a short story, keeping it to five lines, as he was pressed for time, and to number it No. 8, and hand it to him. Ray then asked for a picture, which I furnished, and he blew it up to size 24 by 24 inches. Judge Hawkins' picture and a short news item stating in effect that he had passed away shortly after noon at his home in Marietta: that he had served for 20 years as Judge of the Superior Courts of the Blue Ridge Circuit and Associate Justice of the Supreme Court, having been appointed Associate Justice Emeritus December 30, and that he participated in over 4,500 cases during the 12 years that he served on the Supreme Court.

I contacted Ed Blair of WAGA-TV, Channel 5, and he blew up a picture of Judge Hawkins to be used later as the *Panorama News* of 6:00 PM was over. The next day, after Jane had been contacted, and the family made funeral arrangements, I asked the undertaker to telephone Ed Blair and tell him of the arrangements. The undertaker told me it would be impossible to get that information on TV. I explained that I had already made the arrangements, and that all I was asking him to do was to telephone Ed. On the 6:00 PM *Panorama News* of Friday, June 9, Judge Hawkins' picture was shown and an announcement was made that funeral services would be held Saturday at 11:00 AM in Marietta.

A news item appeared in the June 8 *Marietta Journal*; a news item in detail and an editorial appeared in the *Cobb County Times* of the same date; a detailed news story and editorial appeared in Friday's *Marietta Journal*, along with another story that the courts in Cobb County and all County Offices would be closed for the funeral.

A news item appeared in Friday's *Atlanta Constitution*, as well as in Friday's *Atlanta Journal*, and an editorial appeared in Saturday's *Atlanta Constitution*, together with an obituary notice.

I was one of the active pallbearers along with Dr. W. H. Benson and four others, including two nephews. Judges Head, Candler, Almand, Mobley, Quillian and Grice served as honorary pallbearers. Honorary escort consisted of members of the Cobb, Blue Ridge and Georgia Bar Associations, as well as Deacons of his Church, and Directors of Cobb County Federal Savings and Loan Association, of which he was President.

The obituary in the Marietta newspaper with more complete information appearing on June 10, 1961, reads as follows:

> Friends and relatives of Judge and Mrs. J. Harold Hawkins, Mr. and Mrs. David A. Dosser, Marietta; Mr. and Mrs. Charles Ramsey, Jr., Charlotte, N.C.; Mr. and Mrs. Albert Turner, Atlanta; Mrs. Preston Chaffin, Barnesville; Miss Zilla Hawkins, Milledgeville; Mr. and Mrs. Dick D. Elliott, Decatur and 7 grandchildren, are invited to attend the funeral of Judge J. Harold Hawkins at 11 o'clock this (Saturday) morning at the Marietta First Baptist Church. Rev. I. B. Hall, Rev. George Brown and Dr. Louie D. Newton will officiate. Interment, Marietta City Cemetery. The following will serve as honorary escort and are requested to please meet at the church at 10:45 a.m. Messrs. James H. Dosser, Guy Northcutt, Hines Wood, Grady Vandiviere, Dempsey Medford, Paul Gresham, Earl Medford, Shuler Antley, Henry Troutman, Sr., Judge J. J. Daniell, Dr. Earl Williams, Deacons of the First Baptist Church, members of the Georgia Supreme Court, Blue Ridge Bar Association, Cobb County Bar Association, Georgia Bar Association, The Ten Club, and officers and directors of the Cobb County Federal Savings and Loan Association. Gentlemen selected to serve as pallbearers are requested to please meet at the church at 10:45 a. m. Memorial may be sent to the First Baptist Church Building Fund. Mayes Ward & Co., Marietta.

All of the Atlanta and local news papers were kind in running editorials on Judge Hawkins following his death. Each one was very gracious in their praise of his qualities and accomplishments. Most included the basic history of his life, which has been covered here already. One example of an early editorial in the *Cobb County Times* follows.

Cobb County Times
June 8, 1961

Judge's Death Is A Keen Loss

Marietta lost one of her finest citizens and Georgia one of her most distinguished jurists with the passing of Judge John Harold Hawkins.

The judge was a self–made man. He studied law by reading it in the office of a learned attorney. When he became sufficiently versed in the fundamentals of the profession, he was admitted to the bar. He served the legal profession with distinction for more than 40 years.

In addition to his high regard for the law, Judge Hawkins believed in community service. He gave generously of his time to his church and to local schools, serving both in leadership posts.

More recently, following his deserved retirement from the Georgia Supreme Court, he agreed to head a local commission to make plans for building the new courthouse.

His departure will deny the community of one of the most talented and respected leaders ever to walk our streets.

The TIMES joins others in extending sympathy to the family in their bereavement. Their sorrow is shared by many.

Atlanta Journal
October 12, 1961

Tuesday the Georgia Supreme Court (background) met with members of the Georgia Court of Appeals (foreground) and with other friends of the late Associate Justice of the Supreme Court J. H. Hawkins. A committee reported on a memorial commemorative of the life, character and service of the late justice.

Without reproducing the entire memorial here, which involved several speakers, at least a few remarks from the Chief Justice William Duckworth should be mentioned.

> Justice Duckworth said (that) Hawkins 'made a judicial record seldom equaled and never excelled by any Georgia jurist.' The Mariettan, said the Chief Justice, handed down opinions that were clear, incisive and scholarly. They neither colored nor evaded any point of fact or law.
>
> Undaunted by poverty and limited formal education, Justice Hawkins moved forward to the fulfillment of his ambition to be a good lawyer by wisely utilizing his inherent superior intellect, together with hard work.

An article appeared the next day in the *Atlanta Constitution* covering the memorial of Judge Hawkins on October 12, 1961.

The Atlanta Constitution
October 13, 1961

Sympathy Is Sweetened By a Grateful Memory
Doris Lockerman

In Atlanta this week the old friends and peers of the late Justice J. Harold Hawkins of Georgia's Supreme Court gathered to honor his memory. He was a respected and beloved man, slender, gentle, sweet-faced, yet with an iron reliance upon justice and the law.

He went to work at 10, and found his way, through hard effort, first to the judgeship of the Blue Ridge Circuit. There, though every man knew he would be punished if he appeared, guilty, before Judge Hawkins at the bench, no man would ever offer against him when he ran for office.

Henry Troutman Sr., one of Judge Hawkins' longtime associates and supporters was among those invited to pay him tribute, and in his brief eulogy, Mr. Troutman found this graceful memory to sweeten his words:

Let me quote the words used by the faithful woman who became a part of this fine family. After Judge Hawkins had passed behind the curtain that separated life from death, Mrs. Hawkins was engaged in that melancholy task of writing to some of the many friends who had sought to comfort and share her sorrow, and on one of these days she was somewhat emotional, when this good companion came into the room. 'Miss Irene,' she said, 'don't worry.' You know when you go to the garden to gather some flowers to bring in the house you gets the prettiest and finest ones, and that is what God has done with Mr. Judge. He came down to Marietta and picked the best one there was.'

No letter to the family will be phrased with more delicacy or refinement.

𝕸𝖆𝖗𝖎𝖊𝖙𝖙𝖆 𝕯𝖆𝖎𝖑𝖞 𝕵𝖔𝖚𝖗𝖓𝖆𝖑
April 1967

The Judge Would Be Proud Of His Community Today

By Edna Hawkins

If I could send a message with the assurance that it would be delivered to one who has passed out of this zone of the living, it would be this.

'The community you loved is cheerful and flourishing.' I would sign it 'Country Cousin.'

Edna Hawkins

Just when Judge Harold Hawkins gave me this label I can't remember. But it seemed to delight him and I, in turn, felt he had conferred on me, an honor.

It may have been that Sabbath morning more than a quarter of a century ago when he approached me in the church-yard about teaching my first Sunday school class. With one baby on my hip and attempting to pacify the one I was leading, it was an awkward moment. But his inquiry was brief and to the point.

'The young folks need you; the Lord needs you. Pray about it, then let me know,' he said. A man endowed with such superlative ability was endorsing my own. How could I refuse him who was giving so much of himself?

Gave Her "Ample Time"

Or it may have been in the time we both participated in a program in Canton, Georgia. As he closed his speech, he said, surprising everyone, most of all, me, 'I'm going to shorten my remarks so my country cousin can have ample time.'

The nickname may have first occurred to him at a church dinner when he said to me, 'Country Cousin, if Cobb County women ever serve on juries, I hope you'll be the first.' And sure enough, it happened that way.

But it really doesn't matter when he first uttered it. There have been many Sunday School classes, speeches and jury duties since then for me. But somehow I feel each participation has known a peculiar poverty since he was not a part of them.

Halfway between our house and the city square he sleeps. At first, I wondered why he chose the spot, a few feet up the slope from the railroad, if the choice was his. But then I recall how he always wanted to be 'where the action is.' The train's careless whistle would not cause him to fret for it would mean progress and growth that Marietta was keeping in step. He may have noticed the energy of the stalwart tree nearby, or maybe he chose the spot in early spring when the pink dogwood blooms were fluttering down.

Wore His Title Well

He was a conscientious man, talented yet meek, wearing the much-coveted title, Supreme Court Justice, honorably and well.

Henry Ward Beecher said, 'There are persons so radiant, so genial, so kind, so pleasure-bearing that you instinctively feel in their presence that they do you good; whose coming into a room is like the bringing of a lamp.' Such was his way.

One announcement he made frequently while serving 20 years as Sunday School Superintendent was when we broke the attendance record of 800, he would sing a solo. This was a great challenge to him and we dared him. What would he say if he saw us today? Surely his songs would snap the rafters as he sought to express his appreciation.

Musing on these priceless remembrances as I pass his resting place, do you wonder at my desire to send the message, 'All is well in Marietta' .... 'Country Cousin.'

The Dosser and Hawkins wedding, March 22, 1949.

(L-R) James H. and Elizabeth Dosser, David and Ann Hawkins Dosser, Judge J. Harold Hawkins and Irene Northcutt Hawkins. The beginning of a grand union of two loving families always filled with joy.

Judge Hawkins' Files

CHAPTER EIGHTEEN

True And Faithful Friends Remember

Some fifteen years following the death of Judge Hawkins, he was still remembered affectionately by many in the state. Judge Luther Hames wanted to revive the memory of Judge Hawkins and did something thoughtful and generous. Excerpts from article in the *Marietta Daily Journal* follow.

The Marietta Daily Journal
1976

By Mary Callen

Seldom do political contributions exceed campaign expenditures. But when they do, funds are either kept by the candidate or returned to contributors.

Cobb Superior Court Judge Luther Hames did something different with his extra campaign money reviving a piece of the county's judicial history.

The money, outside of the necessary qualifying fee required for any political candidate, will pay for a color portrait of former Cobb Judge, J. Harold Hawkins.

Judge Hawkins, a native of Forsyth County, served as Superior Court Judge for 18 years back when Cobb was included in the Blue Ridge Circuit. Hawkins presided over court cases in Cobb and rode over to six surrounding counties to hear judicial arguments. That was back in 1931.

When Hames was a young attorney he practiced law in Hawkins's courtroom. 'Judge Hawkins was a genteel man with a quiet sense of humor, once you got to know him well,' Hames Said.

Sen. Herman E. Talmadge, Phil Landrum, former Cobb Judge, James T. Manning, and several other noted legal minds from Cobb said of Hawkins; 'There was no smallness or meanness or ugliness in his nature; no negligence in the performance of his duty; no worldly vanity; no restless ambition.'

Judge Luther Hames commissioned noted artist Robert Meredith to paint the portrait. In April the painting was finished and ready for the unveiling in the Judicial Building of the Cobb County Courthouse.

Scott Edwards, a prominent attorney and loyal friend of Judge Hawkins, was presiding at the portrait unveiling.

The above dignitaries were on hand in April 1977 for the unveiling of Robert Meredith's portrait of Georgia Supreme Court Justice J. Harold Hawkins. The other portrait is that of the late Judge James T. Manning, first Judge of the Cobb Superior Court in Marietta, Ga.

(L-R) Superior Court Judges Luther Hames, James Bullard, Chief Justice Emeritus Bond Almand, Superior Court Judge Howell Ravan, Appeals Court Judge George T. Smith, Cobb Bar Assn. President Irma Glover, Georgia Supreme Court Justice Conley Ingram, Robert Meredith, who painted the portrait, retired court reporter attorney Hines Wood and Georgia Supreme Court Chief Justice H. E. Nichols.

Judge Hawkins File

The family of Judge J. Harold Hawkins' in April 1977 at the unveiling of Meredith's painting of Judge J Harold Hawkins.
(L-R) David A. Dosser, Dan E. Cornett, Mrs. Dick D. Elliott, Dick D. Elliott, Mrs. David A. Dosser, (Ann) David A. Dosser Jr., Mrs. Danny E. Cornett (Jane), Mrs. A.E. Turner, Sue Hawkins Dosser, Mrs. Charles W. Ramsey Jr., Charles W. Ramsey Jr. and Charles W. Ramsey III. Ann Dosser and Jane Ramsey are daughters of Judge Hawkins. Only two of his grandchildren were married at the time. Elizabeth (Betsy) Ramsey was married to James Berry, but unable to attend.

Bill Kinney, Associate Editor of the *Marietta Daily Journal*, attended the unveiling of the portrait of Judge Hawkins and wrote two editorials following the event. Picture from the 1950s.

Bill is a distinguished columnist for the *Marietta Daily Journal*. He has been awarded numerous awards over the years, and his column is read over a large area of Georgia. I remember he was referred to as "Scoop" Kinney in high school. His success has far exceeded that genial title. It is outstanding for him to have become successful but exceptional to have achieved success and remained the same un-pretentious friend to so many.

Photo by Joe McTyre

Bill Kinney

𝔗𝔥𝔢 𝔐𝔞𝔯𝔦𝔢𝔱𝔱𝔞 𝔇𝔞𝔦𝔩𝔶 𝔍𝔬𝔲𝔯𝔫𝔞𝔩
April 27, 1977

Bill Kinney

"You need some help, young man. If you'll sit on my steps, I'll try to explain to you what's happening," he said in a soft, gentle voice.

That's how the late Harold Hawkins took me under his wing as a fledgling reporter more than 30 years ago at the old Cobb County Courthouse where Hawkins presided for so long as judge of the former Blue Ridge Circuit. I had encountered a little difficulty in covering a trial—namely, I had mistaken Solicitor Grady Vandiviere of Canton for the defendant.

Judge Hawkins and Solicitor Vandiviere had been involved in an auto accident near Cummings several years earlier. Grady had sustained some deep facial cuts. Grady's looks—He was stern-faced too—fit my mind's eye image of a defendant.

So you see, my court-reporting days got off to a rather shaky start and did need help from a thoughtful Judge Hawkins.

So thereafter for months when court was in session, I would sit on the steps of Judge Hawkins' elevated bench and listen as he explained court procedure.

Shortly after World War II Cobb was carved from the six-county Blue Ridge Circuit, over which Judge Hawkins presided, and made a separate judicial circuit.

Judge Hawkins himself had never attended law school. He educated himself, then passed the bar.

That's one reason, I'm sure, that he always had compassion for bumbling young reporters like myself as well as for beginning lawyers.

So it was rather a misty-eyed ceremony for me Monday when a portrait of the former Georgia Supreme Court justice was unveiled at the Cobb courthouse before his family, state and local jurists and an array of friends.

To illustrate what a courageous man Judge Hawkins was, he defied all the rules of politics by openly across the state supporting Jimmie Carmichael of Marietta, who was in a bitter race with ex-governors Gene Talmadge and Ed Rivers. Carmichael won the popular vote but lost the governorship to Talmadge via Georgia's then county unit system.

The average politician would have ducked the issue by explaining that it would be up to the people to decide who was governor. But Judge Hawkins wasn't your average politician, man or judge.

In 1947 Judge Hawkins decided he would run for a seat on the state Supreme Court.

The race between Judge Hawkins and Joe Quillian was so close that it required several days to determine the winner. When all the votes were recorded, Hawkins won by the narrowest of margin, 217 unit votes to 193 for Quillian. Hawkins had 338,484 popular votes to 301532 for Quillian, who was a nephew of Sen. Dick Russell and had the backing of the Russell organization.

After that, Hawkins was never challenged again and served on the court until he retired in 1960.

I looked around the courtroom Monday and said to myself that it's a shame some of Cobb's young attorneys hadn't been privileged to practice before as dedicated and really kind-hearted jurist as was J. Harold Hawkins.

One of the most appropriate remarks at the ceremony was made by Bond Almand, Chief Justice Emeritus of the Georgia Supreme Court. Almand said Judge Hawkins didn't legislate the law (which seems the case today in some instances), he interpreted it.

That's probably because Judge Hawkins knew the law thoroughly; having spent all those years reading law books in Solicitor Herbert Clay's office.

Almand also touched on two other attributes of Judge Hawkins – his promptness and his lifestyle. "Judge Hawkins life was marked by clean living and clean thinking." said Almand.

Hawkins was superintendent of the Sunday School at the First Baptist Church for 28 years.

In all the years he served on the State Supreme Court, he was late only once. The bus broke down that he rode daily to Atlanta.

In the earlier picture of the dignitaries in front of the portrait is Hines Woods of Canton. He has not been mentioned in this biography, and I would be remiss if I were to exclude him. Over many years, I knew Mr. Hines as a most spectacular and amiable individual. He was a court stenographer, an attorney, had varied interests, and was never at a loss for a humorous story. He appeared to know everybody every where around the state. He knew no strangers.

Hines Wood

As court reporter in the Blue Ridge Circuit for many years, he became a sincere and faithful friend of Judge Hawkins. He also was a hunting and fishing companion. Mr. Hines had an office in Canton, and it appeared to be a museum of rocks and items regarding the history of Canton.

Annually, it seems, he and Judge Hawkins organized a "Turtle Soup" dinner near Canton, and those invited were long time friends of theirs from the governor's office, senate and house members, attorneys, and others in politics, as well as many non-political associates of both Mr. Hines and the Judge. I am including information in one of the several letters found in his files.

Bill Kinney mentions in another article, "Fond Memories of a Beloved Judge," that Hines Wood was 89 years old. With Mr. Wood and others, Bill Kinney apparently provoked some warmhearted nostalgia at the ceremony. Wood remembers Hawkins bending over from the bench one day to inquire: "Hines, am I going too fast?"

"No, judge," replied Wood, who was taking down Hawkins' charge in shorthand. "I'm two paragraphs ahead of you."

Kinney also reported that attorney Scott Edwards recalled, "For two years Judge Hawkins kept the older attorneys from taking advantage of me and other young lawyers. After that, we were on our own." Edwards said while he was overseas in World War II, Hawkins wrote him a letter about every 90 days, telling him what was going on at the courthouse.

In this same article Kinney recalls a story about Judge Hawkins as told by Morgan Thomas, clerk of the Court of Appeals in Atlanta and one of the most delightful friends a person would want. Morgan rode the bus with Judge Hawkins daily from Atlanta to Marietta and back. He said he had bought a package of sheep manure to carry home.

Trust Company of Georgia
Atlanta 2, Ga.

John A. Sibley
Chairman of the Board

August 11, 1953

Judge J. H. Hawkins
Supreme Court
State Capitol
Atlanta, Georgia

My dear Judge Hawkins:

I appreciate very much your letter of August 10th.

I will accept with pleasure your cordial invitation to have "Turtle Soup" with you at 6:00 P.M. on August 27th.

It will be such a pleasure to see you. I will not be able to spend the night, but I appreciate your hospitality in inviting me to do so.

Cordially yours,

John W Sibley

JAS/hd
cc   Mr. Robert B. Troutman, Sr.
Mr. Henry B. Troutman, Sr.

One of the letters inviting John A. Sibley to "Turtle Soup" dinner.

It was a hot day, and before the bus had gone far, other riders were protesting to Thomas about the smell. With that, Thomas heaved the sheep manure out the window. Forever after, Judge Hawkins dubbed Thomas "The Shepherd."

Again, as revealed in Kinney's article, is a story from John LeCroy, Clerk of Hawkins' Court, and another good friend of Judge Hawkins. According to John LeCroy the story is as follows:

> The Judge was at Blue Ridge, Georgia, for the spring term of court. He had purchased a white seersucker suit, straw hat and low cut shoes
>
> After a good night's rest, he awoke and pulled back the curtains. During the night, it had snowed and there was about four or five inches on the ground. Needless to say, the white suit, straw hat and low cut shoes didn't correspond with the weather.
>
> As luck would have it, he had brought his light raincoat along, so he put it on and ran across the street to find that Saul's Store was closed.
>
> He walked into the courtroom and took his seat without pulling his raincoat off. The judge was asked if he was cold. He said yes, and would keep on the raincoat.
>
> After court he bought a new suit, and wore it the rest of the week.

For many years the Judge's friend John LeCroy (L) was clerk of the Court of Cobb County while Judge Hawkins was Judge of the Blue Ridge Circuit. Attorney Scott Edwards, Jr. (right) was a good friend of Judge Hawkins and officiated at the program for presentation of the painting in memory of Judge Hawkins.

Marietta Daily Journal photo

JOHN LECROY, SCOTT EDWARDS
Warm Remembrances Of Judge Hawkins

CHAPTER NINETEEN

TRULY A GREAT SELF MADE MAN

The designation of an exceptional self-made man has been used several times in this biography. In fact, I said it was my humble opinion that Judge Hawkins was one of few truly self-made men of the century. He was privileged to have received respect and admiration both during his lifetime and after his death. I say modestly that the accuracy of this description is reasonable when his life is reviewed. My judgments were reinforced during the writing of this biography.

Following is a summary of my research and findings regarding this courageous, valiant, and true gentleman. Although the facts speak for themselves, just remember that I had great love and admiration for this selfless gentleman, and my prejudices may show.

One definition of a self-made man is "a man who has risen from poverty or obscurity by the means of his own talents or energies."

Other young men without the privilege of a formal education read law and studied diligently in order to pass the bar examination. There is no reason to believe they were not competent and successful attorneys and more. Nor is there reason to conclude that desire for equal justice and fairness is limited to Judge Hawkins. Of course, many jurists had the same underlying principles as Judge Hawkins, although I do not know of any who had the instinctive qualities and accomplishments of Judge Hawkins, which were by no measure commonplace or routine.

One of his instinctive qualities is tenderly expressed by the Honorable T. Baldwin Martin, who said: "For many years Judge Hawkins and I would meet at the annual meeting of the Georgia Bar Association at the DeSoto Hotel in Savannah, and retire to the spacious veranda where we would review past events, discuss unusual cases and outline our hopes for the future. These occasions are precious in my memory and in a way are comparable to the visit to a beautiful garden."

Chief Justice W. H. Duckworth in his portrayal of Judge Hawkins' time on the Supreme Court said, "Justice Hawkins came to the Supreme Court by the free choice of the people of Georgia. He was richly endowed with a great mind, wide experience and spotless character. These noble qualities permeated his every judicial act, and they are embodied in every opinion he wrote as Justice of the Supreme Court. His opinions were clear, incisive and scholarly. They neither colored nor evaded any point of fact or law. He was a profound thinker, careful and logical reasoner, and entirely fair to all litigants. Many opinions of the Supreme Court, while not bearing his name, were actually decided upon sound principles which he convinced the court should control the case. His good works of service to his fellow man remain with us to guide us in the paths of law and righteousness. His superlative record on the Supreme Court shall endure for all time as one of the brightest pages of Georgia's judicial history."

Nothing could be more admirable than his ability to overcome the many discouraging obstacles that often foiled or delayed his reach for success. The measure of his success, winning distinction and high respect, offers clear evidence of his willingness to endure hardships in order to reach his goals. It also reveals that he had in his nature the fiber and lasting qualities that make a man develop a depth of character, will, morality, and intelligence. He never exploited his humble origin, his lack of early advantages, or difficulties of his boyhood for any purpose.

Clearly the Judge was in no way selfish with his allotment of time for charities, always advancing, especially to young people, the benefits and usefulness of education, the cultivation of independent thought and judgment and a clear regard for those less fortunate than he. By precept and example, he always exemplified the strength and dignity of austere integrity.

From boyhood all through his life, the Judge was steadfast in his heartfelt and unadulterated interests in the nurture of religion and the encouragement of true moral principles.

Judge Hawkins was not rewarded with riches, but he remained faithful to the end to himself, his family, and his mission; He received a more valuable reward in the awareness of duty well and faithfully performed.

I will never forget this wise and gentle man.

CHAPTER TWENTY

SELECTED SPEECHES

A Country Judge
Address
By J. H. Hawkins
Marietta, Georgia
1938

Mr. President, distinguished guests, ladies and gentlemen: I imagine when I came to the speaker's stand; you wondered why I had been put on the program by the executive committee. When requested to appear on the program, I wondered too, but I think I have discovered the real reason.

Ever since I have been a member of the Association, and at every meeting I have attended, I have heard the complaint by those present that the Association had not been able to enlist the country lawyer; that the charge was frequently made that the Association was being run by the city lawyers, and this idea should be corrected, and the country lawyers enrolled and enlisted.

My information is that when this same discussion arose in the executive committee meeting when it met to prepare a program, my good friend, and a member of the Bar of the Blue Ridge Circuit, Hon. William Butt, suggested that in order to forever refute and end the unwarranted charge that the lawyers from the cities were seeking to monopolize the Association, they ask me to appear on the program, and thereby conclusively demonstrate that the country lawyer would have a place in the Association.

When asked by some of the other members of the committee as to just how country I was, my information is that he related a little incident that happened some several years ago.

We have one member of the Bar of our Circuit, who, to put it mildly, is rather eccentric, and always takes any adverse ruling by the court as a personal affront. At that time the Judge of our circuit was Honorable H. L. Patterson, who was a resident of Forsyth County, and in which county I was born. Judge Patterson, a mighty good man and an able lawyer, was advanced in years, wore a beard, and was not one of the handsomest men I ever saw, and was frequently referred to as "Snacks Patterson." Primarily, I think, because I came from the same county originally, he appointed me court reporter, and one day after he had made some ruling against this lawyer to whom I referred, the lawyer went out on the streets and was unburdening himself in something like these words:

"Things have come to a pretty pass when Old Man Snacks Patterson and Harold Hawkins, two men raised up in Forsyth County, twenty miles from a railroad, who never heard a whistle blow until they were grown, and where the hoot-owls holler in the day time, come down into an enlightened community and take charge of Cobb Superior Court. Old Man Snacks ought to be driving a canvas-covered, ox-drawn apple wagon, peddling apples, and Harold Hawkins running along behind with two rocks in his hands keeping the wagon tire knocked on."

Well, as such things sometimes will, this statement got back to Judge Patterson, and the next time this particular lawyer was up strenuously objecting, and arguing his objection after the court had already ruled upon it, Judge Patterson reached up and got hold of his whiskers, and said; "Brother So and So, sit down, I am running this apple wagon."

Any way, I think the committee decided that it would once and for all time demonstrate the sincere desire of the Association that country lawyers take an active interest and part in the affairs of the Association, and invited me to appear.

After I had rather rashly consented to do so, I began to wonder and worry about what I would say. I looked over the program and saw the many interesting subjects to be discussed, the able speakers who were to present them, and the more I investigated, the more I worried. With

Dean Smith, Mr. Justice Warren Grice, Judge Franklin, and other able speakers on the program I just knew that if I undertook to discuss some topic of state, national, or international interest, or some profound legal doctrine, you people would probably reach the same conclusion that one of the trial jurors did in one of our mountain counties recently.

A criminal case was on trial, the defendant being charged with the illegal possession of intoxicating whiskey. The sheriff testified that he raided the place being operated by the defendant, and found nineteen pints of whiskey, with the defendant there in the room. The defendant took the stand and in his statement admitted that the raid was made; that the liquor was found; that he knew it was there, but that it didn't belong to him; that it was left there by a friend of his, with the request that the defendant keep it for him a little while, and that he would come back and get it. At the conclusion of the evidence and the defendant's statement, and the argument of counsel, I instructed the jury that it was not incumbent upon the State to show ownership of the liquor in the defendant, but that if they believed the evidence for the State, or the statement of the defendant, he was guilty under the law, and they ought to convict him.

The jury went out about nine thirty in the morning, and stayed out all day. I called them late in the afternoon, around six o'clock, and asked them if they had been able to reach a verdict, and they said they had not. I stated to them: "Gentlemen, I charged you this morning, and I now repeat, that if you believed the evidence for the State, the defendant is guilty under the law and you ought to convict him, or, if you believe the statement of the defendant, he is guilty under the law and you ought to convict him. Of course, if you don't believe either one, why acquit him. You may retire."

The jury returned to the jury room, and stayed out all night. Next morning, when I came to the court house, I asked the Bailiff who had been in charge of the jury during the night, if they had reached a verdict, and he said that they had not; but that they had certainly been arguing the case all night; that he heard one of the jurors along about three o'clock in the morning say: "Well, I don't believe a thing the sheriff swore; I don't believe anything the defendant said, and I have my serious doubts about whether that damned judge knows any thing about the law of the case."

So I decided I would discuss something with which I was more familiar, country courts. It so happens that a part of our circuit is located just north of and adjoining Fulton County, and naturally quite a good many of the members of the Atlanta Bar have business in our courts, but invariably, when they inquire as to what time court convenes, and are informed that on Monday morning we start at nine o'clock, and during every other day of the week at eight o'clock, run to twelve, take an hour for lunch, and then continue until around five o'clock in the afternoon, they seem dumfounded, and sometimes almost outraged at having to get up so early in the morning, and work such long hours during the day.

Well, there is a reason for that in rural counties, and a good one, that may not have occurred to those gentlemen, and that is the expense of operating a court. I know that in large centers, like Fulton County, Bibb County, Chatham County, this county, and others with a large population, and a large income from taxes, where courts are in session almost continuously, court expenses may not mean much, and certainly not to the average citizen who doesn't take enough interest in governmental affairs to know anything about it. But I call your attention to the fact that holding court is expensive to the taxpayers. Where only the legally required number of Grand and Traverse jurors are in attendance upon court, with a minimum of court bailiffs and other attendants present, it costs from three to five hundred dollars per day to operate the courts.

In one of the counties of my circuit, the total annual revenue of that county from taxes is $19,000; and that was prior to the homestead and personal property exemptions. What the revenue will be this year, I don't know, but it will be considerably less than $19,000; and that county must pay all of its operating expenses for building and maintaining its highways, the construction of bridges, the maintenance of the courthouse and jail, the care of its poor and helpless, the feeding of prisoners, the pay of non-resident witnesses, the cost of its tax equalization board, its jury revisers, board of registrars, cost of elections, purchase of county supplies and materials, and the costs of court out of that fund, and it can be readily seen that a few hours here and there, amounting in the aggregate to a few extra days of court each year would be disastrous to the county's finances. The country judge must keep these things in mind in an effort to save the county money by disposing of as much business in as short a time as possible.

This effort on the part of the country judge may sometimes be responsible for the frequency with which some of us get reversed by the higher courts, for in passing upon difficult legal questions, they must be ruled upon now, without the advantage of mature deliberation, after presentation of arguments and carefully prepared briefs, the presentation of which might consume several hours and sometimes days, for I have had the privilege of presiding in some of the courts in larger counties where arguments on demurrers may sometimes consume a day or two. Then too, in many of the counties, for one reason or another, the State reports furnished to the Clerk and Ordinary are lost, the libraries are inadequate, and legal questions have to be disposed of without access to the authorities, and naturally, under such circumstance one is more likely to err. Well, that sounds like a good alibi, any way.

Another disadvantage faced by rural courts in seeking to administer fair and equal justice to all, is the fact that with comparatively few citizens, everyone knows everyone else; many of the parties and witnesses are related, everybody knows everybody else's business, and in urban communities these conditions do not exist. Then too, local politics are more likely to creep into the courts in the county. In times past it has been said that our circuit had it share of politics. In some of the counties it is said that considerable feeling existed between the Democratic and Republican parties or factions, for in some of them we have the two parties, and it has been said that in times past the jury revisers were appointed from that party or faction which happened to support the then presiding judge, and naturally they selected the members of their own party to serve as jurors, to the virtual exclusion of the members of the other party, and as a result the Jurors undertook to take care of their own party, and give the other party a rather hard deal.

Some several years ago the presiding Judge sought to remedy that situation in one of the counties by appointing an equal number of jury revisers from each of the parties, and thought that he had made much progress, but at the first term of the court following the jury revision under this, he ran into trouble.

A jury was selected to try an assault and battery case, and the evidence introduced by the State made out a most aggravated case. The evidence disclosed that the defendant, while somewhat under the influence of an intoxicant, had been walking along the road and met the prosecutor riding a horse, and challenged him to a fight. The prosecutor tried to avoid any difficulty, had given no provocation, and sought to ride on, but the defendant had pulled him from the horse and badly beaten him. The court charged the jury, and it retired to the jury room along about the middle of the morning. When noon arrived the judge sent the sheriff to inquire if they would likely reach a verdict soon, and on being informed that it was not probable, ordered that they be sent to lunch, and returned to the jury room. Late in the afternoon, no verdict having been reached, he sent for the jury to make some inquiries of them. He asked how badly divided they were in number, and was informed that they stood six and six. He then inquired if they were divided over a question of fact, or a question of law. The jurors looked at one another, and then back at the judge, and finally one of them said: "Judge, it is not either one. Just to tell you the truth about it, we haven't been able to elect a foreman yet."

A little investigation disclosed that the jury was composed of six members from each of the two political parties. Much of that spirit, however, has died out in our circuit, but in the rural counties it is more difficult to keep matters of that sort from creeping into the court proceedings.

However, I know of no phase of human endeavor which brings one in closer touch with the actual, every day lives of the citizens, or which give one a better insight into human nature. In former years, before the days of good roads, the automobile, and the industrial development, which we now have, the litigation in rural sections did not cover a very broad field, but with these things, litigation has increased, and the country courts are now called upon to deal with almost all kinds of litigation. This being true, the country lawyer has developed, the country juror is more intelligent, and the days when a lot of noise on the part of the lawyer, and an appeal to prejudice or emotion was all that was necessary to win a case, has passed. With the widening of the scope of the lawyers activities, both territorially and in volume, the country lawyer has learned that he must practice law in the real sense of the term if he expects to cope with present day conditions, and my observation is, taking them as a whole, they prepare and try their cases as well as the lawyers from the cities.

In my opinion, the revised Constitution, and By-Laws of the Association will do much towards interesting and bringing the country lawyer into the Association and my sincere hope is that in the very near future every member of the Bar of Georgia will be a member of the Association, all working together for the objects stated in Article One of the Constitution, "to advance the science of jurisprudence, promote the administration of justice, uphold the honor of the profession of the law, encourage cordial intercourse among the members of the Bar, and stimulate and coordinate the activities of "the entire Bar of Georgia."

The Commercialite
Southern College of Business
May 14, 1938
Marietta, Georgia

Judge Hawkins Addresses Scobs

Judge J. H. Hawkins, well-known figure in the social and political life of the city, was the principal speaker at the assembly on Wednesday, May 11.

Judge Hawkins told the students both entertaining and informative things concerning his own experiences in business school. He related the amusing incident which helped him overcome his extreme timidity. Short hand was then the same peculiar looking mystery that it is now.

"Business training is the only thing which is invaluable in every job you can undertake. Hardly a day passes that I do not have occasion to use shorthand, typing and other information and practical training which I received in business school.

It is necessary to start at the bottom to learn the fundamental principles of management in carrying on a business. Even at the bottom of the ladder to come in contact with the "higher ups," the people who run the business, and it is up to you to make an impression by conscientious and enthusiastic interest that will please our employer and make him notice the superiority of our work.

The three factors that are absolutely essential to success are honesty, integrity and loyalty. No one wants to employ a person who talks about office problems outside of the office. It is very easy to ruin an employer and even a firm by unguarded and careless expressions. An employer wants the person who works for him to be dependable and loyal to him. Just the ability to do the work is not enough—-there must be a sense of loyalty, honesty and integrity.

Interest may include both honesty and integrity. Certainly if a person is sincerely interested in the work and feels that he is doing something that he has always wanted to do, he has the interest of the firm at heart. This attitude is necessary if you wish to get ahead in the business world. We get out of life what we put into it. It is the same in a position. If you are working just for the money you receive for it, you will never get a promotion. You must have a deeper purpose than that. You must have the desire to do better than just what you consider to be your duty.

The philosophy of success in the business world might be termed devotion to one's work. You must be eager to give service and satisfaction and inspire confidence in our employer rather than over eager to receive your check.

You must keep your business life on as high a plane as you do your social life. The very foundation of success is conscientious endeavor and good character.

A Lawyer's Views on Liberty
July 1952

An address made by Justice J. Harold Hawkins, of the Georgia Supreme Court, at a meeting of the Georgia Bar Association in Savannah.

I am going to follow the pattern of most addresses I have heard recently, and view with alarm. We find the United States of America cast in a role of leadership more powerful and important than was ever before, either by fate or chance, thrust upon any nation. The attendant responsibilities of this hour are trying the fabric of our national strength. The legal profession is largely the architect, guardian, and sponsor of that organized government that reflects more than anything else our way of life. We must ever be mindful of the fact that the legal profession is a living, integral part of what America is, with a definite goal to assume the great responsibility of fostering and preserving the highest order of civilization yet known to history.

There is much governmental extravagance and waste, calling for higher and higher taxes, to the extent that they are becoming burdensome and oppressive. Much abuse has been heaped upon our President, upon Congress, and upon the Judiciary. It may be each branch of our government deserves some part of this criticism, and is partly responsible for the condition in which we find ourselves, but I call attention to the fact, as pointed out in the decision of our Supreme Court in Plumb v. Christie, 103 Ga. 686: "In all independent states and nations absolute power rests somewhere. In this country it is neither lodged with the executive nor the legislative nor the judicial branches of the government, nor with all combined; but sovereignty rests with the people of several states. The ultimate source of legislative power is traceable to them; and, in their sovereign capacity, they have a right to frame laws for their own government, and for the regulation of human conduct on all matters over which exclusive power has not by them been delegated to the federal government. Acting in their organized capacity, and under the forms of existing laws, they can rend asunder all bonds that are thrown as restraint around individual action, unbridled liberty, and make license as free as the winds of heaven and as wild as the waves of the sea. They can, on the other hand, so frame their organic and state laws as to place upon their own necks a yoke as galling as ever serf carried under the edict of a despot. It is eminently in this sense that we live under a free government, which simply means a government created by the people, and which they are absolutely free to change or modify at their pleasure.

If the President has been wasteful and extravagant, it is because Congress by its appropriations has permitted him to be so, and if the Courts have upheld such extravagance and waste, it is because we live under a constitutional government, established by the sovereign people and under written laws passed by the legislative branch of government whose members are elected by the people, and the Courts can enforce only such rights as our laws protect, and remedy such wrongs as they redress.

If the people of this nation want to stop waste and extravagance, it is within their power to do so by ceasing to make so many demands for the furnishing of service and the supplying of benefits by the government. I think it rather inconsistent for us, as American citizens, to criticize and deplore waste and extravagance on the one hand, and on the other to boast of the vast sums of federal funds we have obtained for the carrying out of our pet projects.

The legal profession needs to keep before the people these fundamental facts, and to help them return to the fundamental beliefs of our forefathers in the supreme worth of the individual, and in his right to life, liberty, and the pursuit of happiness; that every right implies a responsibility, every opportunity an obligation, every possession a duty; that the law was made for man and not man for the law; that government is the servant of the people and not their master; the belief in the dignity of labor, whether with head or hand; that the world owes no man a living, but that it owes every man an opportunity to make a living; that thrift is essential to well-ordered living, and that economy is a sound requisite of a sound financial structure, whether in government, business, or personal affairs; that truth and justice are fundamental to an enduring social order; that the rendering of a useful service is the common duty of mankind, and that only in the purifying fire of sacrifice is the dross of selfishness consumed, and the greatness of the human soul set free; in an all wise and all loving God, by whatever name called, and that the individual's high fulfillment, greatest happiness, and widest usefulness are to be found by living in harmony with His will.

A Speech by Hon. J. Harold Hawkins, Associate Justice, Supreme Court of Georgia: To the Georgia Bar Association.
Savannah, Georgia, June 1952

Introduced by Chief Justice William Duckworth.

Introduction: I could present your speaker and do it sincerely, and do it as I think it ought to be done, that is to say, in my honest, candid opinion; he is the nearest approach to a perfect gentleman of anybody I ever knew in this life.

It is my happy privilege to present to you a great man, a great lawyer, a great judge, and one of the finest baby sitters in Georgia. Judge Harold Hawkins.

Address of Justice J. Harold Hawkins

It is with much humility, fear and trembling that I undertake to address this group of distinguished members of the Bar of Georgia. While this beautiful, historic and hospitable City furnishes the greatest inspiration for an address on an occasion like this, I feel utterly incapable of measuring up to what would be expected.

It would seem that the Georgia Bar Association has, with or without an invitation, established this City as its annual meeting place, and I think that is right and proper, for at least two reasons; first, your City is so beautiful and your people so kind, gracious and hospitable, that no other place can compare with it, and, second, this City is cradle of government in Georgia, and the birthplace of the first semblance of an appellate court, where, more than seventy years before the establishment of the Supreme Court of Georgia, the Provincial congress, in 1775, appointed a Committee of fifteen members to hold quarterly sessions in Savannah and to act as a Court of Appeals.

When your President invited me to appear here, I tried to explain to him that he was about to destroy the splendid record he had made as President of the Association, but to no avail.

While deeply appreciative of the honor thus conferred upon me, my hesitancy in accepting the invitation was due to a number of things. In the first place, one of my associates has appeared on the program in each of the past four years, and each of them has done a most creditable job, bringing worthwhile and informative entertainment to the members of the Association, and thereby reflecting great credit upon the Court. I realize that they have established a standard which I could not hope to reach.

After finally accepting the invitation, I became almost as despondent as the man Bob Troutman was talking about the other day. It seems this man frequently became despondent, felt that he was confronted by insurmountable obstacles, that his last friends had deserted him, and he would worry until he would almost blow his top. He visited a psychiatrist, and was advised that when in that condition he should go away out in the orchard, get out under an apple tree, and commune with nature and his maker, and he would, in that way, get relief. Not long thereafter he felt one of these spells coming on and he went out and sat down under the tree. About that time a large bird lit in the tree above him. Looking around, the man took out his handkerchief and brushing off his shoulder, said: "Lord that is what I am talking about. The birds sing for everybody else."

Then too, I was at a loss for a subject. Should I undertake to discuss some profound legal doctrine? I decided against this, for fear you would assume the same attitude that the juror did that Judge Candler told you about.
From some of the motions for a rehearing which have been filed in those cases where I prepared the opinion of the Court, I am afraid that some of the members of the Bar concur in the view expressed by this juror.

But, don't get the wrong idea from that remark. The members of the Court welcome a motion for rehearing if you really think the opinion is wrong. We are more anxious than anyone else to correct an error before it gets in the books. I would like to suggest, however, that a respectful and courteous motion for rehearing serves your purpose much better than one which is disrespectful or abusive. We are all just human enough to resent abuse.

About the only consolation I can get from this effort is a feeling of assurance that I will not have the same experience my associate, Judge Bond Almand, had last year. You will remember that he delivered a most able address and received unstinted praise from those present. It was even suggested that the address be printed at the expense of the Association and copies thereof furnished to every member of Congress. I know that was music in his ear, but it backfired. Following the very next banc, a motion for rehearing was filed in a case in which Judge Almand had prepared the opinion for the Court and it started off this way: "It is inconceivable to counsel that the one who recently delivered that magnificent and scholarly address before the Georgia Bar Association in Savannah and the author of this opinion could possibly be one and the same person," and then proceeded to point out what counsel conceived to be various and sundry erroneous rulings and misinterpretations of the law contained in the opinion.

After much deliberation, I decided to talk primarily to the younger members of the Bar, and to try to give them a more or less intimate view of the members of the Court and of our procedure. That which caused me to do this is my recollection of my own early impressions concerning the Supreme Court and its members. Even when becoming a member of the Court, I approached it with mixed feelings of pride and humility; pride in the fact that the members of the Bar of this State had made possible my elevation to the highest judicial office in the State, for in the Bar and through its influence lies the power to select the member of the appellate courts, and humility in assuming the duties of this most important office, carrying with it such a great and sacred responsibility, and in attempting to measure up to the high standard set by the other members of the Court, and to fill that place on the Court which had previously been occupied by such distinguished and able jurists; as William A. Little, Joseph R. Lamar, J. H. Lumpkin, II, S. Price Gilbert, and our beloved former Chief Justice W. F. Jenkins, at whose feet I sat when he was a member of the Court of Appeals.

I shall never forget my feeling of respect and awe on my first appearance as a practicing attorney before the Supreme Court. My sincere hope is that the Court still merits the respect of the members of the Bar, but I would like to dissipate, if I can, any feeling of awe on the part of the younger members of the Bar. If you could know the other members of the Court as I do, I am sure that any feeling of awe you might have heretofore had would be entirely dissipated. While they may appear, when on the bench and clothed in their judicial robes, to be stern, austere, and unsympathetic, they are, individually and collectively, the most understanding, sympathetic, and human group of men with whom it has ever been my pleasure to associate. In my opinion, the combined, but varied qualifications, of the entire membership, and the way in which cases are taken up and considered, furnish a most excellent background for well considered opinions.

For your information, there does not exist in our Court the practice which prevails in many other States, of the cases being assigned by the Chief Justice to other members. In our Court the cases are assigned by rotation. Each Justice gets whatever case falls to him by number, and not by assignment. This, to my mind, is a far better method for several reasons. If the responsibility for assigning cases to the various members were placed upon the Chief Justice, one would be unable to prevent a feeling of resentment occasionally when some extraordinarily complicated case, with a voluminous record was wished off on him by this Chief Justice. One would just naturally feel like saying, "Why pick on me; why not let some other members of the Court take that case, or keep it yourself," for contrary to the practice which prevails in some States, the Chief Justice of the Supreme Court of Georgia, in addition to his administrative duties, does his proportionate part of the work, and writes the same number of opinions as does any other member of the Court. Under our procedure if you get a difficult case, you just grin and take it, for it has your number on it, and you can blame only old lady luck, and not the Chief Justice.

Then, too, by arbitrary assignment of the cases, there would be a tendency to assign a particular type of cases to a particular Justice, because perchance he had greater experience in dealing with that kind of case, thus creating specialization, which I think would be harmful.

I thought you might be interested in knowing the manner in which cases are taken up and considered after the opinions have been prepared. Both as a practicing attorney and as a trial Judge, I entertained the idea that the opinions of the Court were largely one-man opinions. If so, I want to assure you that such is far from the truth. While each member of the Court prepares his proportionate number of the opinions, they are by no means the sole opinion of that member.

I do not mean to leave the impression that each member of the Court reads and carefully considers every record before the Court. That would be physically impossible with the volume of work we have to do. The present system of consecutively numbering cases was started December 16, 1916, and for the thirty-five year period from 1916 to 1951, over 17,500 cases were docketed, or to put it differently, approximately 500 cases per year.

But where the Court is up with its work, as it now is, there being only three cases pending in the Court which were argued prior to the call in May, and, parenthetically, no one Justice has more than one of those, and where a case is argued orally, all seven members of the Court hearing the argument will get the benefit of your contentions, and will remember them when the opinion is prepared and presented within the next thirty or sixty days. When the Court was from six to twelve months behind with its work, oral arguments were not so beneficial. If your case is not argued orally, and if you will furnish to the Court seven copies of your briefs, then each member can and will read your briefs, and, in that way, be familiar with the questions and authorities presented, and we frequently consult with each other concerning the case in which one of us is preparing the opinion.

At each banc the Chief Justice first reads an opinion which he has prepared for the Court, and thereafter the Justices read in the order of their seniority upon the Court. In passing upon the opinion, each member of the Court is required to state whether he concurs in or dissents from the opinion as presented, and the voting is in reverse order, with the youngest member of the Court in point of service required to vote first. As each member is called upon for his vote, he has and exercises the right to ask any questions he may desire, and to present any view he may entertain with respect to the soundness of the opinion, and to criticize or uphold it. Where there is diversity of opinion, frequently an entire day or more is consumed in the consideration of a single case, and of the various arguments made, and in the examination of the applicable authorities. Sometimes the arguments wax warm and forceful, but I am deeply grateful for the fact that in these arguments there is not, in our Court as now constituted, one iota of personal feeling or animosity. Every member recognizes the right of every other member to present his views just as strongly as he may be capable of doing, at all times being mindful that the opinion is just as much that of the other members of the Court as of the one who prepared it. To my mind it is extremely regrettable that there should ever exist on an appellate court any personal feeling of animosity, or likes or dislikes of a fellow member which could enter into the consideration or disposition of cases pending before the Court.

I can assure you that when an opinion has run the gamut of the brilliant and analytical mind of Chief Justice Duckworth, of the vast experience and store of knowledge of Presiding Justice Atkinson, of the sound deliberate consideration of deep-thinking Justice Wyatt, of the diligent and tireless study and research of Justice Head, of the vast store of legal knowledge and of the good common since of Justice Candler, of the learned and scholarly criticism of Justice Almand, it has been well considered, and the ultimate result is the considered opinion of the entire Court, and not of one man.

The law not being an exact science, and no two cases ever having identical facts, it is not surprising that some times the opinions are not unanimous, but for myself, I have resolved that I shall not dissent unless I can give what to my mind is a valid reason therefore, and that reason I will point out in my dissent. I feel that the Bar is entitled to know upon what ground a dissent is based.

There is one other matter to which I would like to refer, and that is that I have heard some criticism of the members of the Court for asking questions during oral arguments.

May I point out to you that with the work of the Court in its present condition, members of the Court are now enabled to review these records and briefs prior to the call of that case for argument, and in this review some question may be raised in the minds of the Court which is not covered by the Brief. Generally it is for this reason that questions are asked during argument, that the Court may have the benefit of the views of counsel on such questions. There is absolutely no reason why counsel should be embarrassed if he doesn't happen to be able to answer the question when asked. If the one propounding the question knew the answer the question would not be asked, but counsel is thus enabled to know what question is in the mind of the Court, to answer it then if he can and if not, to prepare and present a supplemental brief upon that question if he desires to do so.

There is one other suggestion I would like to make. Don't stay mad at the Court too long after an adverse ruling. We had a member of the bar in my Circuit some years ago who was either damning or praising a Judge, and mostly damning, because he became furious every time a Judge ruled against him, and it didn't make any difference who the Judge was. I recall very well the very first day I held Court as a trial Judge; I carried this lawyer in my car from Marietta to Alpharetta, in an adjoining County. It happened that I directed a verdict against him, and that afternoon when I started home and asked him if he was ready to go, he abruptly told me, "No." I went on home and learned later that he was so mad that he had refused to ride with me, hired a jitney-bus to take him to Atlanta and then rode the street car home, arriving about 12:20 that night, when I would have gotten him there about 6 o'clock.

I remember on another occasion he happened to be on the winning side of a case in Judge Sam Sibley's Court, and on the way home he was praising Judge Sibley to the sky, such a fine character and brilliant lawyer, and commenting that it was a shame that we didn't have Judges like that all over Georgia. The next week he was on the off-side of a case, and Judge Sibley ruled against him about as quickly and emphatically as he had ruled with him the week before. On his way home he was very quiet, and his associate asked him, "Well, what do you think of Judge Sibley now?" His reply was, "Well, I will tell you Sam Sibley is not that little Tin Jesus those darn Presbyterians say he is." However, there was one redeeming feature about him; if you ever did rule in his favor he got in a good humor for the time being, and until the next adverse ruling.

Probably due to the enormous expense incident to maintaining a law library, with so many law books being published, a hue and cry has gone up from the legal profession all over the nation for short and better opinions by the appellate courts.

Well, we have complied with at least one-half of this request. We have definitely made our opinions shorter. The 208th volume of the Georgia Reports, which will soon be published, will cover an entire year's work of the Court, and will contain approximately thirty percent more opinions that the previous volume, and I believe, than any other volume. I hope we are complying with the other half of the request, and making them better. They are at least better to the extent that they are shorter.

In my few closing remarks I am going to follow the pattern of most addresses I have heard recently, and view with alarm. We find the United States of America cast in a role of leadership more powerful and important than was ever before, either by fate or chance, thrust upon any nation. The attendant responsibilities of this hour are trying the fabric of our national strength. The legal profession is largely the architect, guardian, and sponsor of that organized government that reflects more than anything else our way of life. We must ever be mindful of the fact that the legal profession is a living, integral part of what America is, with a definite goal to assume the great responsibility of fostering and preserving the highest order of civilization yet know to history.

There is much governmental extravagance and waste, calling for higher and higher taxes, to the extent that they are becoming burdensome and oppressive. Much abuse has been heaped upon our President, upon Congress, and upon the Judiciary. It may be each branch of our government deserves some part of this criticism, and is partly responsible for the condition in which we find ourselves, but I call attention to the fact, as pointed out in the decision of our supreme Court in Plum v. Christie, 103 Ga. 686: "In all independent states and nations absolute power rests somewhere. In this country it is neither lodged with the executive nor the legislative nor the judicial branches of the government, nor with all combined; but sovereignty rest with the people of the several states. The ultimate source of legislative power is traceable to them; and, in their sovereign capacity, they have a right to frame laws for their own government, and for the regulation of human conduct on all matters over which exclusive power has not by them been delegated to the federal government. Acting in their organized capacity, and under the form of existing laws, they can rend asunder all bonds that are thrown as restraint around individual action, unbridled liberty, and make license as free as the winds of the heaven and as wild as the waves of the sea. They can, on the other hand, so frame their organic and statute law as to place upon their own necks a yoke as galling as ever serf carried under the edict of a despot. It is eminently in this sense that we live under a free government, which simply means a government created by the people, and which they are absolutely free to change or modify at their pleasure."

If the President has been wasteful and extravagant, it is because Congress by its appropriations has permitted him to be so, and if the Courts have upheld such extravagance and waste, it is because we live under a constitutional government, established by the sovereign people and under written laws passed by the legislative branch of government whose members are elected by the people and the Courts can enforce only such rights as our laws protect, and remedy such wrongs as they redress.

If the people of this nation want to stop waste and extravagance, it is within their power to do so by ceasing to make so many demands for the furnishing of service and the supplying of benefits by the government. I think it rather inconsistent for us, as American citizens, to criticize and deplore waste and extravagance on the one hand, and on the other to boast on the vast sums of federal funds we have obtained for the carrying out of some of our pet projects.

The legal profession needs to keep before the people these fundamental facts, and to help them return to the fundamental beliefs of our forefathers in the supreme worth of the individual, and in his right to life, liberty, and the pursuit of happiness; that every right implies a responsibility, every opportunity and obligation, every possession a duty; that government is servant of the people and not their master; the belief in the dignity of labor, whether with head or hand; that the world owes no man a living, but that it owes every man an opportunity to make a living; that thrift is essential to well ordered living, and that economy is a sound requisite of a sound financial structure, whether in government, business, or personal affairs; that truth and justice are fundamental to an enduring social order; that the rendering of a useful service is the common duty of mankind, and that only in the purifying fire of sacrifice is the dross of selfishness consumed, and the greatness of the human soul set free; in an all-wise and all loving God, by whatever name called, and that the individual's high fulfillment, greatest happiness, and widest usefulness are to be found by living in harmony with His will.

If we return to those fundamental beliefs we will restore this nation, and avoid disaster.

The Marietta Journal
December 15, 1957

State Constitution Lightly Regarded,
Too Easy To Amend, Hawkins Says

Justice Harold Hawkins of the Georgia Supreme Court told the Marietta Rotary Club Friday that the state constitution was too lightly regarded and too easy to amend.

A State constitution, Justice Hawkins said, is designed to be a permanent, certain and fixed, document, binding on the courts, and basis protection for all people.

But the Georgia constitution, which was rewritten and adopted in 1945, only 12 years ago, already has been amended 168 times and 15 more amendments are pending to be voted on in 1958.

Only 19 of the amendments have been of general nature, applying to the people of the whole state. All the remainders have been local amendments, applying to certain counties or political subdivisions. Thus, rather than a constitution applying to all the people, it now has been chopped up to the point that it means one thing in one county and another thing somewhere else.

Amendment of the constitution, Justice Hawkins said, is treated the same as a local bill, and this basic document has little more standing than a statute. It no longer is the supreme law of and for the whole state.

He proposed several changes in the method of amending the State constitution. His suggestion was that an amendment having only local application shall be approved by a two-third vote of both houses of the legislature; then submitted to the voters of the area affected within 60 days after adjournment of the assembly; then, if ratified by a majority of the voters qualified to vote, the amendment would be submitted at the next general election to the voters of the whole state.

Under this method, the merits or demerits of the proposal would be threshed out more thoroughly, and the constitution restored to its rightful place in our system of law.

Justice Hawkins emphasized throughout his talk that local amendments means that the constitution does not apply uniformly, but means one thing in one county and something else in another area.

"Today, when the courts rule that a particular county or municipality is pursuing a policy contrary to the constitution all that county or municipality has to do is to submit an amendment to the constitution permitting it to do what the court said it could not do under the constitution — that is, to exercise powers forbidden to all other counties within the state," Judge Hawkins said.

Most of these local amendments, he added, have to do with avoiding or evading the constitutional limitations of indebtedness, which is seven per cent of the total assessed valuation. This is done in various ways through local amendments.

The constitution, he concluded, is designed to protect the individual citizen from the government, and the proposed change in the method of amendment might help this basic document to do that job.

The Law and the Lawyer

Who is the true lawyer?

He is one who devotes himself to maintaining the supremacy of law.

What is law? [May reach conclusion of Mountain Juror; A hand written note to remind him of a humorous story.]

Of law in a general sense it may be said that it has God for its author, the universe for its kingdom, and order and harmony, and truth and justice, for its objects. It holds its benign sway in the realm of the material, the intellectual, and the spiritual. It has to do with all affairs secular and religious, temporal and eternal. We cannot think of God as being without authority, and this involves the ideal of law.

While human law is necessarily imperfect in its enactment and enforcement, it is indispensable to organized society, government, and civilization. It enters into all the affairs of our everyday life, it abides with us in the home; it stands sentinel at the door and protects from the intrusion of the violent and unwelcome. While we sleep it watches. When we awake it is by our side, and goes with us into the highway, the field, the shop, the office and the sanctuary. It stimulates us in our work by assurance that we shall enjoy the products of our labor. It protects us in our amusements and our worship. It has concern for everybody and every interest, not only liberty and property, but life, body, health, and reputation. The most needy are the objects of its special care. It levies tribute to take care of the destitute and helpless. It shields the weak from the oppression of the strong. It protects the strong from the envy and hatred of the weak. It confers rights upon us before we are born. It hovers over our cradle. It guards us all the way to the grave, and even then does not abandon us, but lingers there to protect the grass and flowers love has planted, from the touch of desecration. As far as may be, it is a husband to the widow, and a father to the orphan. Its ears will not listen to falsehood. Its eyes are not clouded by partiality, nor distorted by prejudice. Its hands are a shield for the innocent, and a rod for the guilty. Its feet tread the paths of justice and equity. It speaks, and its voice commands what is right, and forbids what is wrong. Its underlying principles are founded in reason. It makes allowances for human passion and frailties. Its whole being rejoices in the truth; truth in its entirety—the whole truth, truth unmixed—nothing but the truth.

The lawyer's profession is not a trade for barter and sale. His office is not a shop. It is no place for bargain counters. It is rather a school, where by diligent and unremitting study he must qualify himself to instruct the ignorant, strengthen the weak, defend the oppressed, prevent wrongs, terminate contentions, promote justice, inculcate respect for and obedience to constituted authority; and to do this it should be a shrine to truth and right, on which the spirit should reverently kneel, to which the heart should offer its tribute of sympathy and love. Venerable for its antiquity, worthy of the highest respect and admiration for its history, the necessity for our profession springs from the conditions of organized society, and it must continue as long as such society exists.

From the ranks of the lawyers the judge comes; the judge who sits as a minister of justice, representing the power and sovereignty of Government; who is the mouthpiece of the law, pronouncing its decisions, and entering the judgment by which property is taken, liberty is restrained, and life itself is forfeited. An upright, capable, fearless judiciary is the last hope of the people among themselves. The people, the source of all power, wisely recognize the necessity for a written constitution which shall set limits beyond which they themselves can not go; and in times when tumult and passion sway popular thought and feeling, from the bench alone must come the voice of authority which shall curb the spirit that would override these limitations. That rights so sacred have been so well guarded, interests so valuable so well preserved, and power so vast wielded without abuse, is an honor to human nature, weak and imperfect as it is, and an undying glory to the profession which has and must continue to furnish the bench of our country with men and women who will continue to discharge these responsibilities, and bless their country with their services. No greater calamity could befall the State than the infliction of an incompetent and corrupt bench, and the only safeguard against this is a competent and upright bar. The stream cannot rise higher than its source.

[Hand written note; In so far as the Appellate Courts are concerned; it is my conviction that the Bar can control who is elected. Few know or care.]

The lawyer's knowledge must be broad and extensive in the law of real and personal property, of contracts, torts, the administration of estates, corporations, pleadings, practice and evidence, and indeed the whole domain of law, common, statutory, and constitutional, and in these latter days with taxation. In the practice of his profession he must be diligent, orderly, and faithful. These are not just high-sounding terms, for we regard them as necessary and indispensable characteristics of a real lawyer. Diligence, orderliness, fidelity—rightly considered, these are among the highest virtues; they are cardinal. Diligence is more than distinction. The hand of the Almighty stamped the brand of orderliness on the work of creation, and the same law holds the sun, the moon, the stars and the worlds in their places. Orderliness is put in the rank with decency by the great apostle, who wrote, "Let all things be done decently and in order." In the infallible and final estimate of character, fidelity will count for more than fame.

A lawyer as an associate must always be willing to do more than his share of the work. As an antagonist he must be fair and honorable. His demeanor to the court as an institution must always be characterized by that courtesy and high respect, to maintain which is one of the first duties of every lawyer. He should be deeply interested in the local, the State and the National Bar Associations, and always ready to contribute to whatever would promote the honor and usefulness of his profession, to which he should give his unremitting and undivided devotion.

Successful Lawyers do not attain success from sharp practices and questionable methods. The true lawyer secures no clients and wishes and wins no triumphs by ignoble methods in the practice of law; as well as in the conduct of other business, character is one of the most valuable assets.

A lawyer who is honest has no place in his life for the application of the doctrine that says, succeed—honestly, if you can—but at all events succeed.

I know of no profession or calling which demands greater integrity and fidelity than that required of members of the Bar, and according to my observation, the lady members of the Bar fully measure up to these qualifications. [Hand written note; don't get mad at court because of ruling against you, and if you do, don't talk about it in the streets.]

I consider the invitation to speak to you on this occasion a distinct honor, and wish for each of you much success in the practice of your chosen profession.

CHAPTER TWENTY ONE

MEMORIALS

COBB COUNTY SAVINGS AND LOAN ASSOCIATION MEMORIAM TO JUDGE J. HAROLD HAWKINS

Whereas, for the period covering the lifetime of Judge John Harold Hawkins, a faithful and active and conscientious member of this Association, giving freely of his time and talent, now, therefore, BE IT RESOLVED by this Association in regular meeting on July 10, 1961, that we record on the minutes of this Association the accounting of his many services over a period of years.

The record of this man is remarkable when you consider the fact that his formal education consisted of schooling here in Marietta through high school, after which he started his study of law in the office of Herbert Clay. After several years he moved on to secretary of Judge W. F. Jenkins of the State Court of Appeals, an unusual opportunity for a young lawyer, an opportunity which he used to great advantage for several years. He came back to Marietta to enter into partnership with a local law firm where he gained further experience which qualified him for the Judgeship of the Blue Ridge Circuit, where he served with distinction for a number of years, but ever moving forward.

Some of the fine services this man has rendered are:

I. Lifelong membership First Baptist Church where he served as:
    a. A Deacon
    b. Superintendent Sunday School for more than a quarter of a century
    c. Member of Building Committee
    d. Trustee of the Church

II. a. Member of Board of Directors, State Y.M.C.A.
   b. Member of Local Y.M.C.A., being one of two people to show up for the organization of this group.

III. A respected member of the local, state and national Bar Associations.

IV. a. President of the Cobb County Federal Savings & Loan Association.
   b Director of same.

V. Marietta Public School System
   a. Member Board of Education
   b. President of the Board

VI. At the time of his death he was Chairman of the Courthouse Commission where he, along with his co-workers, were [sic] doing valuable service in this direction.

There are many things this man has done for his friends, his community, his state and for the many organizations that called for his service. We think this Bible verse will say of our humble, God fearing, friend all that need be said: "I have fought the good fight, I have finished my course, I have kept the Faith." (2 Timothy 4:7)

BE IT FURTHER RESOLVED that we as members of this Association shall accept humbly the services rendered by Judge Hawkins to the association and to its members and that a copy of these resolutions shall be presented to his family as a token of our love and affection for the past faithful service of this man.

(signed) Robert L. Osborne

(signed) E. D. Williams

(signed) W. P. Gresham

Blue Ridge Circuit Bar Association
And
Cobb County Circuit Bar Association

RESOLUTION

The Blue Ridge Circuit Bar Association and the Cobb County Circuit Bar Association met on this date upon call issued by the Presidents of these Associations, at the court house [sic] in Marietta, and the following resolution was adopted:

WHEREAS, the committee appointed from the Blue Ridge Circuit Bar Association and the committee from the Cobb County Circuit Barr Association appointed to prepare a Memorial commemorative of the life, character and services of Honorable John Harold Hawkins, last Associate Justice Emeritus of the Supreme Court of this State, have submitted their reports and those present were given an opportunity to pay eulogy to Judge Hawkins.

WHEREAS, upon motion made by (signed) A. J. Henderson and seconded by (signed) Herbert Buffington, it was resolved:

(1) That the Memorials prepared by the Blue Ridge Circuit Bar Association and the Cobb County Circuit Bar Association, through their committees, be and the same are hereby unanimously adopted and ordered spread upon the minutes of the said Blue Ridge Circuit Bar Association and the Cobb County Circuit Bar Association records.

(2) That the originals of these Memorials be delivered to Mrs. J. H. Hawkins.

(3) That copies of these Memorials be furnished by the Secretary of the Blue Ridge Circuit Bar Association and the Cobb County Circuit Bar Association to the press for publication.

This the 11th day of September 1961.

(signed) Ralph W. Roper
    President, Blue Ridge Circuit Bar Association

(signed) Ben K. Smith
    President, Cobb County Circuit Bar Association

MEMORIAL

(Blue Ridge Circuit Bar Association)
To

ASSOCIATE JUSTICE EMERITUS
JOHN HAROLD HAWKINS

President Smith, President Roper, distinguished guests, ladies and gentlemen:

Associate Justice Emeritus JOHN HAROLD HAWKINS of the Supreme Court of this State was born May 22, 1892, in Forsyth County, Georgia. He was the son of Mr. and Mrs. Perry Hawkins.

He lived the greater and latter part of his life in the City of Marietta, Cobb County.

He received his educational training in the public schools of Forsyth County and Cobb County.

On April 22, 1914, he was married to Irene Northcutt of Marietta. There are two children: Jane Northcutt Hawkins who married Charles W. Ramsey, Jr. on December 22, 1941; and Elizabeth Ann Hawkins who married David A. Dosser on March 22, 1949. Mr. and Mrs. Ramsey have four children and reside in Charlotte, North Carolina. Mr. and Mrs. Dosser have three children and reside in Marietta.

Judge Hawkins was admitted to practice law on December 26, 1916, at Marietta.

He served as law assistant to the distinguished Judge, W. F. Jenkins, on the Court of Appeals of Georgia from September 10, 1917, until March 1, 1920, when he resigned to enter upon the practice of law at Marietta.

In the year 1920 he formed a partnership consisting of himself; Judge N. A. Morris, former Judge of the Superior Courts, Blue Ridge Circuit; and Campbell Wallace, who married a daughter of Governor Nat Harris of this State. This partnership was dissolved in the year 1931.

On March 1, 1931, he was appointed Judge of the superior Courts, Blue Ridge Circuit, by Governor L. G. Hardman, and served until November 30, 1948. He was later elected to this position four times without opposition.

He was elected to the Supreme Court November 30, 1948, and served until he retired on December 30, 1960. On December 31, 1960, he became Justice Emeritus of the Supreme Court, which position he held until his death on June 8, 1961.

In his youth he became a member of the Baptist Church and remained a member of this church until his death. He served as a Deacon of the First Baptist Church of Marietta for a period of about 35 years, and during a part of this time, he was Chairman of the Board.

In the year 1927, he was elected Sunday School Superintendent of his church and served in this capacity for 27 years. The Christian influences which he left in this section of the State will be more enduring than any monument that may ever be erected to his memory of bronze or marble.

If you forget everything that has been stated in this Memorial, it is my devout wish that you will not forget that he served 27 years as Superintendent of the Sunday School of the First Baptist Church of Marietta. Think of the 27 years which he gave in molding the characters of the youths who attended this Baptist Church! It is my opinion that his service as Superintendent of this Sunday School will in many respects be the greatest service that he has performed for mankind and particularly these children of the City of Marietta and its environs.

The following is a part of the great prayer of St. Francis of Assisi, which illustrates very beautifully and graphically the Christian character of Justice Hawkins:

"O divine Master, grant that we may not so much
seek to be consoled - as to console;
to be understood - as to understand;
to be loved - as to love;
for it is in giving that we receive;
it is in pardoning - that we are pardoned;
and it is in dying - that we are
born to eternal life."

While Justice Hawkins was serving upon the Supreme Court, during his 12-year tenure, there were over 4,500 cases docketed in this court; and of this number 700 were assigned to him. He prepared 541 written opinions for the court. The members of the Supreme Court and attorneys who are familiar with his remarkable and successful career upon the Supreme Court recognize that his opinions constitute hallmarks in the judicial history of Georgia.

From the best information obtainable it appears that the Blue Ridge Circuit was created by an Act of the Legislature in the year 1863, which covers a period of 98 years; and during the existence of this Circuit, we have only had the honor of furnishing two members of this Court: Joseph E. Brown is the first one who was appointed Chief Justice of the Supreme Court by Governor Bulloch; and of course, the second was Justice Hawkins, who was elected to succeed the distinguished jurist, W. F. Jenkins.

It may be said parenthetically that Joseph E. Brown is the only Georgian who ever held the three highest offices within the gift of the people of Georgia: United States Senator, Chief Justice, and Governor of Georgia.

At Canton, in May 1933, the Blue Ridge Circuit Bar Association was organized. Judge Hawkins was elected unanimously as the first president of this Association; and his untiring and devoted service to this position caused the lawyers of the Blue Ridge Circuit to take an unusual interest in it. The statement can be made without successful contradiction that the Blue Ridge Circuit Bar Association is recognized as one of the strongest country bar associations in Georgia.

At the time of his death, Justice Hawkins was a member of the Cobb County Circuit Bar Association, the Georgia Bar Association, and the American Bar Association.

Justice Hawkins was Director of the State YMCA, a member of The Ten Club, and a past president of the Marietta Board of Education. He was an honorary member of the Atlanta Lawyers Club, a member of the Capitol City Club of Atlanta, and the Atlanta Athletic Club. Recently the Marietta Rotary Club named him as an honorary member.

He also served as president of the Cobb County Federal Savings and Loan Association.

Someone has said when John Marshall, the great Chief Justice, entered upon the discharge of his duties, which embraced a period of 34 years, he found the Constitution of the United States a skeleton, and by his great decisions, concurred in by his illustrious associates, he gave it flesh and blood; and at the end of his great judicial career he passed the torch of constitutional government to all the judges, both Federal and State, who were to follow him with the admonition that if the Republic was to endure and the states were to live together as a union, the Constitution was to be the bulwark and the palladium of our liberties, and that it should never be torn down by seeking to appease the different waves of sentiment which could arise from time to time where democracy exists as it does in this country.

The great judicial record which Justice Hawkins made while serving as Judge of the Superior Courts of the Blue Ridge Circuit for a period of 17 years, and as Associate Justice of the Supreme Court for a period of 12 years demonstrates to a marked degree that he loved and respected the Constitution. The torch of constitutional government as received from John Marshall never did flicker or weaken but remained steadfast with him in seeing that every citizen with whom he dealt as a judge was given every constitutional right to which he was entitled, whether it was a civil or a criminal case. This record will take its place along with the record made by other great judges who have served upon the Supreme Court with such distinction and honor.

While serving upon the Superior Court and the Supreme Court, Justice Hawkins was guided and directed in the administration of justice by the polar star - the law. An extended review in detail of the life and character of this great jurist would not be permissible in view of the limited time of each one participating in this Memorial.

Everything he did as a citizen, a lawyer, a profound jurist, and a Christian was crowned with marvelous success, and this is the proper criterion by which we judge a man's greatness.

Bismarck, the great iron Chancellor of Germany, in defining greatness, said:

"A really great man is known by three signs – generosity in the design, humanity in the execution, moderation in success."

A tribute has been paid to another great Southerner, Henry Grady, of whom it was said:

"I have seen the light that gleamed at midnight from the headlight of some giant locomotive rushing onward through the darkness, heedless of opposition, fearless of danger, and I thought it was grand. I have seen the light dome over the Eastern hills in glory, driving the lazy darkness like mist before a sea borne gale until leaf and tree and blade of grass glistened and glittered in the myriad diamonds of the morning's ray, and I thought it was grand. I have seen the light that leaped and flashed at midnight athwart the—storm-swept sky, mid chaotic clouds and howling winds 'til clouds and darkness and the shadow-haunted earth flashed into noonday splendor, and I knew it was grand.

But the grandest thing, next to the radiance that flows from the Almighty's Throne, is the light of a noble and beautiful life, wrapping itself in benediction round the destinies of men, and finding its home at last in the blessed bosom of the Ever-living God. That man is great who has the strength to serve, the patience to suffer, and who, seeking not to conquer the world, masters himself and devotes his life in unselfish service to His fellow man."

Such a man was he to whom we pay tribute today.

This the 11th day of September 1961.

RESPECTFULLY SUBMITTED,
(signed) A. J. Henderson
J. Hines Wood
William Butt
Committee of Blue Ridge
Circuit Bar Association

Capital City Club
Atlanta 3, Georgia

June 27, 1961

Dear Mrs. Hawkins:

On behalf of the Capital City Club, I wish to express to you our sincere sorrow in the passing of your husband and our good friend, who was a valued and beloved member of this Club.

At a meeting of the Governing Board of the Capital City Club on June 20, 1961, the enclosed Resolution was passed and expresses the feeling of the Club in the passing of Justice Hawkins.

If we at the Club can be of service at any time, please let us know.

Sincerely yours,
R. H. Dobbs, Jr.
(signed)
President

Mrs. J. Harold Hawkins
Marietta,
Georgia

RESOLUTION

BY THE GOVERNING BOARD OF THE CAPITAL CITY CLUB

ADOPTED JUNE 20, 1961

WHEREAS, Justice J. Harold Hawkins, was from 1954 to the date of his death a valued and beloved member of this Club, and

WHEREAS, his personality and friendliness added much to the life of this Club during the period of his membership

BE IT RESOLVED that the Board of Governors of this, the Capital City Club take this opportunity to express their regret and that of its members in the death of so valuable a member:

RESOLVED FURTHER that this expression of sympathy be spread upon the pages of the Minutes of the Board of Governors and that a copy of this Resolution be transmitted to the family of the deceased member.

Respectfully submitted,

(signed)
R. H. Dobbs, Jr.
President

MEMORIAL TO
JUSTICE JOHN HAROLD HAWKINS

(Cobb County Bar Association)

In Memoriam, to those surviving Justice John Harold Hawkins,

BE IT REMEMBERED

That Justice Hawkins, late beloved of Marietta, Cobb County, Georgia, was born on the 22nd day of May 1892, in Forsyth County, Georgia, and moved to Marietta at an early age. He attended the public schools of this City and was admitted to this bar on the 26th day of December 1916.

From that all-important date in the life of Justice Hawkins he devoted his life to the furtherance of justice in the Courts of this State. First he served as official Court Reporter of the Blue Ridge Circuit from the 1st day of January 1915, until the 1st day of September 1917. He then served as Secretary of the Court of Appeals from September 10, 1917 until March 1, 1920. He left this position to engage in the active practice of the law in the City of Marietta and over the Blue Ridge Circuit as a member of the law firm of Morris, Hawkins & Wallace for eleven years from 1920-31.

He next served as Judge of the Superior Court of the Blue Ridge Circuit for almost 18 years. His final service to his beloved State of Georgia was rendered as a Justice of the Supreme Court of Georgia, where he served from November 30, 1948, until 1960.

These dates, years and statistics somehow obscure the warm and generous nature of Judge Hawkins. Never could be said about any man any more fervently than of this that his name was long since written in the book of Gold because he loved his fellow man. This line taken from Leigh Hunt's famous poem *Abou Ben Adam* could not have fitted anyone more perfectly than Judge Hawkins. His first concern was to those who most needed his help and guidance. His interest in the coming generations is heralded in the leadership he displayed as a member and President of the Board of Education from 1933 until 1947. It is echoed and re-echoed in his work for the Y.M.C.A., Y.W.C.A., BOY SCOUTS, GIRL SCOUTS, and other Youth groups and organizations. Nowhere was his realization of the verity of Dr. Albert Sweitzer's human equation that each of us is truly responsible for our fellow man more clearly demonstrated than in his lifelong association with the First Baptist Church of Marietta, Georgia. Here he served in virtually every capacity extant in the Church.

Greatly obscured in this brief resume of the life of such a distinguished public servant is the "Blood, Sweat, and Tears" necessary to achieve so much in one life span. He could not have accomplished the task had he not been able to rely so heavily upon his beloved wife, the former Irene Northcutt, whom he married on April 22, 1914, and upon his beloved daughters Jane and Ann. Without them his life would not have been complete.

Judge Hawkins leaves us, the members of the Bar, a priceless heritage of devotion to the profession of the law, to this Superior Court and those succeeding him here a bountiful bequest of justice tempered with mercy; to his family, the precious memory of a beloved father and husband; and to all men everywhere, the fervent devotion to duty, honor, and justice that he gave every day of his life.

Justice Hawkins lives on in these provisions of a will he unconsciously drew as he lived out his span of life.

RESPECTFULLY SUBMITTED
COBB COUNTY BAR ASSOCIATION
MEMORIAL COMMITTEE

By CHAIRMAN_____
(SIGNED Fred W. Bentley, Sr.)
GEORGIA, COBB COUNTY

The grand jury desires to note with regret and sympathy the passing of one of the outstanding jurists that Georgia has produced, a former official of this Court and a most worthy citizen, J. Harold Hawkins. Beginning his Court Career as a court official, he moved on to be admitted to the bar of this Court, served with distinction as the Judge of this Court and with greater honor and distinction as a Justice, Georgia Supreme Court. In his passing, this county lost a most distinguished and honorable servant, citizen and friend.

GEORGIA,
COBB COUNTY.

I, JNO. T. LECROY, Clerk of the Cobb Superior Court, do hereby certify that the foregoing is a true, correct and complete copy of paragraph thirteen of the interim presentments returned by the August-September Term, 1961 Grand Jury, as the same appears of record in this office. Witness my hand and official seal of office, this 11th day of September 1961.

(Signed)
JNO. T. LECROY
CLERK, COBB SUPERIOR COURT, C.J.C.

MEMORIAL TO
JUSTICE JOHN HAROLD HAWKINS

In Memoriam, to those surviving Justice John Harold Hawkins,

BE IT REMEMBERED

That Justice Hawkins, late beloved of Marietta, Cobb County, Georgia, was born on the 22nd day of May 1892, in Forsyth County, Georgia, and moved to Marietta at an early age. He attended the public schools of this City and was admitted to this bar on the 26th day of December 1916.

From that all-important date in the life of Justice Hawkins he devoted his life to the furtherance of justice in the Courts of this State. First he served as official Court Reporter of the Blue Ridge Circuit from the 1st day of January 1915, until the 1st day of September 1917. He then served as Secretary of the Court of Appeals from September 10, 1917 until March 1, 1920. He left this position to engage in the active practice of the law in the City of Marietta and over the Blue Ridge Circuit as a member of the law firm of Morris, Hawkins & Wallace for eleven years from 1920-31.

He next served as Judge of the Superior Court of the Blue Ridge Circuit for almost 18 years. His final service to his beloved State of Georgia was rendered as a Justice of the Supreme Court of Georgia, where he served from November 30, 1948, until 1960.

These dates, years and statistics somehow obscure the warm and generous nature of Judge Hawkins. Never could be said about any man any more fervently than of this that his name was long since written in the book of Gold because he loved his fellow man. This line taken from Leigh Hunt's famous poem *Abou Ben Adam* could not have fitted anyone more perfectly than Judge Hawkins. His first concern was to those who most needed his help and guidance. His interest in the coming generations is heralded in the leadership he displayed as a member and President of the Board of Education from 1933 until 1947. It is echoed and re-echoed in his work for the Y.M.C.A., Y.W.C.A., BOY SCOUTS, GIRL SCOUTS, and other Youth groups and organizations. Nowhere was his realization of the verity of Dr. Albert Sweitzer's human equation that each of us is truly responsible for our fellow man more clearly demonstrated than in his lifelong association with the First Baptist Church of Marietta, Georgia. Here he served in virtually every capacity extant in the Church.

Greatly obscured in this brief resume of the life of such a distinguished public servant is the "Blood, Sweat, and Tears" necessary to achieve so much in one life span. He could not have accomplished the task had he not been able to rely so heavily upon his beloved wife, the former Irene Northcutt, whom he married on April 22, 1914 and upon his beloved daughters Jane and Ann. Without them his life would not have been complete.

Judge Hawkins leaves us, the members of the Bar, a priceless heritage of devotion to the profession of the law, to this Superior Court and those succeeding him here a bountiful bequest of justice tempered with mercy; to his family, the precious memory of a beloved father and husband; and to all men everywhere, the fervent devotion to duty, honor, and justice that he gave every day of his life.

Justice Hawkins lives on in these provisions of a will he unconsciously drew as he lived out his span of life.

All of us, the members of his family, members of the Supreme Court of Georgia, The Court of Appeals, Blue Ridge Circuit Bar Association, Cobb Judicial Circuit Bar Association, The First Baptist Church, the Cobb County Federal Savings and Loan Association, must perpetuate more than a beautiful memory of Judge Hawkins. We must dedicate our lives to continuing the promulgation of his ideals and his untiring efforts to restore the dignity and brotherhood of mankind to this earth.

Respectfully Submitted,

COBB JUDICIAL CIRCUIT

by_____
      (SIGNED Fred W. Bentley, Sr.)
      CHAIRMAN

I, JOHN T. LECROY CLERK, COBB SUPERIOR COURT do hereby certify that the within and foregoing is a true, correct and complete copy of the MEMORIAL TO JUSTICE JOHN HAROLD HAWKINS as appears of record in Minute Book 3-V page 438 Cobb County Records.

Witness my hand and the official seal of this office this 21st day of August 1961.

(Signed)
CLERK, COBB SUPERIOR COURT,
MARIETTA, GA.

SEAL

SUPREME COURT OF GEORGIA
Atlanta, August 18, 1961

The Honorable Supreme Court met pursuant to adjournment

The following order was passed:

It is hereby ordered that the following committee be appointed to prepare a memorial commemorative of the life, character and service of Honorable J. H. Hawkins, late Associate Justice of this Court, viz.: Honorable Robert B. Troutman, Sr., Chairman; and Honorables F. M. Bird, J. Lon Duckworth, H. B. Troutman, Sr., John L. Tye, Jr., Shuler Antley, L. M. Blair, John P. Cheney, Scott S. Edwards, Jr., Luther C. Hames, Jr., A. J. Henderson, Jr., James T. Manning, J. G. Roberts, Garvis L. Sams, James R. Shaw, Harold M. Walker, Dr. Louie D. Newton, Honorables F. Frederick Kennedy, Vance Custer, Ben F. Carr, William Butt, T. H. Crawford, Charles L. Gowen, R. A. Bell, Ronald F. Chance, Sam P. Burtz, A. J. Henderson, Sr., H. G. Vandiviere, John S. Wood, J. Hines Wood, B. H. Chappell, Leon Boling, R. Carter Pittman, James C. Davis, Carl K. Nelson, Herbert R. Edmondson, R. Wilson Smith, Jr., Phil M. Landrum, Hatton Lovejoy, Herman E. Talmadge, L. Harold Glore, Charles J. Bloch, Claude Joiner, Jr., T. Baldwin Martin, James Maddox, E. T. Averett, Edwin A. McWhorter, John W. Davis, Henry G. Neal, and Kontz Bennett.

It is further ordered that the report of this committee be received at eleven o'clock a.m. on Tuesday, October 10, 1961. After presentation of the committee's report, addresses may be delivered by individual members of the bar.

Supreme Court of the State of Georgia Clerks' Office, Atlanta, August 18, 1961

I certify that the above is a true extract from the minutes of the Supreme Court of Georgia.

Witness my signature and the seal of said court hereto affixed the day and year last above written. (signed) K. C. Bleckley, Clerk.

IN MEMORIAM
JUSTICE JOHN HAROLD HAWKINS

IN THE SUPREME COURT OF GEORGIA

OCTOBER 10, 1961.

Chief Justice W. B. Duckworth: The Supreme Court has convened for the purpose of receiving the Report of the Committee appointed to prepare a Memorial commemorating the life, service and character of our deceased Associate, Mr. Justice Harold Hawkins. I now recognize Mr. Robert B. Troutman, Sr., the Chairman of that Committee.

Honorable Robert B. Troutman, Sr.: May it please the Court; Members of the Court of Appeals, Mrs. Hawkins, Jane and Ann, and the other members of Judge Hawkins' family; and friends of Judge Hawkins:

The undersigned, members of your Committee, respectfully submit the following as a Memorial to Justice John Harold Hawkins.

REPORT OF THE COMMITTEE APPOINTED
BY THE COURT.

Justice Hawkins was born in Forsyth County, Georgia, on May 23, 1892. He was the son of Mr. and Mrs. Perry Hawkins. His paternal grandfather was the Reverend Frederick M. Hawkins, a prominent and distinguished Baptist minister. His maternal grandfather was Cicero Bramblett. These pioneer families played important roles in shaping the religious, political and business developments in North Georgia.

Measured by present day standards, his formal education was brief and limited. But he relentlessly pursued his education through study and observation, until his untimely death on June 8, 1961.

Upon completion of his schooling in the Marietta Public Schools, he learned shorthand and became a secretary in a law firm in Marietta, which had become the family home when he was a small boy. There he spent the remainder of his useful life.

In 1914 he married Miss Irene Northcutt of Marietta. They were blessed with two fine daughters, Jane Hawkins (Mrs. Charles W.) Ramsey and Elizabeth Ann Hawkins (Mrs. David A.) Dosser, and in turn they brought seven grandchildren to his family. All survive him. His was a long and beautiful family life, where the simple but eternal reign of love prevailed. He was a devoted husband and father, and his deep affection was returned to him manifold, by each member of the family. It was, indeed, a family to inspire all who seek genuine happiness.

His training for admission to the Bar was likewise informal. He could not afford to attend a law school, but he studied law at night and in his spare hours and was admitted to the Bar in 1916. His subsequent career demonstrates how he utilized his every talent and opportunity to prepare himself for his great career as a Member of this court.

First, he became secretary to Judge W. Frank Jenkins of the Court of Appeals of Georgia, later Chief Justice of this court. What an opportunity it was for this neophyte to learn at the feet of one of Georgia's great lawyers and judges the lessons which every truly successful lawyer and judge must learn: industry, integrity, selfless devotion to the cause of truth and justice. He was an apt pupil. Well did he learn not only the principles and rules of substantive law, but also the means of applying them to the case at hand, under orderly procedure.

In 1920 he became a member of the firm of Morris, Hawkins & Wallace in Marietta. Its practice carried him into all seven counties in the Blue Ridge Circuit, and into many beyond its limits. It was a varied practice, which involved cases of almost every nature. And he learned from all of them. He learned that justice is rendered by human beings—judges and jurors—and that the rules of logic are not always applied. It is a soul-searching process which reaches deep into the consciences and souls of men seeking to do "right," as God gives them the vision to see the "right." His successful career at the bar served well in his training for the bench.

In 1931, he was appointed Judge of the Superior Court of his circuit. For 17 years he presided over that court, elected four times by his people without opposition. To the daily task of doing justice to all who came before him, State and citizen alike, he dedicated himself without restraint. He established a reputation for fairness, impartiality, compassion, and firmness, with a profound respect for the rule of law, which remains today throughout the circuit.

In 1948, he was elected by the people of his State to this court, to succeed his friend and mentor, Chief Justice Jenkins, who had voluntarily assumed the role of Chief Justice Emeritus. For twelve years he adorned it, until his retirement in 1960 to become Justice Emeritus. His career as an appellate judge and his work with his associates on the bench will be dealt with today in the response of the Chief Justice. In this Memorial, however, on behalf of the Bar, the Committee desires to record that in Justice Hawkins the people of our State had on their highest court a man whose whole life and talents were dedicated to the administration of justice, not only according to the highest ideals, but also in its practical day-to-day application to the lives and affairs of the people.

From the simple environment of his boyhood among the mountains he always dearly loved, Justice Hawkins received early convictions on fundamental principles, which never left him, as he moved into ever-widening circles of opportunity: deep religious faith; respect and love of family as the basic unit of our society; compassion for his fellow man and recognition of his status as a child of God; the obligation to meet, as a man made in God's image, the responsibilities which life places upon him; the recognition that the administration of justice is the supreme duty of government, and that the people have set apart the members of our profession to see that justice is done to each and all who come before the courts, and that when man assumes the duty of sitting in judgment upon others, he approaches some of God's prerogatives.

In a rapidly changing world, he was never shaken from those principles. In fact, he never removed himself from the mountain scenes of his youth. All of his life he lived in sight of them and constantly revisited them as if to renew the strength they brought to his character.

He never flagged in his devotion to his religion and his church. A deacon in the First Baptist Church of Marietta for 35 years, he was Sunday School Superintendent for 27 years. He gave leadership and strength to all its activities and received in return grace and the blessings which flow to the faithful.

Not only to his church but to his community, he gave of himself to public service. He served for years as a member of the Board of Education in Marietta, part of the time as its chairman. He was active in the Y.M.C.A., both local and state, and in the Boy Scout movement. Thus, he sought in every way to help guide the youth of Georgia into useful lives as upright citizens.

He contributed to the business life, by serving as president and a director of a Savings & Loan Association in Marietta, and other enterprises.

To the Ten Club, of which he was a beloved member, he contributed the fruits of his scholarship and his capacity for making loyal friendships.

He brought to his professional life the products of his fundamental convictions: love of God and neighbor, devotion to truth and justice, not only in the abstract but in the arena of man's struggles with life in this world. As a lawyer and as a judge, he was guided by the highest ideals of our profession. He inspired his fellow lawyers, his associates on the bench, and the people at large, to love justice and to respect the law as the foundation stone of our system.

To those of us who had the privilege of knowing him intimately, he was a devoted friend, gentle, cheerful, kind, generous, with a keen sense of humor and understanding. Truly, he was a Christian gentleman. He shall live in our memories as long as they last.

There is a Chinese proverb: "The ear cannot hear unless the heart will listen." When King Solomon succeeded his father, the Great King David, to the throne, God appeared to him in a dream and inquired what he asked of God to guide him in his new and important role as king. He replied that he did not desire wealth or power, even over his enemies, but what he needed above all was an understanding heart with which to judge his people. And God granted his request.

He also gave to Judge Hawkins an understanding heart. And thus his ear could and did listen to all who asked justice, and with it came humility, which is the mark of true greatness. There was no smallness or meanness or ugliness in his nature; no negligence in the performance of his duty; no worldly vanity; no restless ambition. Instead, there was in all his life, professional and private, the overwhelming desire to serve mankind wherever he was—in the home, in the church, in the community, in the halls of justice—whether he be a lawyer or judge.

A truly beautiful life of a dedicated lawyer, filled with love of neighbor because of his great love of his God.

Respectfully submitted, Your Honors,
By the Committee you have appointed:

Shuler Antley
E. T. Averett
R. A. Bell
Kontz Bennett
F. M. Bird
L. M. Blair
Charles J. Bloch
Leon Boling
Sam P. Burtz
William Butt
Ben F. Carr
B. H. Chappell
Ronald F. Chance
John P. Cheney
T. H. Crawford
Vance Custer
James C. Davis
John W. Davis
J. Lon Duckworth
Hubert R. Edmondson
Scott S. Edwards, Jr.
L. Harold Glore
Charles L. Gowan
Luther C. Hames, Jr.
A. J. Henderson, Sr.
A. J. Henderson, Jr.

Claude Joiner, Jr.
Frederick Kennedy
Phil M. Landrum
Hatton Lovejoy
James Maddox
James T. Manning
T. Baldwin Martin
Edwin A. McWhorter
Henry G. Neal
Carl K. Nelson
Louie D. Newton
R. Carter Pittman
J. G. Roberts
Garvis L. Sams
James R. Shaw
R. Wilson Smith, Jr.
Herman E. Talmadge
H. B. Troutman, Sr.
John L. Tye, Jr.
H. G. Vandiviere
Harold M. Walker
J. Hines Wood
John S. Wood
Robert B. Troutman,
Chairman

I would like to add just a personal word in addition to
the report of this Committee. Judge Hawkins was a friend
for many years; a loyal friend, a devoted friend; one whose
life inspired me tremendously. My life has been enriched
because of the friendship of Judge Hawkins. I would like
to add this personal tribute to the Report of The Committee.

Now, Your Honors, there are several members of the Committee whom I have asked to make some remarks, and there may be others at this time who wish to say a few words. I would like to call on Dr. Louie D. Newton, Pastor of the Druid Hills Baptist Church, who is a member of this Committee.

ADDRESS BY DR. LOUIE D. NEWTON.

May it please the Court, Members of the Court of Appeals, this dear family, distinguished fellow Georgians:

JOHN HAROLD HAWKINS
A Good and Just Man

In the Gospel of Luke, chapter 23 and verse 50, we read: "And, behold, there was a man named Joseph, a counselor; and he was a good man, and a just. The same had not consented to the counsel and deed of them [who condemned Jesus to death]. He was of Arimathea...who also himself waited for the kingdom of God. This man went unto Pilate, and begged the body of Jesus. And he took it down, and wrapped it in linen, and laid it in a sepulchre that was hewn in stone, wherein never man before was laid."

"A good and just man." The context is cited to support this eulogy rarely found in the Scriptures. I find in the tribute to Joseph a happy parallel of the good and just friend in whose memory we are gathered today. Joseph was a lawyer, whose character and ability accounted for his seat in the Sanhedrin, the supreme court of the Jewish nation, dating back to Numbers 11:16-17. His courage in refusing to consent to the condemnation of the Son of God reveals his inflexible sense of justice, and the recorded statement that he "waited for the kingdom of God." This documents his unwavering faith in the ultimate triumph of justice and righteousness and truth.

When we examine the record of Judge Hawkins' life, whether in his home, his church, his community, his long tenure as Judge of the Blue Ridge Circuit, or here on the Supreme Court of our State, we discover, at every step of the way, the qualities of true goodness and integrity, reflecting his love of God and his unerring purpose to do justly. I fancy that Joseph of Arimathea and John Harold Hawkins of Marietta are often together, walking along the River of Life, fulfilling the beautiful proverb:

"The path of the just is as the shining light,
That shineth more and more unto the perfect day."

MR. TROUTMAN: Thank you very much, Dr. Newton.
At this time I would like to call on Honorable T. Baldwin
Martin of the Macon Bar.

ADDRESS BY HONORABLE
T. BALDWIN MARTIN

May it please the Court:

I am grateful to this court for naming me as a member of the Committee, and it is a privilege for me to pay tribute to Judge J. Harold Hawkins.

The report filed by the Chairman is comprehensive and does not need elaboration. I do want to say a few words, however, from a personal angle as to my thoughts concerning our departed friend.

One of the many compensations that a lawyer receives from the practice of law is the opportunity of coming into contact with men like Judge Hawkins and had it not been for the fact that he served on this Honorable Bench, I feel reasonably certain that our paths would not have parallel and that I would have been deprived of a friendship which I value highly.

If I were called upon to name the two outstanding characteristics of Judge Hawkins, I would say that they can be characterized as clean living and clear thinking.

From reading his decisions and from trying cases before this court, and in our personal contacts, I am sure that he approached each case with the sole question of "What is right?" and that every outside influence was excluded from his mind.

For many years Judge Hawkins and I would meet at the annual meeting of the Georgia Bar Association at the DeSoto Hotel in Savannah, and retire to the spacious veranda where we would review past events, discuss unusual cases and outline our hopes for the future. These occasions are precious in my memory and in a way are comparable to the visit to a beautiful garden.

This court has always been known as a great court, and the people of Georgia have learned to feel that a decision from this court represents that which is right and just. There is no doubt in my mind but that Judge Hawkins' tenure of office contributed to this feeling of confidence and respect, and he will always be remembered for that reason.

Thank you.

MR. TROUTMAN: Thank you, Mr. Martin.

At this time, may it please the Court, I would like to call on Honorable J. Lon Duckworth of the Atlanta Bar, a long time friend of Judge Hawkins, and a member of this Committee.

ADDRESS BY HONORABLE
J. LON DUCKWORTH.

May it please the Court, members of the Court of Appeals, members of the family, and our mutual friends:

It is a signal honor to have the opportunity on this occasion to say a word in memory of my good friend and such a distinguished gentleman as was Mr. Justice Harold Hawkins. However, I find my capacity to express my own feelings totally inadequate and unequal to the occasion.

I first knew Judge Hawkins when he became Judge of the Superior Court of the Blue Ridge Circuit. Soon after he became Judge he presided as visiting Judge in the DeKalb Superior Court. It was on this occasion that I first witnessed, as a practicing attorney, the opening of court by prayer. This procedure was typical of the life and official conduct of Judge Hawkins. I soon learned that Judge Hawkins had a fast rule never to enter upon the transaction of court business or the making of an important decision of any kind without first invoking the guidance of Almighty God.

Judge Hawkins was a friend to men in all walks of life, both in and out of court. In his court a man was never so depraved nor a youth so delinquent that they did not get a sympathetic hearing and a well-reasoned judgment. He sought to rehabilitate the person and at the same time do justice to society. In civil matters his judgment was never slanted because of the position or prestige of a litigant, or the lack of such. He was as firm and positive in his judgments as was his sympathy and understanding. Out of court he took a positive and fearless stand in all political and civic affairs and was always found on the side he conceived to be the right side of every issue.

As a Justice of the Supreme Court of Georgia, he faced and decided every question legitimately raised without giving consideration to the popularity of the decision, the litigants involved, or the repercussions. He was guided by an enlightened conscience. He had the enviable capacity of finding all the law on the issues involved, clearly understanding it and properly applying same impartially to the facts at hand, and of expressing his conclusions and reasons in opinions that were clear and convincing.

He would have been the first to move the reversal of any decision based upon an opinion which he wrote once he found a mistake had been made or an error committed. Future courts may criticize some of his opinions, and even reverse some, but I am sure no court or lawyer can or will ever find occasion or reason in one of his opinions to question his judicial honesty.

Judge Hawkins was a true pillar of his church in every sense of the word. Few men have worked longer, more faithfully, or more conscientiously than did he for his church. He was a true friend, a fine citizen, a great trial judge, and a distinguished Justice of the Supreme Court because his life was built upon the ever-enduring foundation of an unfaltering faith in Almighty God. In fact he was truly a Christian gentleman. To paraphrase from the Holy Scripture, "Surely goodness and mercy followed him all the days of his life and now he resides in the House of the Lord."

MR. TROUTMAN: Thank you very much, Mr. Duckworth.

May it please the Court, I am happy to state that all sections of this State are represented here today in this memorial to our friend. Members of this Committee have come from the northwestern part of our State, the western part, the eastern and the south, and the whole State is here to pay tribute to Judge Hawkins. This concludes the formal report of our Committee, Your Honors. I am very happy that I have been a part of this occasion, although it is indeed a solemn one.

CHIEF JUSTICE DUCKWORTH: I now recognize Judge Nichols of the Court of Appeals.

ADDRESS OF JUDGE H. E. NICHOLS.

Mr. Chief Justice Duckworth, Mr. Presiding Justice Head, Eminent Associate Justices of the Supreme Court of Georgia, Members of the Memorial Committee, Members of the Family, and Friends:

The hands of the grim reaper were never laid upon a son of Georgia soil more truly loved and universally respected; the shaft of death never struck down a leader of the legal profession to whom his brother lawyers were more implicitly devoted and for whom their eyes could yield more copiously the tearful tributes of affection than the man whose life we are gathered here this day to memorialize.

I shall not attempt to offer additional eulogy upon the life of this great and good man. Certainly I have not the ability or the words to express the many fine qualities of this outstanding jurist. Any attempt to do so would only tend to gild the lily. All knew him to be an able and honorable man—a just and upright judge, but speaking from a very personal standpoint, if I may, there was one particular trait of Harold Hawkins' life that made an indelible and everlasting impression upon me as a young lawyer, and that was his tremendous consideration and uniform kindness to all people and more particularly to the young—the scared and inexperienced neophytes at the bar who had the very good fortune to begin the practice of their profession in a superior court over which he presided. I was one of those so fortunate. I began the active practice of law in the old Blue Ridge Circuit—a judicial circuit comprising at that time six counties over which Judge Harold Hawkins presided for better than 17 years without opposition—that within itself is an eloquent testimonial of the respect and esteem in which this outstanding Georgian was held by his fellows. On the bench he was never tyrannical or dictatorial, but always extended kindness and courtesy to all members of the bar, parties litigant and witnesses alike. If he ever raised his voice to anyone I never heard of it. His obvious concern and sincere consideration for any defendant who stood convicted in his court would move a heart of stone;

he never spoke harshly or excoriated a defendant when, under the law it became necessary to impose a sentence of servitude, but rather in his soft, gentle, dulcet voice that is now stilled and silenced, he would speak words of encouragement and often times evince a deep sense of sorrow at the thought of having to do what the law compelled and directed to be done. Although blessed with the wonderful attribute and virtue of compassion for others, yet he was a fearless judicial officer; he was conscientious, always striving to see that justice prevailed in every case.

As a member of the Supreme Court of this State, he has engrossed upon the history of our jurisprudence his own imperishable record. In his passing the State of Georgia has lost one of its most valuable citizens and a devoted public servant. No man ever gave more of himself to the service of the people of Georgia.

On behalf of my colleagues on the Court of Appeals and myself I should like to say in conclusion that the example set by Harold Hawkins when he walked this earth among us as a judge and as a Christian gentleman will ever stand as an ideal and a challenge to which all of us might well aspire. He was truly one of God's noblemen. May his soul rest in peace.

Thank you.

CHIEF JUSTICE DUCKWORTH: Are there others who wish to speak?

REMARKS OF HONORABLE
HENRY B. TROUTMAN, SR.

May it please the Court: I would like to add a few words to these remarks.

The accumulation of years and events that accompany them, both are of great value to those of us who have stored them away in the archives of our minds.

During the passage of time many men and women cross our pathway. Some are endowed with qualities that make them superior to others, and in this category we find among those at the top, one of the truly great men that I had the good fortune to know—Justice J. Harold Hawkins.

During most of his life he was surrounded by three of the finest and most gentle of women—his wife, whose charm was helpful and conducive to inspire him to achieve his goal in life, and this he did, and became one of our best lawyers and judges. The other two who added to his success were his lovely and charming daughters.

But let me quote the words used by the faithful colored woman who became a part of this fine family. After Judge Hawkins had passed behind the curtain that separates life from death, Mrs. Hawkins was engaged in that melancholy task of writing to some of those many friends who had sought to comfort and share her sorrow, and on one of these days she was somewhat emotional, when this good colored companion came into the room and said: "Miss Irene, don't worry. You know when you go into the garden to gather some flowers to bring in the house you gets the prettiest and finest ones, and that is what God did. He came down to Marietta and picked the best."

Thank you.

CHIEF JUSTICE DUCKWORTH: I have a telegram here from Mr. Charles J. Bloch. I wish to read it and order it be made a part of this Memorial.

TELEGRAM OF CHARLES J. BLOCH

I regret very much that having to be in Chicago on an assignment by the American Bar Association President prevents my participating in the exercises honoring my departed friend Justice Harold Hawkins. I had hoped to be able to add to the prepared memorial my personal tribute to a great American and a great judge. As you and the other Justices who were serving with him know, his counsel and assistance to the committee of lawyers known as the Supreme Court Rules Committee of which I have the honor to be chairman are perpetuated in the amendments to those rules which he and the other Justices on your committee strive so to perfect.

RESPONSE FOR THE COURT BY
CHIEF JUSTICE W. H. DUCKWORTH.

Mr. Chairman, on behalf of the Supreme Court I wish to thank you and each of the participants for the beautiful and richly deserved tributes to the memory of our dearly beloved former Associate, Mr. Justice Harold Hawkins. Your factual portrayal of his life and achievements is a vivid and impressive illustration of the eternal virtues of a free society in which every American is privileged to live.

Undaunted by poverty and limited formal education Justice Hawkins moved forward to the fulfillment of his ambition to be a good lawyer by wisely utilizing his inherent superior intellect, together with hard work. In his struggle to succeed he was aided immensely by an abiding faith in his country, his fellow man, and the God that gave him life. Having thus become a great lawyer he crowned his legal career by serving nearly 20 years as a trial judge and 12 years as a Justice of the Supreme Court where he made a judicial record seldom equaled and never excelled by any Georgia jurist.

At this critical hour in the history of the world when the human race is seriously threatened with extinction; when powerful atheistic nations are devoting their resources to an effort to enslave all mankind into an ungodly world, and when we constantly hear of men in public office betraying the trust reposed in them, it is indeed reassuring and wholesome to meet as we are here to recount the deeds of honor of one of our own who served long in high and responsible public office, and whose official record is one of constant faithfulness to the trust reposed in him. His fidelity to every trust, and fulfillment of every duty strengthens our faith in humanity and is a challenge to all who don the judicial robe to keep it unsullied and to merit the honor which it symbolizes.

Justice Hawkins came to the Supreme Court by the free choice of the people of Georgia. He was richly endowed with a great mind, wide experience and spotless character. These noble qualities permeated his every judicial act, and they are embodied in every opinion he wrote as Justice of the Supreme Court. His opinions were clear, incisive and scholarly. They neither colored nor evaded any point of fact or law. He was a profound thinker, careful and logical reasoner, and entirely fair to all litigants. Many opinions of the Supreme Court, while not bearing his name, were actually decided upon sound principles which he convinced the court should control the case. All of his associates were comforted when a difficult and important case fell to Justice Hawkins to write the opinion for the court, for we knew he would approach it with an open mind, and devote his great ability to a full discovery of all relevant facts and all applicable law, and then prepare an opinion based upon these alone, utterly indifferent to public clamor for any given result.

He cheerfully and patiently conferred with all of his Associates on the cases assigned to them, and in this way contributed greatly to the soundness of their opinions. He was too modest to volunteer advice, but never too busy to give it when requested. In every phase of the work on this court, Justice Hawkins was the equal of any Justice that has ever served here. He was honored, respected, and genuinely loved by all of his Associates, and every one connected with the Supreme Court. He was highly intellectual but not conceited; firm and fearless, but kind and modest; filled with compassion and mercy, but he steadfastly refused to allow these to divert him from deciding cases upon the law and the facts as he understood them to be; deeply sympathetic with the unfortunate, but sympathy neither controlled nor influenced his judicial acts; pure in thought and act but not self-righteous. He put his Lord first in all things, and his conduct at all times revealed this fact. His great achievements were made with a full recognition of the eternal truth found in sacred writings that; "Except the Lord build the house, they labor in vain who build it."

While man is given life on earth for an extremely short time, yet his good works live after him to serve and bless the generations that follow him. The spirit of Justice Hawkins has departed this earth and now mingles with the Saints and Angels in Heaven, but his good works of service to his fellow man remain with us to guide us in the paths of law and righteousness. His superlative record on the Supreme Court shall endure for all time as one of the brightest pages of Georgia's judicial history.

The Justices of the Supreme Court, I am sure, are joined by his countless friends throughout this State and by his loved ones, in solemn thanks to Divine Providence for the life and services of this great and good man.

It is ordered by the court that a page of the minutes of the Supreme Court be set apart to be inscribed with the dates of the birth, death and service of Justice Hawkins on this court, together with all that has been said this morning. It is further ordered that a copy of all of these proceedings be published in the official reports of the Court, and that a copy be given to the family of Judge Hawkins. And now in further respect for our deceased beloved Associate, Justice Hawkins, the Supreme Court is adjourned for the day.

THE TEN

ORGANIZED 1898

ATLANTA

July 3, 1961

Mrs. J. Harold Hawkins
709 Church Street
Marietta, Georgia

Dear Mrs. Hawkins:

At the meeting of The Ten, July 30, the enclosed resolution, prepared by Bishop Arthur J. Moore, was adopted unanimously, after the members present stood in silent tribute to our dear and cherished friend.

I enclose three copies of the resolution, so that you may pass copies on to the two daughters.

May I say again that Judge Hawkins was loved and honored by every member of The Ten, and we shall treasure his fellowship through all the years.

With continued prayer and appreciation for you and the lovely daughters and the grand-children.

Sincerely yours,

(signed)

Louie D. Newton

LDN:jb

256

JOHN HAROLD HAWKINS
A Good and Just Man

In the Gospel of Luke, chapter 23 and verse 50, we read: "And, behold there was a man named Joseph, a counselor; and he was a good man, and just. The same had not consented to the counsel and deed of them (who condemned Jesus to death).

He was of Arimathea, who also himself waited for the Kingdom of God. This man went unto Pilate, and begged the body of Jesus. And he took it down, and wrapped it in linen, and laid it in a sepulcher that was hewn in stone, wherein never man before was laid."

"A good and just man." The context is cited to support this eulogy, rarely found in the Scriptures. I find in the tribute to Joseph a happy parallel of the good and just friend in whose memory we are gathered today. Joseph was a lawyer, whose character and ability accounted for his seat in the Sanhedrin – the supreme court of the Jewish nation, dating back to Numbers 11:16-17. His courage in refusing to consent to the condemnation of the Son of God reveals his inflexible sense of justice, and the recorded statement that he "waited for the Kingdom of God," documents his unwavering faith in the ultimate triumph of justice and righteousness and truth.

When we examine the record of Judge Hawkins' life, whether in his home, his church, his community, his long tenure as Judge of the Blue Ridge Circuit, or here on the Supreme Court, we discover, at every step of the way, the qualities of true goodness and integrity, reflecting his love of God and his unerring purpose to do justly. I fancy that Joseph of Arimathea and John Harold Hawkins of Marietta are often together, walking along the River of Life, fulfilling the beautiful Proverb:
"The path of the just is as the shining light,
That shineth more and more unto the perfect day."

-Louie D. Newton

Some adjectives thrust themselves on you when you are thinking of certain people. This is especially true when one sets out to evaluate the life and labor of Judge J. H. Hawkins. Somewhere in his writings John Milton affirms that "when God would create a strong and beautiful society He begins by raising up for His will and work men of rare abilities with more than common industry; men who can not only look back and revise what has been taught heretofore but go on to some new and enlightened steps in the discovery of truth."

We of The Ten Club who for many years have walked at the side of Judge Hawkins are convinced that he qualified as one of these rare and gifted souls. He lived all of his days as a friend of good men, and the supporter of good causes. His life was a day-by-day demonstration of a type of rare and rugged spirituality. He was faithful to his friends and supremely loyal to his church and his Christ. We will not soon forget his swift assent to duty, his gentle courage or his winsome smile.

His life was an open book of unmistakable integrity. As a lawyer in private practice he honored his profession and as Judge of the Blue Ridge Circuit and later a member of Georgia's Supreme Court he was a master of a trained mind and did all of his work with the precision of a skilled workman. In short he was an unobtrusive specimen of a cultivated American, a dedicated public servant and a sincere Christian [sic]. He has left to his family and friends a rare and lasting example of flawless fidelity to every trust committed to his care. His friends will dwell on his name lovingly and from such a memory gather strength of nobler living. In that country where God lets us go when the sun goes down we shall companion with him there as we have here.

We the members of the Ten Club record in this simple fashion that we are better because Judge Hawkins was here, and today grief is in our heart because he is not here. To Mrs. Hawkins and the children we convey this inadequate expression of our sympathy and record our faith that we shall meet him again in the heavenly company.

CHAPTER TWENTY TWO

A TEN CLUB PAPER PRESENTED
BY JUDGE J. HAROLD HAWKINS

The subject assigned to me is -

SUMMARY OF OUR FOREIGN POLICY – Department of State

I have heard and enjoyed very much the able discussions presented by Mr. Troutman on "Relations with England, France and Spain, 1789 - 1815"; by Dr. McCain on "The Monroe Doctrine, 1823 to Date"; by Dr. Pressley on "Spanish-American War and Our Island Possessions"; by Bishop Moore on "Far Eastern Policies, 1868 to Date"; by Dr. White on "U.S. World Responsibility after Fall of British Empire"; by Dr. Newton on "Struggles with Russia over the Spread of Communism," and by Mr. Gellerstedt on "Some Notable Secretaries of State and their Contributions," he having selected and given a most interesting paper on Mr. Cordell Hull. I was not privileged to hear the other papers in this series. Those which I did have the pleasure of hearing evidenced an enormous amount of work on the part of their authors, and since I began to try to prepare this paper, I can appreciate the vast amount of study that was necessary in the preparation.

To make anything like a comprehensive summary of our foreign policy would require a lifetime of work. The activities of the Department of State during the very brief period between 1950 and 1955 requires two volumes consisting of 1,245 pages to record them.

During recent years I have been guilty of joining in the criticism of our present Secretary of State, who now lies desperately ill in the hospital. While I regret exceedingly his illness, that has not been the cause of a resolution on my part to refrain from further criticism, but my study during the past few weeks has convinced me that criticism from one who knows so little of the vast field covered by the Department of State, and the responsibilities imposed thereby upon the Secretary of State, arises from an abundance of ignorance, and comes from little grace from one so handicapped.

To me the most striking phase of our present foreign policy is the complete about face, or reversal, of our position which has come about within the last forty years.

On September 17, 1796, President Washington, in his Farewell Address, had this to say:

"Against the insidious wiles of foreign influence (I conjure you to believe me, fellow-citizens) the jealousy of a free people ought to be constantly awake, since history and experience prove that foreign influence is one of the most baneful foes of republican government. But that jealousy, to be useful, must be impartial, else it becomes the instrument of the very influence to be avoided, instead of a defense against it. Excessive partiality for one foreign nation and excessive dislike of another cause those whom they actuate to see danger only on one side, and serve to veil and even second the arts of influence on the other. Real patriots who may resist the intrigues of the favorite are liable to become suspected and odious, while its tools and dupes usurp the applause and confidence of the people to surrender their interests.

"The great rule of conduct for us in regard to foreign nations is, in extending our commercial relations to have with them as little political connection as possible. So far as we have already formed engagements let them be fulfilled with perfect good faith. Here let us stop.

"Europe has a set of primary interests which to us have none or very remote relation. Hence she must be engaged in frequent controversies, the causes of which are essentially foreign to our concerns. Hence, therefore, it must be unwise in us to implicate ourselves by artificial ties in the ordinary vicissitudes of her politics or the ordinary combinations and collisions of her friendships or enmities."

The spirit or doctrine of isolationism remained a fixed policy of this government down to and extending beyond the First World War. During the early days of our national existence it was possible to carry out this policy with more or less success, but during that War we found that we could not remain a nation apart and unaffected by occurrences in other parts of the world. Some, even before that time, could visualize the part our nation would be called upon to play in world affairs, formerly half a century ago Theodore Roosevelt said: "The United States of America has not the option as to whether it will or will not play a great part in the world. It must play a great part. All that it can decide is whether it will play that part well or badly." With the benefit of hindsight, we can now see that we played the part badly following the First World War when the spirit of isolationism on the part of many of our leaders in Congress defeated the League of Nations, which had the effect of destroying one of our greatest Presidents, Woodrow Wilson, and of laying the foundation for the Second World War.

The world has been so shrunk by the developments of science and technology that events anywhere affect men everywhere, and international communism, seeking its "one world", operates against us on a global basis.

Lenin wrote, "First we will take Western Europe; next the masses of Asia; and finally we will encircle the last bastion of capitalism–the United States. We will not have to attack it–it will fall like overripe fruit into our hands," and it is apparently this policy which Khrushchev is now following, although he continues to rattle the saber on occasions.

Mr. Francis O. Wilcox, Assistant Secretary for International Organization Affairs, recently said: "I venture to say that the most remarkable development of this century is the assumption over the last 17 years by the United States of its present role of responsibility and leadership in world affairs. This is a role we did not play during the previous 150 years of our existence as a sovereign state."

Indeed, the United States has been going through a revolutionary period since 1941 in our relations to other countries. In this brief period we have moved from relative isolationism to internationalism, from a policy of no entangling alliances to a system of complex political, economic, and security alliances with more than 40 nations.

We have only to recall our extreme reluctance to participate in some of the meetings of the League of Nations, even in the modest role of observers, to realize how times have changed.

Clearly this dramatic shift has been impelled by considerations of the national interest. It is often forgotten that every important more in foreign policy is based on one overriding consideration–whether it will advance the well-being and security of the American people. The effectiveness of our policies must be judged on how well they accomplish this end.

In no country is foreign policy more constantly under review than in the United States. In no country do the people have a greater voice in foreign affairs. Our budgetary process alone assures such annual review. To be sure, this process often dismays our friends and allies, who may not understand our system of checks and balances. Yet it has the great virtue of insuring that our policies, once arrived at, are backed by a majority of the informed leadership in the Congress, in the executive branch, and among the public. This again insures that they will be carried out with vigor and confidence. It also insures, and I think this is of vital importance, that our policy is morally defensible, for our people will tolerate no other.

I should like to say a word here about the unique nature of American leadership in international affairs. Through the centuries other countries have grown in influence, expanded their borders, and carved out empires because of personal ambitions of leaders, for religious reasons, for the advancement of trade and the accumulation of riches or because of some other compelling sense of mission. Most who succeeded, at least temporarily, in carrying out such policies were able to count on the compliance of disciplined citizens, either because the governments were autocratic or because their people were also imbued with some particular sense of mission in the world. In the process some of them have brought blessings along with oppression and have planted the seeds of future self-government and independence.

The new American leadership, on the other hand, was not sought but was largely thrust upon us by a sick and frightened world. Its objective is neither conquest nor territorial aggrandizement but the preservation of freedom. It identifies the well-being of the world community, under freedom with the security and welfare of the American people. In essence it seeks for other peoples the blessings we enjoy at home. The vast resources that we have poured into other countries in support of these convictions are sometimes mistaken as generosity of the "do good" variety—or a belief that all problems are susceptible to economic solutions. This is to misinterpret the deep wellsprings of our belief, tested since the day of our independence, that men are created equal and that life, liberty, and the pursuit of happiness apply to mankind, not just to the people of one land, if we are all to prosper in peace.

Public support for United States leadership has been strong and consistent for a period of years now, despite surface fluctuations. Support has been especially strong for the United Nations, which was born of American initiative and continues to receive the approval of the overwhelming majority of our people in both political parties and in all sections of the country. It is based on the increased awareness of the American people that the United Nations has served the interest of the free men everywhere. It has served the cause of peace, security, and well-being for mankind.

I think we all have a responsibility to help preserve the unique quality, high purpose and practical application of the American concept of leadership lest it deteriorate into a new isolationism or be tempted to control where it cannot persuade.

During the period following World War Two, 21 new nations have been granted political independence, and others are on the threshold of independence. Since World War Two the communists moved on two fronts to extend their influence: The military, as by the takeover of the new satellite countries, and the aggression or threat of aggression against Greece, Turkey, Iran, and Korea, and the politico-economic, as demonstrated by their propaganda and subversion among the peoples of Asia and Africa, many of whom were in various stages of revolutionary ferment.

The United States countered these two moves by military assistance and economic aid. Contrary to the views of some, these are not "give-away" programs, but cooperative endeavors designed to help people who are free to remain free. Much has been accomplished through the United Nations organization, brought into being largely through the efforts and influence of the United States. The United Nations has a record of solid accomplishments, although it has had many disappointments, due to the subversive acts and influence of the Soviet Union and its satellites. It played a major role in the withdrawal of Soviet troops from Iran in 1946; helped bring to an end the Communist war in Greece; condemned the Chinese Communists as aggressors in Korea and fought to roll back aggression there; brought about a truce between India and Pakistan in Kashmir; avoided a major war in the Suez crisis by bringing the pressure of world opinion to bear for a quick end to hostilities; condemned the Soviet Union's invasion of Hungary and revealed its brutal repression of the Hungarian people's efforts to achieve freedom; cleared the Suez Canal and reopened it to the commerce of the world; created an International Atomic Energy Agency for the peaceful development of the atom; has fought poverty, hunger, disease, and ignorance in many lands in order to improve the general well-being of mankind and remove some of the basic causes of war.

The aim of our foreign policy today is to secure the blessings of liberty and freedom, not only for ourselves, but for the world.

That freedom is still a magnet that attracts is evidenced by the following facts:

Of the Chinese Communist prisoners taken in Korea, two-thirds rejected repatriation.

From Communist China the people flee to Hong Kong and Macao.

In Korea about 2 million have gone from the Communist north to the south.

In Vietnam nearly 1 million went from the Communist north to the south.

During the Hungarian rebellion, 200,000 escaped to freedom.

In Germany over 3 million have gone from east to west.

Within the past five years there have been violent outbreaks in East Berlin, East Germany, Poland, Hungary and Communist China.

It was stated in the newspapers the other day that Mr. Dulles, since he became Secretary of State on January 20, 1953, has traveled 559,938 miles for conferences, ceremonies, and speeches, all over the world.

When we realize the wide diversity of interests of the numerous countries and governments with which our Department of State is forced to deal, we marvel at even the limited success which our Secretary of State and the Department of State have been able to achieve.

In the mid-20th century we no longer have a choice about our position in the free world. It is merely a question of how effectively and how well we lead.

If we will understand the long-range nature of the Communist threat and do our best to meet it;

If we will continue to support the United Nations and the cause of which it stands;

If we will work closely with our allies and continue to avoid going it alone;

If we will demonstrate to the uncommitted nations of the world the enduring qualities of democracy and freedom;

If we will take our stand always as a nation on high moral grounds–then we can face the future with confidence that the cause of free men will prevail.